Unlocked

Unlocked

An Irish Prison Officer's Story

DAVID McDONALD
WITH MICK CLIFFORD

SANDYCOVE

an imprint of

PENGUIN BOOKS

SANDYCOVE

UK | USA | Canada | Ireland | Australia
India | New Zealand | South Africa

Sandycove is part of the Penguin Random House group of companies
whose addresses can be found at global.penguinrandomhouse.com.

First published 2022
001

Copyright © David McDonald with Mick Clifford, 2022

The moral right of the copyright holders has been asserted

Set in 13.5/16pt Garamond MT Std
Typeset by Jouve (UK), Milton Keynes
Printed and bound in Great Britain by Clays Ltd, Elcograf S.p.A.

The authorized representative in the EEA is Penguin Random House Ireland,
Morrison Chambers, 32 Nassau Street, Dublin D02 YH68

A CIP catalogue record for this book is available from the British Library

ISBN: 978–1–844–88619–7

www.greenpenguin.co.uk

Penguin Random House is committed to a
sustainable future for our business, our readers
and our planet. This book is made from Forest
Stewardship Council® certified paper.

For Matthew

Contents

Prologue   1

1 The Town That Made Me   11

2 All the Familiar Faces   22

3 Learning the Job in 'The Joy'   28

4 Dying Men Walking   39

5 Back Home in 'The Bog'   47

6 The Defaulters   59

7 Getting to Know the Heavies   70

8 The Border Fox, the Cop Killers and
   the Garlic Man   85

9 Love in a Cold Climate   101

10 The Night They Drove Old Dixie Down   111

11 Moving On, Moving In Next Door   120

12 Here Comes the Night   131

13 John Daly Talks to Joe   140

14 Three Heads of the New System   147

15 Face to Face   159

16 Bad Apples   173

17 Getting a Handle on the Gangs   187

18 Ear to the Ground   205

19 Blocking Out and Listening In   217

20 Deep Sea Fishing   229

21 Shining a Light in Dark Corners   243

22 The Murky Depths of The Bog   256

23 Away With You   271

24 Looking In Through the Out Door   283

    Acknowledgements   293

Prologue

We Want a Head

I was in the screening area of the Midlands Prison when the call came through. It was 5.20 p.m. on 28 December 2012. 'Get down to the circle,' I was told. 'We have a situation.'

In that instant I was torn between the high of an adrenalin rush and the sinking feeling that the evening was not going to unfold as had been planned. After a straight month at work I was already halfway out the gate. Having missed any kind of a break over Christmas, I had a few days off coming to me. The highlight of the down time would be an upcoming Tommy Tiernan gig in Vicar Street.

In my head I was already sitting there at one of the tables, surrounded by family, a creamy pint in front of me, and everyone wired for laughs. Now, with the door in sight, I was being hauled back to the present with a bang.

When I arrived at the circle, I was met by one of the governors. He told me that all the prisoners in D division were out on the landings. They were tooled up and refusing to go into their cells.

'What do they want?' I asked.

'They want you gone, out of here, transferred,' I was told.

D block in the Midlands Prison housed some of the most notorious prisoners in the state, the kind of gangland figures who often feature in the media. Some of them had murdered. A few of them were at the level where they ordered murders. Before being imprisoned, these men had run mini empires. Inside, they still managed to maintain their status as significant players in the drugs business.

And that was their problem with me. I was in charge of the OSG, the Operational Support Group, in the Midlands. One of our main tasks was to stop the flow of contraband into prisons. The two big items are drugs and phones. Both multiply in value once they make it inside a prison's gates.

As on the outside, the season of goodwill is celebrated in prison. Not being in a position to stroll down to the local pub for a few extra pints, prisoners make do with drugs other than alcohol.

The volume of the stuff flowing into prisons ratchets up at this time of year, as for other big events like an Ireland soccer match. These occasions take on an even greater significance inside. They relieve for a short time the mind-numbing boredom and tedium that passes for life in prison. For those who deal in drugs, Christmas is a time to make a killing.

Phones also jack up in value in prison at this time of year. Naturally, prisoners want to be in closer contact with loved ones, and that's understandable. But it is against the law – and for very good reason. Phones can, and are, used on the inside to run crime gangs outside. They are also another lucrative form of contraband for the gang leaders who have control in prison. A phone can be rented out for anything between €50 and €100 a night. But if it is discovered and forfeited, the cost is around €1,800 in compensation, which has to be paid to the gang leader. That can be the start of months of hell for both the prisoner and his family. Effectively, the prisoner becomes a slave.

Our job was to intercept, disrupt, frustrate the flow of drugs and phones into and around the prison. By 2012, the OSG had been in operation for four years as a separate dedicated unit in the Irish Prison Service. It takes time to build up a unit from scratch, but by then we had resources and confidence, and we decided to put down a marker. All the stops were pulled out to make sure that, this Christmas, Santa wouldn't be coming for those who oversaw the drugs trade. We put plans in place. We were relentless in disrupting the flow of drugs by coming down hard on the known channels, especially visitors.

For us, the results were very satisfying. We confiscated what amounted to a whole truckload of drugs that December. Upwards of 10,000 tablets were seized. I'd been liaising with gardaí in Portlaoise, where the Midlands Prison is located, and they arrested fourteen visitors. Four were arrested on Christmas Eve alone. Now, in the anticlimactic days that followed, tensions had risen. The big boys were pissed off that their Christmas market had been ruined. They were intent on wreaking some form of revenge. They blamed me – and they wanted me out.

So, I'm standing there, digesting the news that I am the focus of what is building up to be a riot. There were about 150 prisoners on the three landings in D division and 80 staff in the whole prison at the time. Naturally, I was far from relaxed about what was happening. On one level, I could have enjoyed a little pat on the back for myself. The prisoners' anger was as a result of me, and the men and women I oversaw, having done a good job over the previous few weeks. But there and then, shaken out of my gate fever, I had to concentrate on how to rescue a situation that was on the brink of getting out of hand.

There was no way we could let the men stay out on the landings all night. That would have been a concession. Their protest was a show of strength, and it was important that we regained control. There was every possibility of violence. The officers who had been on the landings reported that the prisoners were tooled up with the usual weapons. Somebody saw one of them waving a pool ball in a sock. We didn't know but assumed that they also had a good share of chivs: home-made knives in which razor blades are melted into toothbrush handles.

Rescuing the situation rested with the OSG. We were in charge of security and, crucially, we had the dogs. My direct boss, a chief officer in the OSG, Ben Buckley, was based in Cork but operated throughout the country. In the Midlands I reported directly to him rather than to the prison governors.

First thing I directed was the monitoring of the internal phones. Now that the prisoners on D division had the run of the place, they would be using the opportunity to call home. Intelligence garnered from the calls would help assess what we were up against, and what exactly they wanted – apart from my head.

The calls were as we had expected:

'It's kicking off tonight . . .'

'We're tooled up and ready for them . . .'

'That bastard McDonald is going to get his . . .'

'We'll show them that we're not taking their shit . . .'

The tone of the calls sounded like the prisoners were united. There were three landings on D division, so if the calls had suggested that most of the boys looking for trouble were on just one, then we could isolate that landing, cut the head off the snake. But the intelligence coming back from the calls was that all three landings were involved. That was going to make our job a lot more difficult.

The other bit of intelligence we took from the calls was that they really had it in for me personally. In their enclosed

4

world, I had graduated from party pooper to the devil incarnate.

I rang the chief. 'Ben, we have a situation.'

It was the last thing he needed to hear at this time of year but, true to form, he clicked into work mode straight away. He told me he'd organize to get people to us. He then got on the phone to our colleagues in prisons around the country to see who could be mobilized.

Over the following hour, men and women in the OSG got into cars in Dublin, Cork and Limerick. At each prison, we had to strip the unit down to a bare minimum and divert whomever we could to assist us in the Midlands. All roads led to Portlaoise. As most people were picking over the last of the turkey, tippling through the beer and wine in a warm seasonal glow, these men and women were driving through the dark, not knowing how dangerous was the situation that would face them on arrival.

Ben Buckley also organized the dogs. They are a vital asset in any conflict situation in prison. We had a number of them on site in the Midlands, and Ben called in more from Mountjoy in Dublin. German shepherds, lovely fellows who would literally jump through hoops for their handlers but are capable of taking the head off you, if commanded. They don't distinguish between prison officers and prisoners. Apart from their handlers, everybody is fair game. They used to be called guard dogs but, as with much else in life these days, we have a brand-new shiny title for them. They are now conflict resolution dogs – but, as you might have guessed, nobody urges the dogs to, 'Go in there, lads, and resolve the conflict!'

We put together a plan. Since Victorian times, prisons have mostly been designed to the same model. This involves a centre – the circle – which is really a general assembly area from which the prisoners are excluded, with the blocks (as they are known) projected out from there, like the spokes on a bicycle wheel. This design is primarily for security. Any problems that arise can be isolated on the block in question, and the whole prison does not come under threat.

In the Midlands, A, B and D blocks housed the general population of prisoners, while C block was reserved for the protection of prisoners under threat of attack from other prisoners, as well as sex offenders. D was where the most serious criminals were held.

Each block has three landings on three different floors. The ground floor is just a corridor, with cells lined up on each side, and on the two floors above there are landings, or walkways, outside the cells. A net is attached to the walk-ways on the first and second floors, to prevent anything potentially dangerous being thrown down.

After consulting with some of the other officers, we came to the conclusion that the best way to attack was to go across the attic, to which we had access but the prisoners didn't. There was a walkway in the attic where the service ducts and cables ran. At the far end, there was a spiral stair-case winding down, with a locked door giving access to each of the three landings.

The prisoners had barricaded the main entrance from the circle on the ground floor, so a full-frontal assault could get very dangerous. Coming across the attic meant we could pour out into the ground-floor landing from that end. The regular Midlands staff could then come out from the circle and herd the men in.

By 7.15 p.m. we were ready to go. We had forty OSG officers all togged out in full riot gear – helmets, body armour around the chest, shoulders and elbows, even a groin guard for that area. Some of the prisoners we were facing were good with their fists and feet. We had thick leather-type gloves and knee guards, hip guards, shin guards and fire-retardant boots. We carried batons and perspex shields. We all had been through full control and restraint training, but some of the men on D block were capable of anything. As a form of defence, our riot gear was perfect and all sealed up. You wouldn't be going dancing in it, and you wouldn't want to be togged out for too long. It was deadly uncomfortable, and we knew that once we hit the attic walkway the heat would be nearly unbearable.

We had five dogs: the main event. If we were using the dogs in an ordinary situation, we would face each other in two lines, with our long shields held aloft and linked together, creating a tunnel. Then their handlers would free the dogs, who would rip down through the tunnel and attack the target. We had to be sure that we were behind the shields and out of reach because the dogs would as likely turn on us. When the dog sees a man with a weapon in his hand, he's trained to go for that hand and take the man down. These creatures cost up to €50,000 each to train, but as a weapon they're hard to beat.

Once we got them into the building, they began to bark like they had seen the end of the world. Experience has taught me that one thing which can put fear into even the hardest of hard chaws is the sound of those German shepherds spitting anger. We knew that, in all likelihood, the prisoners on D landings would have bleach ready to throw into the eyes of the dogs. But even at that, the prospect of these shepherds tearing into them must have been getting inside their heads.

There was a slight delay before we kicked off. Lockdown was at 7.30 p.m. and we wanted to make sure that all the other prisoners among the 800 or so in the prison were in their cells when this kicked off. When all other blocks had been locked in for the night, we stepped forward. All of the officers began beating batons off their perspex shields. The dogs responded with gales of angry barking. The volume cranked up. Prisoners in the other blocks – who knew, by now, what was happening – began shouting and roaring, taunting us, trying to egg on the big boys in D block.

The result was a racket that could wake the dead. Steel on steel, baton on shield, human voices roaring beyond reason, and the deafening, threatening sound of animals straining at the leash to inflict violence on anyone who got in their way. All of this compressed and contained within the walls of the prison, removed from the world outside.

We climbed the stairs and took off across the attic. The heat was sauna-like as we moved in single file, staying well out of the way of the shepherds and the handlers. Below, the hard men could hear us. And while I don't pretend to know what was going through their heads, I'd take a safe bet that the sound of our shepherds wasn't doing them any good.

We descended the steel steps, the adrenalin now pumping. Even with our physical power, and protected in full riot gear, there will always be the prospect of facing into the unknown when it comes to this kind of confrontation. We passed the door to D3 and down to D2. Then on the ground floor we came out, batons raised, full of fight.

There to meet us was an empty landing. We looked up at the catwalks above and instead of missiles of shit or pots of piss, we were met with silence. They had surrendered before we showed up for the fight. Every single prisoner was back in his cell. I breathed a long sigh of relief and hurried to get on with the counting and the lockdown, just tearing to get out of the bloody suit before I fainted from the heat. I was still wired, but a big tank of pressure within me was being released. We had faced them down. They wanted my head, but in the end they had accepted that they would not be running this prison.

Five days later and the whole episode was disappearing in the rear-view mirror. We were on the road to Dublin: myself, Valerie, our son and daughter and their partners. At last, I was getting some quality down time with the family. All of us were in the mood for a proper evening in Vicar Street in the company of Mr Tiernan.

Sailing along on the motorway, just after the turn-off for Kildare Town, I got a call on my mobile from one of the prison governors.

'We've just got word that you're the subject of a category five death threat.'

That threw me, taking my good mood. I wasn't sure what a category five threat exactly was.

As we hit Dublin, I pulled over and got out of the car to phone a friend of mine who was a detective in Portlaoise. I told him what had been relayed to me.

'What exactly does it mean?' I asked my friend.

'Where are you?' was his response.

'Just hitting Dublin on the way to Tommy Tiernan. What does it mean?'

There was a pause on the line.

'It means they're going to shoot you. If I was you, I'd get back into that car, turn it around and come home. You're going to have to do a serious ramp-up on security from here on in.'

1. The Town That Made Me

The biggest influence on my opting for a career in the prison service was growing up in Portlaoise. My father, Michael McDonald, is a pure Dub, a native of Pearse Street in the inner city. He was known far and wide as the Gateaux Man, due to his job in confectionary sales, in which he delivered cakes throughout the Leinster area. My mum, Claire, was from Co. Meath and was working in Dublin when they met.

I was born in the National Maternity Hospital in Holles Street, on 11 May 1963. My only sibling, Matthew, was born four years later. Frank McCourt, who wrote *Angela's Ashes* about growing up in Limerick, once noted: 'The happy childhood isn't worth your while.' According to that principle, my childhood was completely unremarkable. I grew up in a loving home. There was none of the alcoholism, violence or dysfunction that might make for great reading but does nothing for a child's development. Our family has always remained close but has been marked by tragedy, more of which later.

My parents' decision to move to Portlaoise when I was four had a crucial impact on me. They decided to do so largely because that was the best place for my father to locate himself for work.

Portlaoise is a garrison town that was established by the British Crown in 1557. Originally, it was called Maryborough in honour of the reigning queen at the time, but soon after the Irish state achieved independence it was renamed

Portlaoise (though many older folk who grew up pre-independence called it Maryborough to their dying day). It is the biggest town in the Irish midlands, with a population of around 22,000.

The only thing that separates the town from others of its size around the country is the presence of not one but two prisons. Portlaoise Prison was built in the 1830s. For the longest time, it was used as an overflow from Mountjoy in Dublin or to house prisoners from the country. In 1999, a second prison, the Midlands, was built on land adjoining the original prison.

Throughout much of the nineteenth and twentieth centuries, the original Portlaoise Prison wasn't terribly significant. But then an event in Dublin, on 31 October 1973, changed everything for the prison and the town.

On that day, a helicopter landed in the yard of Mountjoy Prison and scooped up three leading IRA figures. This was at a time when the Troubles in the North were wreaking havoc and costing lives on a daily basis. Those who were convicted of crimes associated with the political violence were known as subversives (because they were trying to subvert the state). They served their sentences in either Mountjoy or the military prison in The Curragh.

The helicopter escape made worldwide headlines and was highly embarrassing for the government. A drastic response was needed. The outcome was a decision to relocate all subversive prisoners to Portlaoise, where it would be possible to create a genuine ring of steel around the prison. The plan included deploying both the army and gardaí to guard the prisoners. One of the first moves in fitting out Portlaoise Prison was the installation of nets over the exercise yard, to ensure there would be no more helicopters dropping in.

The move was to have a transformative effect on the

town. In a short space of time there were hundreds of new, very well-paid jobs pumping money into the local economy. On the negative side, the changes also brought some tensions to Portlaoise.

It took a while for the new regime to fully ramp up. In the meantime, the Provos managed another spectacular escape. On 18 August 1974, a number of officers at Portlaoise Prison were overpowered by nineteen prisoners in the main cell block. They took the officers' uniforms and the keys to an adjoining roof. From there, they made their way to one of the gates and blew it open with sticks of gelignite. Outside, some of them hijacked two cars and disappeared from the town into the jagged network of country roads that fan out across the midlands.

Politically, this was another disaster. It led to a further ramping up of security and, it would later emerge, a harsher regime in which there were allegations of brutality. Two hunger strikes were undertaken in the following years in protest at the harsh conditions, but both were abandoned.

We lived on the Dublin Road, a few hundred yards from the prison's main gate. The breadwinners among most of our neighbours were prison officers. There was a whole row of prison houses, built specifically for those working in the prison, down one side of the road.

At school in the town's Christian Brothers School (CBS), a good share of my classmates were the sons of prison officers.

The Dublin Road was known locally as Hardware Boulevard. On the right-hand side you had the prison officers, known as the screws. Across the road, in St Fintan's psychiatric hospital, the residents were unkindly referred to as the nuts.

Prison officers were a different breed in those days. I could see, even as a child, that these were hard men. Playing in the neighbourhood, or in the homes of some of my school pals, I have memories of being a little scared of their fathers. Some of these adults had an edge to them which conveyed that they knew what trouble looked like – and they'd meet it head on. Many among them were also physically big men.

Socially, they were a very tight bunch. They hung out with each other. They drank together. They even holidayed as a group. I have memories of my friends heading off with all of their families, busloads of them, to the seaside town of Tramore, Co. Waterford, for the summer holiday. As a child there was a part of me that was filled with jealousy at such a sight. As an adult that kind of a set-up now looks like hell on earth. Rather than getting a break from the job, they were bringing the prison on tour.

Despite the impact of the prison on the town, I hadn't a clue, growing up, what it was like behind the high walls. I suspect few outside the prison service did. It was never mentioned in general conversation, or in socializing locally, by officers who were fathers of friends of mine. Even my own dad knew next to nothing about it, despite being a regular in the prison club, where he played darts. What went on behind the walls stayed among those who worked there. To that extent, the prison was like its own little island, with the town washing up against its outer walls.

Much later, I was to learn that, at that time, there were various tensions, not least between prison officers and the gardaí. For every two prison officers on duty in the prison there was one garda. Yet they didn't get on. Resentment played a role in this. I think it's fair to say that many among the gardaí saw themselves, socially and professionally, as a cut above prison officers. Yet financially the prison officers were doing much better. The only bar to overtime was the clock. They could work all the hours God gave, and then some. The same opportunities weren't available to the gardaí in the town.

The tension was ramped up with the odd arrest of a prison officer for drink-driving. In reality, if the laws were being applied with any kind of rigour, there should have been a lot more arrests. Notwithstanding that, resentment swelled among prison officers whenever one of them was collared for being above the limit.

The other element that frequently ratcheted up tensions in the town was the staging of protests on behalf of subversive prisoners. These were frequent and involved crowds marching down the Dublin Road with placards, chanting slogans that were anti-government and noticeably anti-prison officers. At one stage there would have been some of them dressed up as the blanket men who were on the dirty protest in Long Kesh prison, in Northern Ireland. That was confusing for us kids. Somebody tried to explain that this was what was going on in the North, but we didn't realize how easily the same thing could have happened in Portlaoise. While the British government made an issue over the political status of the prisoners, down south the cabinet thought it better to allow some leeway rather than cause further confrontation.

When the protesters arrived, the gardaí had it organized that they would only be allowed so far down the Dublin Road, stopping at a point that was close to where we lived. They were often out there on the road, hostile, loud and making it known that they had no time for the fathers of my friends.

Despite all these tensions, I naturally had more pressing issues on my mind as a child and a teenager. One of these was sport. I went to the local CBS primary and secondary schools, but I wouldn't claim to have been a great man for the books. Sport was a different matter.

Gaelic football was the main sport in the midlands, but we were also into rugby. I was handy enough at the latter, skinny and fast with the ball in my hand. I also took up the shot-put in school and represented Leinster at schools' level in the sport. Matthew was the real footballer in our house. He went on to play for the county and the local club team, Portlaoise, and helped them to win county and Leinster titles.

While I was at secondary school I took up a part-time job in a local pub, The Hare and Hound. That brought me into touch with another aspect of life behind the prison walls. Some of those officers could put away enough drink for a camel. It was a huge part of the culture, from what I could see. They would come in nearly always wearing the uniform, which I found odd. As with the other aspects of their lives, they drank in packs.

Sometimes, a call would come through to expect a big crowd of them in around closing time. If there had been a search in the prison, a whole platoon would arrive in, thirsty after their stressful hours confronting the subversives.

At closing time, there would then be a lock-in and I'd be kept on hand to serve into the wee small hours. That was fine with me because I was making extra cash. A few of the officers would drink through the night and head off to work again in the morning. If there had been a breathalyser at the gates of Portlaoise Prison in those days, there would have been serious staff shortages.

When the governor came in for a pint, it was quite a spectacle to behold. We'd know he was on the way because some minutes before his arrival two plain-clothes detectives brandishing Uzi sub-machine guns would enter the pub and check out thoroughly who was there and who was not. This would include searching the toilets and backrooms. The governor would then be allowed to come in. He'd sit with the detectives, having a few pints. The town's only restaurant was next door and, if he was in the mood for some food, it would be brought in from there for him. On one level, you might think the man was being treated like a king, but if all he was interested in was a few relaxing pints, it must have been something of an ordeal.

Looking back, the whole drinking culture couldn't have been healthy, but it was also understandable. These men were working in very stressful conditions. And they had to watch their backs outside the prison – to an extent that wasn't necessary anywhere else in the western world. Prisons and prisoners were a big part of the IRA's campaign of violence. In the North, prison officers were being targeted for assassination. In those days, Portlaoise was the most secure prison in Europe.

The gravity of what was going on, and how it spilled out into the town, hit home on the night of 25 March 1983. Brian Stack, who was a chief officer in the prison, attended an amateur boxing tournament in the National Stadium in Dublin. Stack was a keen boxing fan. I knew him to see from coming into The Hare and Hound, but from memory he wasn't among the most hard-drinking of the officers, many of whom I would have known well.

He was returning to his car on the South Circular Road when a man came up behind him and shot him in the neck. The man escaped on the back of a motorcycle. Brian was taken to hospital in a coma. He never recovered and died eighteen months later.

Thirty years after he was shot, when Brian's family were making headway in attempting to identify his killer, the IRA provided them with a statement. 'In Portlaoise a brutal prison regime saw prisoners and their families suffer greatly. This is the context in which IRA volunteers shot your father.'

No doubt, it was in the IRA's own interests to attempt to justify shooting a prison officer in the south of the country, but it is also true that there was a harsh regime in the prison. Was it any wonder that some of the officers drank like fish to relieve stress and find temporary respite from what was going on?

These were not matters that greatly occupied me at the time. One that did was the awakening of my interest in girls, but even here there was no getting away from the prison. In my teenage years, I was briefly seeing a girl from the town. Her father was a detective, part of the inflated complement of guards who were now stationed in Portlaoise.

One night, she had a free house, and we were back there in all our innocence. Suddenly, the beam of headlights came through the front windows. If you've been a teenager in that situation, you will be familiar with the sense of panic. I took off out the back door. Moving cautiously around the side of the house, I thought for an instant I heard something in the darkness.

Then I heard those dreaded words. 'Don't move.' There was a gun pointed at my head.

My girlfriend's father had crept around the side of the house after hearing a movement – and who could blame him? In his mind, the disturbance was as likely to be an active service unit of the IRA as young McDonald enjoying his daughter's hospitality. As a way to get rumbled by your girlfriend's irate father, it doesn't come much scarier than that. Still, the lads in school were impressed with my exaggerated version of it the next day.

Another time, I was seeing the daughter of one of the prison governors. As with all teenage couples, the local cinema was the location for one of our dates. Except this was a date with a difference. While we sat there with our eyes on the screen, two armed detectives were at the back of the theatre with their eyes on us. They were detailed to protect the governor's family from the threat of kidnap. That was a night at the movies I remember well – for all the wrong reasons.

Once my Leaving Cert was done, I was all set to see Portlaoise through the rear-view mirror. The bright lights of Dublin were calling. Towards the end of my time in secondary school, I developed an interest in hotel management. From this remove, I don't remember what exactly sparked that interest, but I applied for a course in the College of Marketing and Design, part of the Dublin Institute of Technology, and got accepted.

The student life was all I wanted. Plenty of socializing and not enough time concentrating on the books. Despite that, I was still reaching for distant horizons. I left halfway through the course and headed for France, taking a year out. A friend had told me about this co-op in the town of Pau in the Pyrenees, where casual work was available, and the craic was only mighty. I headed there and had a blast for the year. It was a completely different experience for a young lad who had grown up in the midlands of Ireland. The campsite where I stayed was full of young people from all over Europe and beyond. For some reason there was a good share of them from the Lebanon, and the mix of cultures was a real eye-opener.

Every morning, we were picked up at the site and brought to one of the large farms scattered throughout the area.

We'd spend anything from a day to a few weeks at each farm, usually harvesting maize crops. We were well looked after on all the farms. In the evening, we cooked our own food and sat around. More often than not, somebody would pick up a guitar. There were no pubs near the site, just a café up the road. The whole place – the atmosphere, what passed for socializing – was completely different to what I had been used to at home. It was a year well spent.

Once I got back to Dublin, I finished the course in college. Following that, I did a spell as a sales rep for a drinks company. It was torture. Every day, I trotted off to work – visiting pubs, making my pitch – in formal shirt and tie, carrying a briefcase. That was bad enough, but my competition was lads from the big companies in Ireland, like Guinness. I'd arrive into a pub all smiles, with a few free T-shirts. The Guinness rep would have been there already, handing out a trip to Paris for the rugby. You can't compete with that.

Anyway, it just wasn't me. But through the job I met Liam O'Dwyer, who owned a pub in Mount Street, in Dublin. We got on well and when I decided to chuck in the repping job, he offered me a slot in the pub. Working behind the bar suited me better and had a big impact on my life. It was there that I met Valerie, from Roscommon town. She was nursing across the road in the National Maternity Hospital, in Holles Street, and earning a few bob extra working part-time in the pub. We hit it off – and the rest is history.

We got married, bought a house in Drumcondra, and before long a baby was on the way. The prospect of family life threw up a few questions for us. Do I stay in the pub business? What were the prospects? What about the unsociable hours? And how would that fit in with Valerie's work?

During my time in Dublin, I often ran into friends and

former classmates from Portlaoise who had joined the prison service. They appeared to be happy with their lot. The money was good, and there was a great sense of camaraderie among them. In 1988, the service began a new recruitment drive. I was alerted to it by a friend from school. What did I have to lose?

The interview was straightforward – and handy, too, as it took place in offices that were just across the road from O'Dwyer's. In fact, when it was over, my interviewers arrived in for lunch to the pub a few hours later. Maybe that was a good sign.

In any event, I got the letter telling me I was in. A new career beckoned. My life behind prison walls was about to begin.

2. All the Familiar Faces

On the morning of 2 February 1989, I kissed Valerie good-bye, left our home in Drumcondra and walked the short distance to Mountjoy Prison. My training was about to start. Heading towards the prison on the North Circular Road, I had an odd feeling that I was in some way going home. Later that day I would be heading back to Portlaoise where the training took place, but it was more than that.

I had broken out and seen a bit of the world. I had tried a few different lines of work. Yet it was as if I'd been destined to enter the service ever since I was a teenager growing up among the sons and daughters of prison officers. My family had no direct involvement in the prison service, but it was as if the town that shaped me was calling me back.

After entering Mountjoy, I was brought to a room where the new recruits were meeting up. Once inside the door, I saw all the familiar faces. Around a third of the class were from Portlaoise. Some I'd been in school with, others were brothers of schoolmates, or neighbours. Many among them were going into the family business.

We were brought down to the stores to get our uniforms. The fitting out consisted of the man in the stores sizing us up with a sideways glance and handing out what he considered to be the correct size. After that, we were sworn in, signed paperwork and filed on to the bus heading south.

Then, as now, training took place in the college attached

to Portlaoise Prison. When I joined, the building was known as Beladd House but has since been renamed Stack House in memory of Brian Stack.

The college was an eight-minute walk from the home where I grew up and where my father still lived. In late 1987, my mother died after a battle with cancer, so Dad was living alone when I was in training. On the first day, I made a pitch to the supervisor to allow me to stay at home while we were based in the college. He agreed, so that night while my fellow recruits were billeted in the college, I was tucked up in my old bedroom.

The following morning, I arrived down to the college to find the front door locked. It took me over five minutes to get in, and as a result the start of the day was delayed. The supervisor lay down a marker by telling us that a five-mile run was the punishment for the whole class. Needless to say, I wasn't Mr Popular on the first day's training. I got the message. At lunchtime I approached the supervisor and told him that I was grateful for the chance to live at home, but I'd decided to stay in-house. 'I thought you might,' he replied.

There were twenty-three of us in the class. Most were a similar age to me – in their mid-twenties or so. At the time, the service wanted to recruit men – and it was nearly all men – who had a small bit of life experience, rather than taking them directly from school. That changed over the years, but I can't say for the better. Entering the prison service at eighteen or nineteen is not healthy, to my mind. You do need some life experience in the bag in order to deal with all that the job can throw at you, not least the capacity to interact with the prisoners.

Just two of the class were women. Some might find it difficult to believe today that the ratio of men to women just over thirty years ago, even in a job like that, was ten to one. It is completely different now but, back then, sexism was an accepted way of life in the service. Women were assigned to a limited number of jobs. You would hardly ever see a female officer on the floor of one of the prisons, apart from the women's prisons in Mountjoy and Limerick. They might be assigned to a job in the governor's office, working as a secretary. Another typical assignment at the time was to put a female officer in charge of the cleaning party sent out every morning to pick up the 'bombs' of human waste thrown out through cell windows during the night. Another favoured role for female officers was to oversee the card decks, an ancient system of records where prisoners' names and numbers were arranged.

Things have changed hugely since then, but one constant remains – prisoners in general treat and regard female officers with a degree of respect not afforded to their male counterparts. It is a kind of badge of honour, even among some of the most notorious criminals in the system. That is not to say that female officers have never been physically attacked or hurt, but there is definitely a different attitude towards them from most inmates. Many of these prisoners grew up in homes with strong women. They have respect for their mammies and their sisters. A degree of that respect is retained in prison for women who are in a position of authority.

Apart from that, it is the case that female officers do bring some unique qualities to the job. They have the right instincts for what is required in a confined space where male feelings are intensified. They are better at making a connection with prisoners, and they often have a greater ability to strike the best balance between care and security. This is important. It makes life easier for everybody, including the prisoners, and helps reduce the stress which is an occupational hazard.

Anyway, back at Beladd House, we got cracking. On day one we were told we'd have to get into shape. The first item on the agenda was the short back and sides. We were all dispatched to Rocky Scully's barber in the town. I took off for a quick jaunt down memory lane. I was back in short trousers, my mother taking me through the door of Rocky's into this new world. Of course, I wasn't the only one. When the barber saw all the familiar faces from the town coming in, he must have thought it was a day from *Back to the Future*.

After that, we were straight into it. The training was intense. All day we had either classes or physical exercise of one sort or another. And despite the intense exercise, all of us – including me – put on weight over the three months. I entered training weighing in at eleven stone and gained two stone before passing out day. Much of that could no doubt be put down to the three square meals a day we got. We were well fed.

The classes brought us through everything we were likely to meet on the job, with a big emphasis on our obligations and duties under the prison rules. The rules dated from 1947, which tells you plenty about the lack of advance in penal matters over the decades, certainly up to 1989.

Looking back, some of it was off the wall. For instance, we were told how much milk a prisoner was entitled to and the weight of the meat that he could receive.

Then there was what passed in those days for control and restraint. C&R is a basic function in prison. Prisoners will resist. Some of them will sometimes become violent. One of a prison officer's basic functions is to exercise control and restraint. It does what it says on the tin: the prisoner must be brought under control and restrained from doing damage to himself or others. Today, with the advance of the concept of human rights, there are strict and sometimes sophisticated processes involved in C&R. Back when I was in training, it was all fairly primitive. You were shown a baton and how to use it, where to apply it with force, and where to refrain from using it at the risk of inflicting serious injury – or worse.

Every morning, we were subjected to a parade to get us into the habit of scrubbing up well. We were drilled in marching, in the importance of discipline, in basic stuff like putting out a fire using a shield. Then there was the legal side of things. Barristers were brought in to give a few lectures, and we also had a visit to the Four Courts in Dublin. We were taken around as if we were a class of wide-eyed schoolkids on a day out. We learned about warrants. Every prisoner committed must be on foot of a warrant, the legal document directing incarceration.

We got to know the different kinds of courts, from district up to the Central Criminal, which dealt with significant crimes such as murder and sexual assault. The barristers demonstrated how we would be expected to behave in the courts, including the removing and applying of cuffs. Then there was a tour of the holding cells in the Four Courts: small rooms where many of us were destined to spend hours freighted with boredom over the years.

The crucial aspect to court work from our point of view was the escorts. The worst thing that can happen to an officer outside a prison is to lose a prisoner. Security is paramount while the prisoner is engaging with the courts. Huge precautions have to be taken, and we were well drilled in all that.

One element of the training in which I developed a particular interest was the lectures from a psychologist. She explained to us the different kinds of prisoner we would come across, as well as the state of mind they were likely to be in at times – for example, just after committal. We were also told about the kind of dysfunctional family backgrounds most prisoners came from, and how that would feed into their psychological make-up.

During the three months of training, everybody spent a week each at four different prisons: Mountjoy, Arbour Hill (in Dublin 7, like Mountjoy, and close to Heuston Station), St Patrick's Institution for young offenders, and the training unit. The last two were both attached to Mountjoy but treated as separate institutions. At each prison you were assigned to an officer and shadowed him for the day. It's fair to say it was a petrifying experience, the first introduction to the inside of actual prisons. Here I copped a lucky break. Three of the institutions were in Dublin and I was able to go home and stay with Valerie. Most of my classmates had to book into B&Bs for the week, as I did for the stint in Cork Prison.

After three months, we were considered trained. The passing out was not the kind of affair you see for the gardaí in Templemore, with a minister in attendance, family invited, and the hats thrown in the air. It was instead very tame and just among ourselves. When it was over, we simply headed off down the town and went on the tear for the day.

We were fully fledged prison officers. Now, all we had to do was the work.

3. Learning the Job in 'The Joy'

Newly trained recruits apply for the posting of their choice. More often than not, they don't get it because the sought-after numbers are grabbed by those already on the job. As a third of my class were from Portlaoise, most of them applied to go home to their mammies. But there were no vacancies in that prison. Portlaoise was a choice posting where you could work all the hours God gave, but its unique function in housing subversives also meant that they didn't want to know you unless you had experience.

There was no mad rush among the class to head for Mountjoy. We had all been there on familiarization during training, and, if truth be told, it was a frightening place. Even during our brief week, the prison reeked of organized chaos. If I hadn't been settled in Dublin, I wouldn't have picked Mountjoy either. But I was living in Drumcondra, a fifteen-minute walk from the gates of the prison. Valerie was happy in her job, and we were at the early stages of family life. So, 'The Joy' was top of my list of postings. I knew I'd get it, because nobody else in the class applied.

Most of my classmates were packed off to Spike Island in Cork Harbour. There were always vacancies on Spike. Everybody who was on the island wanted to get off. The first thing you did if sent to Spike was put in for a transfer – even the lads from Cork did that. The big problem was that your workplace was removed from civilization. Every morning, you'd get the early ferry out to the island. Times varied according to the tides, so that was the first blow to routine. Then once you were on Spike you were there for the day, waiting for the tide to get the evening ferry off again. There was no popping down the town for a few pints at lunchtime: there was no town and no pub on Spike. Neither was there anything else that might pass for normality. Spike was Cork's version of Alcatraz, the notorious prison in San Francisco Bay. Because of its unpopularity, the place was often top heavy with the new boys and girls. It's most likely where I would have begun my career if I hadn't put in for Mountjoy.

While Mountjoy had its obvious drawbacks, a posting there did present one advantage. If you wanted to learn the ropes of the job, there was no better place. Throughout the service, those who had served in The Joy were highly regarded. Practically every day something happened, all adding to your store of experience. You could go a week in the more sedate prisons like Arbour Hill without ever having your adrenalin pumped up. In The Joy you went to work every morning wondering what the day ahead would bring. A posting there would also show you the ropes on court and escort work, as it was then the main committal prison in the state.

My abiding memory of my first years on the job in Mountjoy, which in some ways sums up the place in those days, is of the alarm going off. This would happen frequently, often several times a week. Once it sounded, all officers would rush to a little key room located near the circle, where cardboard boxes full of batons were stored. Somebody would already be there, emptying the batons out on to the floor. You'd grab a baton and follow the herd to whichever block was the source of the trouble. It could be two prisoners fighting, or an officer being threatened. You simply didn't know until you arrived at the scene.

These were the days before CCTV cameras everywhere. When I ended my career in the Midlands Prison in 2020, there were 1,200 cameras throughout the prison. When I started in Mountjoy in 1989, I could count on one hand the number of cameras. Off you went to the trouble, knowing only that a colleague had called and it was your duty to respond. Control and restraint in those days meant nothing more than swinging your baton and connecting with wherever you felt would make the greatest impact.

Afterwards, you just trotted back to your post. The gas thing about that system was that up to half the batons went walkabout after an alarm call. Stealing batons (or maybe 'misappropriating' is the better word) was all the rage in those days. We weren't issued with batons, and everybody liked to have their own personal one at hand.

Mountjoy is located in Phibsboro on the northside of Dublin. It was opened in 1850 and had the traditional design of the circle with four blocks branching out at right angles. There are three landings on each block, and another in the basement. Most people who know the prison at all will tell you it is long past the day when the demolition crews should have been invited in. Back in 2005, there were plans to abandon it for a spanking new prison out in north Co. Dublin. The site was bought and plans put in train, but it hasn't happened yet – although there has been speculation at various times since that the Irish Prison Service is looking at possibilities for the site.

When I started off there, the complex also housed the training unit for young offenders, St Pat's, as well as the female prison. Today, St Pat's is gone and the female prison has been completely reshaped into the Dóchas Centre for women. Back then, there was no real distinction between the institutions. You could be assigned to any one of them, depending on daily needs.

On my first day in The Joy, I was put shadowing a class officer, Mr Clear. Officers all address each other as Mr or Miss (except in Portlaoise where, for security reasons, and to this day, first names are used). Each landing has its own class officer, who is effectively in charge. All of the landings on a block are overseen by an assistant chief officer, or ACO.

My memory from that first day was an incident with a prisoner who was a small-time recidivist criminal whom I'll call 'Carrots Kelly'. Carrots and three others had robbed glue from the workshop, barricaded themselves in a cell and wouldn't come out. The first thing I learned was that they'd be left in there all day, until after lockdown. Any incident like this was to be dealt with only once all the other prisoners had been locked up, so there would be no distractions.

Just after lockdown some of the lads who were used to this kind of situation arrived on the landing. They were dressed in green overalls and wore helmets, just like the headgear you'd see on motorcyclists at the time. This was the wrecking crew. They went into the two adjoining cells and began swinging sledgehammers to break into the cell containing Carrots and his mates.

You can well imagine the kind of terror that was building up in the prisoners' minds. They were high on glue and the walls of their cell were literally falling in on them. Once the walls came down, the prisoners removed their barricade and ran for the door, desperate to get out. They knew what awaited them in the cell: there was going to be no escaping a beating. As Carrots came through the door, one of the officers swung a baton down on to his head. Now, Carrots was as bald as a coot, and his other outstanding feature was that he had a glass eye. Once the baton made contact, the eye popped out and bounced across the landing.

A medic was on hand throughout, as would have been standard during this kind of operation. Some of the officers began kicking the eye around. The medic was tearing after it with a tissue, shouting that it cost £300 and they should be careful. The officers' reaction to that was to smirk and kick the eye further along the landing. Carrots and his mates got a few more slaps and were then moved to another cell until the walls were rebuilt over the coming days. The incident kind of shocked me as an introduction to the system, but that was The Joy for you.

My first specific job, which Mr Clear assigned me, was to stand at the end of a landing in the morning as the prisoners came out with their overnight pots full of urine. These were poured into this big trough to be taken away. A glamour gig. Later, I was briefly put in charge of the cleaning crew. There was no in-cell sanitation, so if prisoners needed to do a number two in the night, they would wrap up their waste and throw it out the window into the yard. In the morning, a cleaning crew of prisoners, armed with shovels and wheelbarrows, went around picking up the 'parcels', as they were known.

An officer oversaw this crew, which was usually composed of Travellers. I have seen elsewhere that some believed the detailing of Traveller prisoners to this job was an example of bigotry or racism, but my memory is different. For the greater part, they volunteered to do what was a filthy job because the reward would be a few more cigarettes or a few extra pounds on their weekly cash allowance. They were willing to literally put up with the shit for that small bit extra.

The sanitary system was just one aspect of The Joy that

showed how far removed it was from society. The absence of in-cell sanitation was tolerated in a country that was becoming completely modernized, growing wealthy and gaining in self-confidence. This was around the time of the 1990 World Cup, the emergence of a highly educated work-force, lots of well-paid jobs, the throwing off of the shackles that had existed for decades. Yet behind the walls of the country's biggest prison, it might as well have been the 1940s.

The other outstanding feature of The Joy was the smell. It had its own unique pong, even compared to prisons in general. It's difficult to describe but it was a mixture of paint, dirt, urine, body odour and the musty smell of an old building. The smell actually got in on you. When I arrived home in the evening, Valerie would tell me to take off all my clothes as if I had been working in a radioactive facility. Like everything else, though, you got used to it. It's only in hindsight – after you've moved on – that it strikes you just how awful it was.

In those early days, it was inevitable that you would make mistakes. In the first week, I did something really stupid. Each evening the prisoners were given their supper, con-sisting of a currant bun and a glass of milk. They queued up to be served, with the milk being poured into cups from a large jug. I was handing out the buns and when it came to an older prisoner, he asked me for a second one. I told him he couldn't get it: the regulations stipulated that it was one bun per prisoner. He got a bit ratty, and some of the other prisoners made a few noises about me being mean. The senior man who was there with me told them to shut it and backed me up.

Afterwards, we were cleaning up and I was disposing of the leftovers, which consisted of maybe four dozen buns. I was scooping the buns into the bin when a senior officer came over and put a hand on my shoulder. 'What do you think?' he said. Here I was, throwing out all this food. What difference would it have made if I'd given an old fella an extra bun? It might have made a marginal difference to him, and it would have meant a bit less waste.

'That wasn't very clever of me,' I said.

'No,' he replied. 'But you learn from it.'

The point was that, despite my stupidity, the more experienced officers all backed me up. One of them could have intervened and told me to sort out the old lad, but once I had imposed my authority on the situation, they weren't going to undermine me in front of the prisoners. It was a small incident, but telling – and hopefully I did learn from it.

The culture of The Joy also made itself known to me from early on. There was a very 'us and them' attitude towards the prisoners, as if we were in a low-grade war of sorts. The character and background of most of the prisoners were very similar. They were mainly from Dublin's inner city, often having been reared in difficult circumstances, nearly always in poverty. Their range of choices in life was narrow. When that's the start you get, one of the more attractive routes for some is to turn to crime, a career in which imprisonment is part of the gig.

To these lads, we were the enemy. For them, maybe we represented the state, society, all the institutions that had conspired to send them down a road paved with disappointment and resentment. For our part, we were just doing a job, and it was important that lines were drawn early on to demonstrate who was in charge and that no threat to our authority would be tolerated.

*

One of the most enduring aspects of life as a prisoner became apparent to me from those early days. In society in general there is often talk about 'how easy they have it' and all that malarkey. The reality is that life on the inside is weighed down with the kind of boredom that can drive you out of your mind. You'd have to see it to appreciate the sheer tedium that fills every day. That is not to say that some, if not many, of these fellas don't deserve to be locked up, but to suggest that they have it easy is completely wide of the mark.

I became aware of the grinding routine during those first months when I 'floated', or was moved around, between jobs.

After slopping out the night's waste in the morning, the prisoners went down and collected breakfast. Contrary to what is portrayed on TV, in Irish prisons they eat in their cells not in a communal dining room.

After breakfast, they were locked up again and the officers went off to their breakfasts. Prisoners were given fifteen minutes to clean up their cells, bring down the breakfast trays, that sort of thing, then they were off to workshops, the exercise yard or recreation halls. Somewhere between a third and a half of the prisoners had some sort of workshop, training or education to go to. The rest just hung out in the halls or the yard. Many spent a good deal of time doing laps of the yard, just walking around in circles. In the halls, they might play pool or watch TV. The pool table was obviously popular, but there would have been one table for about every fifty prisoners, so getting on it was a bit novel. A small number of prisoners were kept on the landing to do the cleaning.

As officers who were floating, we would be given tasks by the ACO for that particular day. This could be supervision of visits, or carrying out duties in the yard, the recreation room or on one of the landings.

The visits started at 10.30 a.m. Remand prisoners were entitled to a fifteen-minute visit every day while sentenced prisoners had a half-hour per week. Time limits for the visits were strictly adhered to in order to keep the system ticking over.

At 11.50 a.m. all prisoners returned to their landing and the noise volume went through the roof, with lots of roaring and shouting and just general chat in that confined space. When it comes to noise in prison it's either near silence or a complete racket. The prisoners were then lined up to go down and get their dinner. If something was going to kick off, it would most likely start here. In The Joy it wouldn't have taken much for something to kick off: a stray comment, a resentment kept hidden for hours or days, or even something to do with the food. That was the time of day when we were most on alert, tension simmering just below the surface.

Getting through the dinner service itself was a smooth operation, with each block of about 150 prisoners getting their meal and being back in their cell within twenty minutes. Typically, in those days, dinner was fried chicken and chips or, on the odd day, sausage and chips. Once the prisoners had been locked up to eat, the numbers were checked and given in by the class officers. A chief officer then stood in the circle and called out the landings: A1, A2, A3, B1, etc. If the numbers were incorrect, it had to all be done again.

Counting prisoners is a big part of prison life. The men have to be counted every day to make sure that all are present. Whenever the numbers don't tally, all blocks have to be recounted. Everybody is held up, so getting your sums wrong means you are not going to be popular.

After dinner, it was back to workshops or exercise for the afternoon until teatime at 4.15 p.m. when the eating and counting were done again. One thing that struck me about the meal routine was that it was a long spell from four in the afternoon until eight the next morning with no food, apart from a glass of milk and a bun for supper.

After tea it was what was called a reserve period that was basically a few hours of down time, although many of the prisoners were on down time for the day in the recreation halls. Then at 7.30 p.m., they'd be locked up for the night. That was the routine: seven days a week, fifty-two weeks of the year.

It wasn't all fun and games for us officers either, but we were there to do a job rather than serve a sentence. Our days were filled with a combination of boredom and tension. Most of the time there wasn't a lot to do, beyond counting and keeping your eyes open. And then, every so often, you could nearly smell trouble on the way, so the tension cranked up.

There was another aspect to the job that I became aware of from early on: the power. It first hit me when I was on duty in the exercise yard, and it was time to bring everybody back in. I just let out a roar at the men to fall in, as I'd been told to do. The first few times, I was petrified, me barking instructions at these fellas. Some of them were hardened criminals who, in different circumstances, mightn't think twice about beating the lard out of me – or worse.

But they just responded to my barking at them by doing what I instructed. Similarly, on the landing at lockdown the same routine applied. I roared out that it was time and they just moved into their cells. Of course, there is a sense of power in that, no matter what way you look at it. There must be a similar feeling for young guards, who are given huge powers to use in the name of their jobs.

You are aware of the power that goes with exercising your authority – and some will no doubt abuse it – but that is the system. Anyway, I didn't have too long to dwell on the kind of power that came with the job in my first months in The Joy. Before long, I was assigned to a new duty with a category of prisoner that, even today, sometimes still haunts my dreams.

4. Dying Men Walking

By the time I started in Mountjoy, the AIDS virus had become a serious issue in the prison system. As with other global phenomena in those days, Ireland was a bit behind the curve, but by the late 1980s it had well and truly arrived, particularly among the groups in society on whom it really impacted.

One of the principal means of infection was the sharing of needles for intravenous drug use. Crime and addiction go hand in glove, so the prevalence of AIDS in the prison system ballooned in a short space of time. At first, everybody was scared stiff as there were all sorts of urban myths about how easily the virus could be transmitted. HIV, which led to full-blown AIDS, was reputed to be transmissible through actions such as hugging, touching, kissing, coughing or sneezing. Many people feared they could be at risk by even sharing a public or communal toilet, or by sharing a glass, cup or eating utensils. Little of this was based on fact, but in the early years, with so much widespread ignorance, it was understandable that such notions would take flight.

Put that in the context of a confined prison environment, which included unstable and sometimes violent individuals, and the sense of despair among those infected – and the potential for chaos – is obvious.

The virus and all it spawned changed prison life in some fundamental ways. When I started in the service, the most common and frightening weapon a prisoner could come at you with was the bog-standard chiv. This was typically fashioned from the handle of a toothbrush into which blades would be melted on two sides. Soon after the arrival of AIDS, the chiv was replaced as the deadliest weapon by the needle. Being stabbed or even just pricked by a needle containing infected blood could be a death sentence. Even if any test for AIDS came back negative, there was the psychological damage inflicted while waiting for the result.

Close physical contact with prisoners was reassessed. For instance, before AIDS there had been a standard response if prisoners refused to come in from the exercise yard – a not infrequent occurrence. You asked, then maybe cajoled, and finally, if that didn't work, you went out and forcibly brought them in. Confrontation of that kind presented a whole new threat if a prisoner could simply lunge at you and break your skin with a needle.

The response to that threat was to instead use water cannon when there was a stand-off in the yard. That got the prisoners moving and ensured you weren't taking your life in your hands. Alternatively, you just left them there until the night came on and they got cold. Eventually, they would be happy to get back to their cells.

The prevalence of the virus in Mountjoy was set out in an academic paper from a group of medical professionals based in St James's Hospital in Dublin.*

The paper reported that between January 1987 and January 1991, 168 known HIV-infected prisoners were held in Mountjoy. The figure represented 16.6 per cent of the total HIV-infected population in the state at the time, even though prisoners in general accounted for less than

* Murphy, M., Gaffney, K., Carey, O., Dooley, E. & Mulcahy, F. 1992. 'The impact of HIV disease on an Irish prison population'. *International Journal of STD & AIDS*, 3 (6), 426–9.

0.1 per cent of the total population of the Republic of Ireland.

Just under two-thirds of infected prisoners were diagnosed HIV positive while they were serving sentences, the average length of time served being a little over three years. The vast majority of infected prisoners who answered the questionnaire said they were imprisoned for drug-related crimes and that they had also been involved in drug use since entering prison.

'As the HIV epidemic unfolds in Dublin, increasing numbers of prisoners with symptomatic HIV disease will spend time incarcerated in Mountjoy,' the paper read. 'This will pose a considerable burden on prison and hospital medical services.'

I was somewhat fortunate in that I had far greater knowledge of the virus than most people in the prison. Valerie was employed in public health, so she filled me in, separating the facts from the urban myths and rumours. She calmed my worst fears. That kind of insight turned out to be hugely valuable when I was detailed to work with the infected prisoners, about eight months after I started in The Joy.

Early on, a decision was made that any prisoner diagnosed with the virus had to be segregated. There would have been huge potential for violence, and even chaos, if infected prisoners remained in the general prison population. But the problem was where to put them?

The answer was in the basement located under B block, a horrible place, where they would be far removed from everybody else. It had been used to house committals overnight until they were assigned a cell on the remand landing. As such, it was an awful introduction to prison, but at least it was for one night only.

41

There was room for about thirty prisoners down there. The place was dark and dank and rodent infested. The recreation room was very basic, with no pool table, just one small communal TV. There were no TVs in the cells, and no in-cell sanitation. The prisoners didn't work. There was no education or workshops. Even the basic cleaning of the landing was given to other prisoners brought down for the task.

The men spent most of the day locked up, alone with their thoughts which must have been filled with dread of the future. There was precious little integration or socializing among themselves. Meals were brought to them from the main kitchen, served on paper plates with paper cups and plastic utensils. Everything was disposed of after every meal. Exercise was taken in their own private yard, about twenty-foot square.

Apart from the awful conditions, a sense of dread permeated the air among the infected prisoners. How could it be otherwise? There was no effective treatment for the virus, so they all knew they were dead men walking. For those who weren't on short sentences, their final months until eventual transfer to hospital or hospice were to be spent in here, removed from family and friends, removed from the general prison population, living with the rodents.

The other location for AIDS prisoners was the separation unit, a small standalone block on the campus, which was a short walk across a yard from the basement. For years, the unit had been used to house prison officers' accommodation, but all that changed when it became necessary to find a location for this new category of prisoner. The unit when it was renovated had five landings with five cells on each and a small recreation room.

Naturally, it was the last place on the campus where any

staff wanted to work, so the gig was handed to the newest recruits. Eight months on the job and somebody decided that young McDonald would be well suited to take up the role.

I spent the best part of two years working between the basement under B block and the Separation Unit. Prison is a tough place at the best of times, but there is always some chink of light. Despite it all, you can have the craic, as you might in any workplace. Sometimes you can even have the craic with the prisoners.

All of that was very difficult in the basement. There were no redeeming features about any of it. Most of the men were addicts, yet their access to their illegal drug of choice was highly restricted. The entry and distribution of drugs in prison depends on the capacity to move around, pass the stuff on, share it. When a prisoner is removed from the general population, all the routes are effectively blocked. That greatly added to the heightened sense of despair being felt by these sick men as the darkest of futures rushed to meet them.

It is said that two things make a prison work on a basic level – food and visits. For the AIDS prisoners at that time, neither of these were in any way satisfactory. The food was awful, brought down from the kitchen in the main prison, often a long while after it had been cooked. Visits were very restricted, taking place in separate visiting boxes with a screen between the prisoner and their visitor. The news received from the world outside was also frequently dark. These prisoners were practically all addicts whose partners and friends were similarly dependent on drugs. Every now and again, word might filter through about somebody who had died from either an overdose or the virus.

We weren't given any training in how to deal with the

prisoners. Between the effects of the virus on them and the conditions in which they were being held, they were going half crazy. That, in turn, impacted on how they interacted with us. The possibility of violence breaking out was ever present, and few days were without some tension. On the one hand, we were aware that these were condemned men and we had to have sympathy for them and attempt to put our most humane foot forward. At the same time, their circumstances ensured that they were likely to lash out for the most innocuous reason – or none at all.

One of the more depressing aspects to what was a depressing job was the escorts across the North Circular Road to the Mater Hospital. That was where many of the men got the final diagnosis that they were in the latter stages of the condition, and it was time to get their affairs in order. Sometimes a prisoner just broke down on receiving the news. He might have been the hardest of men on the street, or even inside, but faced with his own mortality much of that melted away. Others simply reacted with rage, lashing out even there in the hospital, raging against where life had landed him.

Once, I was in the hospital with a prisoner and the doctor asked could I leave the room. He said he had news he wanted to deliver to his patient privately. The office was on the ground floor and there was a window through which the prisoner could have escaped. I was handcuffed to him and I addressed him rather than the doctor.

'You know I can't leave you here,' I told him.

The prisoner turned to the doctor. 'Am I fucked, Doc?' he said.

The doctor said things weren't good. He went through how the treatment wasn't working, that the man's liver was now in a bad way. He asked the prisoner how long he had to

44

serve, and the answer was three years. I could see by the look on the doctor's face that there was no way this man was going to see out his sentence. The doctor didn't tell him he'd be dead in a few months, but everything he said pointed towards that. The prisoner got the message. He knew that this would be his last visit.

Being present when a young man is given that news is no joke. It's an intimate conversation, yet you have no relationship with the person on the receiving end. You can offer the comfort of a stranger, for what it's worth. But even that is complicated by the fact that your job in that moment is to ensure that this man does not break free to spend some of his remaining precious time out in the general population.

On the long walk back to the basement the prisoner spoke about his kids – he had three of them, despite being only in his early twenties – and how he'd never get to see them grow up. What do you do in a situation like that? I listened and said very little, because there was nothing of comfort I could offer him. And at the same time, I had to remain alert in case he snapped and lashed out, as frequently happened when a prisoner was given his final diagnosis.

That man eventually went down the route that many others did. When he got too weak, he was granted temporary release, to be spent in a hospice out in Blanchardstown, in the west of the city. That was how most of the AIDS prisoners left Mountjoy. Each time, their going was marked by a darkening of the mood in the basement. Usually, a few weeks later, word would drift back that the released man had died, prompting another period of sombre reflection by the staff and the prisoners, the latter group no doubt wondering whose turn would be next.

Looking back now, it was all wrong. Those men were treated in an appalling manner. But people infected with

AIDS in society at large were also cast as some form of lepers at the time. With that sort of attitude prevailing outside the prison walls, the men inside were never going to be treated with empathy and due compassion.

A few years back, I ran into a female officer who had served with me in those years. She went on to have a stellar career in the service and was no shrinking violet. But as we chewed over the old times, casting our minds back to our younger days, working in the midst of so much wasted human life, she broke down. Some things can't be left at the prison gate.

5. Back Home in 'The Bog'

After two years or so in The Joy, I put in for a transfer. With the birth of our son, Simon, Valerie and I were giving serious thought to the future for our family. Did we want to stay in Dublin? We were living in a smallish two-bedroom house in Drumcondra. For what the house was worth we could buy a much bigger home down the country. We came to the conclusion that a move down to the midlands would be the way to go.

There was always a need for experienced officers in Portlaoise, so the fact that I had worked in The Joy would stand to me. The chaos, the constant action and the variety of work had given me a level of experience that it might have taken at least twice as long to arrive at in one of the other prisons. My transfer request was granted within two days of applying.

Apart from experience, the other reason I got transferred so quickly was that, being from the town, I would have been known by some of the staff in Portlaoise. If I had been from, say, Mayo or Kerry, and little was known about my background, further checks would have been made. With Portlaoise housing the subversives who were involved in political violence, there was always the huge fear that an officer would have Republican sympathies.

So, I was heading back home to 'The Bog', the name by which we knew Portlaoise in the prison service – it was in the midlands, a place that was full of bogs, many miles from The Joy in the heart of Dublin.

On the first day I turned up at my new posting, the chief officer asked where I had worked. I said at The Joy.

'That's grand, so,' he said. 'You know the job.'

On arrival in Portlaoise, in March 1991, we moved into one of the prison houses on the Dublin Road. This was really back to the future for me, as I knew these homes – they were where many of my childhood friends had grown up. We resolved from the outset that this was only going to be a temporary stop for us. Some officers lived in those houses for the whole length of their careers, but you would want a particular mentality for that.

The reality was you would be taking the job home with you. There was even an arrangement in place that some very low-risk prisoners – known as trustees – would come along every week to take out the bins, keep the grounds clean and generally service the place. You couldn't even get away from the prisoners at home. That life was never for us.

Even before we moved down, we had decided that we wouldn't live in the town. I knew from my own childhood that there would be simply no escaping the prison in Portlaoise. Doing basic stuff like shopping, or bringing the kids to an event, and particularly socializing ourselves, it was inevitable we would be encountering fellow prison officers on a regular basis. Back in those days, many officers wouldn't even change out of their uniform when going for a few pints after work.

Naturally, some of my best friends are people I have met on the job, and we do socialize. But that is different from engaging in constant casual encounters with fellow officers when you are off duty.

Even at that stage of my career, I knew that you had to consciously take steps to ensure you weren't consumed by the job. You could be working anything up to eighty hours a week, certainly before a brake was applied to overtime in the 2000s. You *become* a jailer. We have our own mentality, including a dark, even black, humour that lurks in most conversations. Paranoia is also a part of the jailer's condition. In work, dealing with potentially violent or unstable individuals, the possibility of violence is a constant threat. That keeps you looking over your shoulder, and when your day is done the mentality clocks off the job with you.

Whenever you meet up outside work, you inevitably talk about the job. That's the life, and if you are living in a relatively small place like Portlaoise – where the prison is a huge part of the town's infrastructure – things can get fairly claustrophobic if you're not careful. Valerie and I decided that removing ourselves from that environment, to somewhere within easy reach, was the way to go.

Our daughter, Róisín, was born soon after the move, and we spent most of those early months house hunting. Eventually, we found a lovely home a good twenty-minute commute from Portlaoise, with great access to schools and a really nice community.

Despite growing up in the town, and among officers' sons and daughters, I'd never got to know the prison. You simply didn't, unless you worked in there, and nobody ever spoke about what went on behind the walls.

The first thing that hit home was the level of security. In Mountjoy, you went through the main gate and three other gates and you were on to the landing in a matter of minutes. In Portlaoise, there were a total of fourteen security gates in order to reach the same place. There was a gate maybe every fifty yards, all of them manned. Some of the gates were solid steel, others had bars; some were sliding and others operated on an airlock system. Each gate could only be opened when the one behind was closed. This ensured that if an officer was taken prisoner there was nowhere to go.

At the main gate, you were subjected to a search. In those days, it was the only prison where officers were searched on turning up for work. The gardaí and the soldiers who worked there were also searched. If anything was found on the soldiers, they were arrested by military police. As far as the government was concerned, the subversives' reach was potentially all around.

The search was the standard pat-down of your body, but every so often you'd be brought to a room and swab samples for explosives would be taken. To be fair, this wasn't really paranoia. There had been escapes in the years immediately after the subversives had been transferred to the prison (following the helicopter escape in Mountjoy). Any attempt would not involve just a couple of prisoners but was likely to include dozens. In 1983, a total of thirty-eight prisoners had escaped from the Maze in the North. Anything of that scale in Portlaoise would be a political scandal and would probably attract accusations that the southern state was somehow complicit in supporting the IRA. For those reasons, in particular, Portlaoise was, throughout the 1980s and into the 1990s, the most secure prison in Europe, possibly even in the world.

Staffing levels were about three times higher than in any other prison in the state. There were twice as many officers in Portlaoise as worked in Mountjoy, even though The Joy was much bigger. For every two officers in Portlaoise there was one garda. Then you had the military, whose job it was to secure the perimeter of the compound, both on the ground and on the roofs. There were about a hundred soldiers there at any one time: one third on duty, another third on backup, and a third at rest.

There was no mixing or great sense of camaraderie between the three security arms of the state. Resentment usually simmered between gardaí and officers. As far as I could see, the gardaí considered themselves superior; but with overtime taken into account, the prison officers were earning far more. And then you had the soldiers. Their big resentment was being searched. Sometimes, one of them would inadvertently have something on him – even a bullet, which wouldn't be unusual in the army. Yet that would be recorded, and a big deal made of it, resulting in a black mark against his name. That was the extent to which security was iron-clad in Portlaoise, in those days.

While The Bog was guarded as if it held some of the most dangerous criminals in the world, the regime inside the walls of the compound was like no other prison, possibly in the entire world, at the time. Portlaoise did not have the classical design: a circle and spokes of a wheel. When I arrived, just two blocks – E and D – were operational. These were separate buildings in the compound. E block held the subversives and the heavies. The main subversive group was the Provos, kept on E3 and E4 landings. E2 was for the INLA and others who were non-aligned to the main subversive groups. These would have included the three men convicted of murdering two gardaí in Castlerea in 1980: Peter Pringle, Colm O'Shea and Pat McCann. (Pringle's conviction was later set aside, which means the guilty verdict is overturned, but the person can be tried again. As it turned out, Pringle was not put on trial for a second time.)

On E1, the landing at ground level, there was the crowd we called the heavies. These were the most serious ordinary criminals around at the time. It was decided they should be housed in Portlaoise due to the extra layers of security.

Among them were crime gang leader John Gilligan, serving a long sentence for drugs offences, and his associate Brian Meehan, who was convicted of the murder of Veronica Guerin, the *Sunday Independent* crime journalist shot dead in 1996. Also on E1 were two other garda killers, Peter Rogers and Michael McHugh, who had been involved in separate murders.

D block was a very different place altogether. It housed prisoners who were there specifically to carry out cleaning and maintenance duties around the prison. Unlike in other prisons, the men in E block in Portlaoise did not work. The subversives refused to work on the basis that they were political prisoners; and it was decided that organizing work for the heavies would be too much hassle from a security point of view.

As a result, these other, low-threat prisoners – the 'trustees' – were brought to Portlaoise to do that work. The incentive was extra remission: anybody who served on D Block got a third of their sentence off, instead of the standard quarter. They deserved it, because D block was a horrible place in which to live or work. It was the last remnant of the original Victorian building. The waft of the place alone was awful – musty, damp, leaden, as if the past was throwing up all the smells that had been part of life in the nineteenth century. Some of the cockroaches scurrying around were as big as mice. There were around forty prisoners kept there, four to a cell, on the ground-floor landing, D1. This was well beyond its capacity, but most of D block was in such a state it was uninhabitable.

These lads worked in the kitchen, kept the grounds maintained – including the prison houses on the Dublin Road – and did the cleaning on the landings. Occasionally, a trustee didn't behave himself or got into trouble of some kind or another. When that happened, he was simply put in a van and packed off back to one of the other prisons. For those who completed their allotted time in D block, usually between one and two years, the reward was relocation to an open prison with their extra remission secured. D block was demolished a few years ago – and not a moment too soon.

The subversives were largely left to their own devices. On each landing they had an officer commanding. All communication between prisoners and staff was conducted through him and the assistant chief officer for the landing. (In Portlaoise, every landing had an ACO, whereas in all other prisons there was only one ACO for a block, which would include three landings.)

When any problems arose, it was dealt with through those channels. The subversives took care of disciplinary matters themselves, with the officer commanding deciding on whether a prisoner deserved a punishment and what it should be. It wasn't unusual to see one of the subversives cleaning a toilet with his toothbrush, which was one of the punishments handed out. But it was their own leader who decided on the punishment, not the staff. There is a standard sheet – known as a P19, in the prison service – which records disciplinary offences among prisoners. Ordinarily, you could issue anything up to half a dozen in a week. In my seven years in Portlaoise, I never handed out a single one.

The subversives, through their officer commanding, had a say on who was allowed on their landings to do the cleaning. If they had a problem with one of the trustees, this was communicated to the ACO. At least once, I recall the problem being simply that the trustee in question was a Traveller, and they didn't want him on the landing. In such a scenario, changes were made to accommodate their wishes.

They locked themselves in their cells at night. Anywhere

else, an officer stood on the landing and roared that it was lockdown time. In Portlaoise, the staff member would just stand at the end of the landing and wait until their officer commander called them to attention and issued instructions, in Irish, to turn and march into their cells. And off they went. On E2 landing, which housed the non-IRA subversives, there could be three or four factions, all with their own officers commanding. They would each do the lockdown routine and, to be fair, they all had respect for each other, even if the scenario was a little surreal.

In other prisons, if there had been an issue of some sort during the day, the prisoners on a particular landing might decide they weren't going into their cells at lockdown. This would lead to them being forcibly put in. Not in Portlaoise. If a stand-off developed, they were just left out on the landing. In that respect, they were treated with kid gloves.

While security was obviously top of the agenda, a certain amount of leeway was given to the subversives. There was an unspoken agreement on temporary release, because the governor knew it would be honoured. When a prisoner was let out for a funeral, or if a close relative was critically ill, there was never a question of absconding.

A few tried it. And on those occasions, the prisoner would be sought out by the IRA and forcibly returned to the prison. There were times when a car would pull up at the gates of the prison with a few men inside. They would get out and open the boot, where the errant prisoner was confined. He would be walked to the door and handed over. Everybody played along, as if this was just the way things were done. Once inside, that man would then most likely be subjected to discipline from his own officer commanding. All of this was on the basis that anybody acting the maggot would spoil it for everybody else.

There were other liberties. It wasn't unknown for an order of two hundred steaks to be sent out to the local butcher on a Friday night. These were then cooked up – to specific instructions – and handed out. The whole thing was paid for out of funds the prisoners were provided with by their organization. This, of course, was usually acquired through robbing banks and protection rackets. Some of that money, obtained through criminal activities, was contributing to easing the plight of their political comrades who were locked up.

Similarly, if there was a birthday, a cake would be ordered and handed over. Then there were the times when we had some local team or other in to play a football match. An arrangement was in place that the visitors would be taken back to the recreation room on the subversives' landing for tea and sandwiches and a chat. This would be a complete no-no with any other prisoners, but it was done on the basis that no harm would come to the visitors, no hostages would be taken, and the event would not be used as a cover for an escape attempt. As with everything else, it was honoured because the prisoners viewed it all as easing the burden of serving their time.

Probably the biggest concession the subversives enjoyed was conjugal rights. If a prisoner was meeting a wife or girl-friend, you were told to bring a newspaper with you into the visiting box. You would know what was coming because the prisoner would be dressed in loose clothing, such as track-suit bottoms. (These were the days before half the country habitually wore tracksuit bottoms all the time.) You'd take out your newspaper and hold it in front of you to block the view of the couple. On the other side of the paper, they would get to it, having sex, but doing so in a manner that at least attempted not to be too obvious. There was no mad passion across the table, with cries of ecstasy, as you might get in a movie. Instead, he might sit on the chair and she pop down on top of him, trying, in the most bizarre circumstances, to be as discreet as was humanly possible. And behind my copy of the *Star* I would try hard to concentrate on the runners and riders for the 3.30 at Kempton, or become immersed in the latest transfer dealings in the Premier League, as if all this was the most normal thing in the world.

In that strange atmosphere, the relationship between staff and prisoners was also different. We didn't get to know each other on the kind of casual basis that was typical in other prisons. Relations weren't cordial, as we were part of the security apparatus of a state that these people didn't recognize. But at least things had improved hugely since the days when I was growing up in the town.

Claims of abuse in custody, whether in police stations or prisons, was often considered a propaganda tool by the Provos – and it may well have been. But it is the case that, in the first decade or so after Portlaoise began housing the subversives, a harsh regime was in place. This was referenced at a Prison Officers' Association conference in 1984, where it was alleged that staff in Portlaoise were being forced by senior management to use excessive force against the prisoners. One delegate to the conference was reported to have said, 'If Hitler wanted generals today he would find plenty of them in Portlaoise. After the war, the Nazis said that many of them were just doing their duty, and that is what the management in Portlaoise are saying today.'

This was before my time, but I heard the stories. And it's probably no coincidence that relations had begun to improve by the 1990s, as events in the North were moving slowly towards some resolution. By then, Sinn Féin delegates often visited the prison and were allowed to enter without being searched. Again, this was highly unusual, but it formed part of the unspoken agreement that if anything untoward was attempted, concessions such as these would be instantly withdrawn.

By the time I arrived, it's arguable that the power dynamic between staff and the subversives had shifted. Even in the weird atmosphere of minimal interaction between staff and prisoners, little things can happen: an ill-advised comment maybe, or an overly aggressive approach when searching a prisoner. After such incidents, the staff member might hear a few words, often delivered in passing, sometime later. 'Your young fella is doing well at left back in the under-13 team,' or, 'So it's Thursdays the wife hits Tesco for the weekly shopping.' The message is conveyed. Don't mess with us. We know where you live.

That kind of power was also on display if there was any issue with the heavies on E1. It might be as innocuous as a radio playing too loudly, but word would be sent down from the upper landings. *Stop it now.* And if it didn't stop, messages about family or interests on the outside would be conveyed. The heavies were hard men on their own patch, but they lived in constant fear of the subversives.

As officers we had to be extra vigilant about security. Small adjustments were made at work. As I've mentioned already, in every other prison, fellow officers address you by your surname in front of prisoners: 'Mr McDonald, you and Mr Murphy go to E block.' In Portlaoise, it was first names only: 'David, you and John take care of . . .' The less information conveyed to prisoners, the better. But, in reality, they knew everything they needed to know about all of us.

Then there were the escorts, nearly always to Dublin, usually to the Special Criminal Court in Green Street. The non-jury court had been set up to deal with the subversives and was located in an old courthouse, a ten-minute walk from the Four Courts.

More often than not, three vans would set off from Portlaoise, two of them decoys just in case there was an attack by the Provos. Part of the convoy also included soldiers. On the outskirts of Dublin, we would be met by motorcycle outriders and escorted all the way to the city centre, sirens blaring. Inside the back of the van, the usual inflated staffing levels applied. There would be three officers to guard the prisoner. The conversation would always be between ourselves, as the subversives wouldn't engage with us, even when going to and from court.

At the courthouse, you'd step from the van and the whole place would be as if the US president was in town: street cleared, army snipers on the roofs. And there you are in the middle of the whole operation, cuffed to the star of the show.

That was the work environment I joined when I moved back down to The Bog. There was a different kind of tension to what I'd experienced in The Joy. There was also a fair amount of boredom – a result of the circumstances in which the prisoners were held, as well as the inflated staffing levels. But now and again, things exploded, or new prisoners were brought in, and that was when the sparks flew.

6. The Defaulters

On Saturday 4 January 1997, six prisoners locked themselves into the recreation room in my old stomping ground of the separation unit in Mountjoy. Among them were Paul Ward, who was convicted of murdering Veronica Guerin (a conviction subsequently overturned), and Warren Dumbrell, probably one of the most notorious figures in Irish penal history. I had plenty of dealings with Warren, and few of those were of a convivial nature. There were also Éamon Seery, Edward Ferncombe, Stephen Galvin and Joseph Cooper. The last four were not as notorious, or dangerous, as Ward and Dumbrell, but all were involved in the siege that developed.

The whole thing appears to have begun with an attempt to stage a rooftop protest. But once the prisoners broke through the false ceiling in the separation unit, they encountered the concrete roof and were forced to abandon the plan. Instead, they just barricaded themselves into the recreation room in the unit.

Crucially, they held five prison officers hostage, releasing one of them within an hour. The prisoners quickly let it be known that if there were any attempts to storm the room, they would stab the officers with HIV-infected blood-filled syringes. Officers who were quickly on the scene spotted the syringes and noted that the prisoners were armed with iron bars.

A siege then commenced that would resonate down through the service, and the lives of those involved, for years afterwards. Once barricaded in, the prisoners began making demands. John Lonergan, the governor of Mountjoy at the time, described the episode in his memoir, *The Governor.*

'I knew after a short time that the prisoners were not an organized or unified group. Their demands were all over the place. Because of this it was a very dangerous situation; a group with an agreed set of objectives or demands is more straightforward to deal with than a group of individual mavericks. It was impossible to gauge what was really wanted and why they were holding officers as hostages.'

The officers were being terrorized. Ward was stomping around the room, wielding a syringe. At one point, he threatened to hang one of the officers if he wasn't given chocolate. Dumbrell put another syringe to one officer's neck and said the blood was infected with HIV. 'I have the virus since I was fifteen years old,' he told the officer. 'I don't give a fuck. I'll make you drink my blood.' He also threatened to 'slash and slaughter' the officers, telling them, 'You have ten minutes and you'll be done. I'll do one more every twenty minutes.' He forced some of the officers to kneel on the floor in what was later described in court as 'execution style'.

All of this was taking place in an atmosphere where the prisoners had a container of blood which they topped up from time to time. At one stage, Dumbrell was walking around the room with a syringe behind each ear.

On the second day of the siege, the prisoners made a rope out of shoelaces and sheets and slipped it around an officer's neck. One end of the makeshift rope was tied to a radiator pipe and the other to the main door into the recreation room. The door was locked but if an attempt was made to force it – and this was being considered outside – the prison officer would have been choked.

Later that day, Sky News broadcast that Ward was the leader of the gang. He told negotiators he would start beating the officers unless the report was changed. He also threatened that he would stab one of the officers with the blood-filled syringe unless he was handed in a copy of the *Irish Independent*. The prison officer was so scared, believing that the blood was infected, that he begged Ward to break every bone in his body rather than stab him with the syringe.

Eventually, the men made it known that they wanted transfers to another prison. They need have had no worries on that front. After what they had engaged in, they weren't going to be kept in Mountjoy. They also wanted a nun who was known to them to be present when they came out, to ensure they weren't beaten up. A solicitor was also called to the scene.

By Monday evening, they had enough of it. After eventually speaking to Lonergan, they agreed to give themselves up. Again, from Lonergan's memoir:

> First they released the prison officers one by one. They were told to throw away their weapons and come out with their hands up, which they did. They were escorted individually down the two flights of stairs. I walked down with the prisoners who had asked for me. On the ground floor they were searched by prison officers and placed in single cells. The siege was officially over. It was shortly after 11 p.m.
>
> The released officers were examined by a doctor and then seen by a team of psychologists led by Mountjoy's senior psychologist, Colm Regan. Shortly afterwards they were taken to a private room and reunited with their families. They continued to need counselling for many months. They paid a high price for doing their jobs as prison officers.

They certainly did. The siege had lasted over fifty-two hours. Afterwards, it was established that one of the syringes was filled with Hepatitis C-infected blood. Three of the four officers who had been subjected to the ordeal left the service soon after. The fourth never worked in close contact with prisoners again.

Down in Portlaoise we were keeping a close eye on events over that weekend. Naturally, the focus of much of our thinking was on the fate of our colleagues. The notion of being taken hostage by prisoners, not to mind some of the most dangerous specimens in the system, was terrifying. In those days, with the contraction of AIDS most likely delivering a death sentence, there was nothing that struck greater fear into the heart than a blood-filled syringe.

Once word of the siege filtered through to Portlaoise, I and many others volunteered to go to Mountjoy to help out in any way possible. I still had friends in The Joy and was on the phone to them constantly over the weekend, looking for updates. Sure, some of it was just being nosy, but we all did have huge concerns for the officers who were being held.

Our offer to assist – which I'm sure was replicated in other prisons across the country – was not taken up. That's the nature of prisons in this country: the management and staff in each are very self-contained. They don't want outsiders coming in to sort their problems, as if it might be seen as some kind of weakness. So it went that weekend, despite the obvious emergency that was unfolding in Mountjoy.

The other thing that heightened my worry was the fact that I was familiar with some of the prisoners involved and knew they were extremely dangerous individuals – capable, I believed, of almost anything. The end of the siege, when it came, was a huge relief right across the service.

The following day, five of the six prisoners involved were transferred to Portlaoise. Cooper was the exception. He was granted bail at one point and did a runner to the UK, only to return six years later.

When they landed in Portlaoise, the five men were initially put on E1 with the other heavies. I remember seeing two of them soon after their arrival, sitting on the landing, smoking and drinking tea. When some of the other prisoners passed there would be a high five for them. It was like, 'Well done, lads, you showed the fuckers.' The scene really got up my nose, and it was obvious that my irritation was shared by all the staff.

Within hours, everything changed. Calls were made and a letter drawn up by the Prison Officers' Association. The defaulters, as we knew them, were to be segregated away from E block on their own. Special arrangements were to be made, which would facilitate staff dealing with the men in a way that minimized danger. The management was informed that if this wasn't done by dinner time the following day, there would be a walkout from the prison.

I've never seen anything happen so fast. There was no way the management, or even their bosses in the Department of Justice, were going to face us down on this. The poor old trustees on D1 were cleared out of their cells that afternoon and shifted on to D2 and D3. Tradesmen were then sent in to clear out the cells in D1 of all furniture and fittings, to render each one completely bare. All that remained was a bed, table and chair. By 2 p.m. the following day, the five were moved on to that landing.

We had won that battle with management. Now, a regime was going to be put in place that would show these men they would not be getting away with their actions lightly. Nothing was said, officially or otherwise, but everybody knew that the usual standards would not be applied in any duty of care to these prisoners. In plain language, they would be taught a lesson, designed to ensure that no prisoner would ever again subject one of us to the kind of terror that had been inflicted on our colleagues in Mountjoy.

I worked on D1 with the defaulters for the best part of a year in what was a kind of surreal experience. The staff were based in the Portakabin next to D block. There were eight of us on at any one time, as every interaction with the prisoners required the presence of four officers. We wore riot gear for all interactions with them. As I mentioned earlier, the gear was horribly uncomfortable, consisting of full body armour, fire-resistant boots, shin guards, thigh guards, chest armour, pads for shoulder and neck, thick gloves and, most importantly, a helmet with a visor. We had to tog out every time we went on to the landing, as if we were entering premises full of radioactive material.

They were the only five prisoners on the landing which had capacity for twenty-five. Each was kept in their own cell for up to twenty-three hours a day. The only time they were allowed out was for exercise. This was supposed to be for one hour, but sometimes it was cut short. Other times, they were left out in the yard, sometimes in the rain, even if they wanted to come in before the hour was up.

The exercise yard had been made specifically to accommodate them. It was about thirty feet square in area, enclosed in steel panels. All you could really see was the sky. In the cell there was nothing to occupy or distract. After six months, the only concession was that they were allowed a transistor radio.

Whenever a prisoner was taken from his cell, he was handcuffed with rigid cuffs. These are specially designed cuffs with a steel bar which, if twisted, results in a huge bolt of pain shooting up the prisoner's arms into his body. Usually, they are used with a prisoner who has a record of being violent or unstable. The rigid cuffs were in everyday use with the defaulters.

When going to the yard, they put their hands through a hatch in the cell door to be cuffed. The same routine applied when they arrived at and left the yard. They were cuffed before leaving the cell for a telephone call and then accompanied by four officers to the telephone. There, the prisoner was uncuffed for the call, but the officers then stood around the prisoner while he spoke on the phone.

Meals were brought to their cells, often having been made hours before. Some of the delay was down to getting the meals across from the kitchen to D block. More of it was wanton disregard. Sometimes the food arrived over and we just held on to it for a while before bringing it in. *Fuck 'em.* That was the attitude.

Presenting the prisoner with his meal was an operation in itself. One officer would enter the cell with a webbed rope attached around his waist. In the event of the prisoner attacking him, the other three could then pull the officer back out to safety. This was not being dramatic, as attacks were regular. One time I brought Paul Ward his meal, he lashed out and kicked the tray from my hands. I was pulled back out by one of the officers while the other two ran in to subdue the prisoner with a few belts of a baton.

Mass was provided for the men on Sundays. At least two of them would attend and you have to assume that, as with the general prison population, the attraction of Mass was a break from the boredom rather than religious conviction.

Mass for the defaulters consisted of bringing a kind of mobile cage up to the door of the cell and walking the cuffed prisoner into it. The contraption was then wheeled along the landing to where the Mass was celebrated. This was one of the few times that the defaulters actually saw each other. The priest said the Mass and they stood in their cages listening. At Holy Communion, the Eucharist was passed in through the bars of the cage.

For the first few months, they weren't allowed any visits. But when that changed, the visits were a stilted affair, even by prison standards. The prisoners sat cuffed about eight feet away, across a table from the visitor. No physical contact of any sort was permitted. Two officers were in the visiting box at all times. As usual, the officers were fully togged out in riot gear. Apart from visits, the only engagement these fellas had with other human beings was through officers in riot gear. Hannibal Lecter would know the feeling.

We didn't engage with them. There was no conversation, apart from issuing instructions, and any requests were ignored unless deemed absolutely necessary. We were slowly driving them mad, inflicting constant and relentless psychological damage.

The reaction, more often than not, was violence. Warren Dumbrell, in particular, was constantly up for a fight. Often, he simply wouldn't come in from the yard for no other reason than he wanted a dust-up. He would just stand there, his body language saying, 'Come and get me.' And four of us would pile out in our riot gear and take him on. He appeared to enjoy the battle, as if it was the best form of escape from the grinding boredom. When we had him under control, he would be telling us where exactly to grab him in order to move him, as if he was an instructor rather than a prisoner out of control.

He was one of the strongest men I ever came across.

More than once, it occurred to me that if he had been born into a family in, say, a nice south Dublin suburb, he would in all likelihood have ended up playing rugby for Ireland. I could see him as an unstoppable tearaway back row forward, rampaging through the opposition. But he was born where he was, did what he did, and caused some horrendous damage to his victims. He was, and is, a very dangerous individual.

Then there was the time that I got scalded. In the evenings, the prisoners were entitled to two cups of hot water in order to make tea. On this occasion, I brought the paper cups into Éamon Seery and handed them over to him. He reacted by throwing the boiling water at me. Now, I had been careless in that I hadn't sealed the visor on my helmet, which left some of my neck exposed. He must have spotted that and decided he was going to exploit a weakness. The pain was horrendous. Immediately, I roared out and one of the lads pulled me back out of the cell with the rope while the other two ran in and gave him a hiding. They cuffed his hands and ankles and left him lying there on the floor overnight. I was off work for a few days and received £800 in compensation. The incident served as a painful warning that you must be on your guard at all times with these fellas.

That was life working with the defaulters: spending most of the day sitting around, interspersed with surreal encounters dressed fully in riot gear, awaiting an outbreak of violence.

The regime being imposed was known throughout the service and, I assume, throughout the prison population in the state. On one level, that was the purpose – send a message that what these men did will not be tolerated.

The conditions were raised during court appearances by

the five when they were prosecuted for the siege. During Dumbrell's trial the court was told that the European Convention on the Prevention of Torture, which operated under the Council of Europe, had complained in writing to the government about the conditions in which he was being held.

In 1999, Ferncombe's trial was told that he was being held in 'surreal circumstances'. He was locked up and handcuffed for twenty-three hours a day, which was described as 'pure punishment'. A psychiatrist gave evidence that during visits by him, Ferncombe was surrounded by four or five prison officers in full riot gear, even though the psychiatrist detected no aggression from him. Ferncombe had alleged to him that he was being held in these conditions on the instructions of the Prison Officers' Association, which had threatened to go on strike if he was not held handcuffed.

As is often the case with prisoners and prison conditions, little media or political attention was paid to these statements. By then, though, the situation had begun to ease. The point had been made; the defaulters had been dealt with.

Most of them were allowed to go back to E1 landing to be housed with the heavies. Even then, Dumbrell continued to cause trouble on a constant basis and was regularly transferred to a punishment block in Cork Prison. The others slowly integrated back into the general population.

Years later, I was on a course with officers from across Europe which was dealing with human rights in custody. I remember, at one point, being highly embarrassed when conditions in some notorious prisons were raised: I couldn't help thinking about the defaulters. I was afraid of telling the conference about the experience, which must have ranked with the worst examples raised by my fellow attendees.

But I've given an honest account of what happened. I

can say now that it was wrong, completely wrong. We didn't have to be so brutal. We were acting on our feelings towards those men, not our professional obligations. With hindsight, there is no doubt but that we could have shown them a little more humanity. I didn't feel like that at the time. I was part of the system that was determined to grind those men down, to make them suffer for the terror they had inflicted on our colleagues, to drive it home that nothing like that would ever be tolerated again.

7. Getting to Know the Heavies

In 1994, I was approached by the governor in Portlaoise to join the prison's education unit. As with many other things in the Irish Prison Service, the education unit doesn't necessarily do what it says on the tin. The role would involve me becoming a sort of jack of all trades, basically performing a whole raft of duties that fell outside the standard roles for officers. This would include helping out with education, but also involvement in the censoring of material coming into the prison, and in running the prison library. All of that would contribute also to introducing me to another aspect of prison life – getting to know on an individual basis a whole range of prisoners, particularly those who were removed from the general population.

By that time, I had already shown a bit of initiative by helping with the computerization of records. Computers were new to prison in the early 1990s – as they were, to a large extent, to society in general – and I had an interest in the area. It wasn't that I was madly ambitious to start doing new things but, as I've stated before, the long hours and the nature of the work in The Bog meant that boredom was constant. I just grabbed the chance to do something different.

When computers were introduced, two other young officers and I offered to help transfer all records from hard copy on to the new Prison Records Information System (PRIS). Many people today might find it hard to believe, but as recently as the 1990s all of the records in prisons were entirely paper based. We got to know the system and then became de facto trainers for the rest of the officers.

A lot of these lads didn't know how to turn on a computer, not to mind find their way around the PRIS system. They had been in Portlaoise for long years and were probably more focused on their career finishing line, rather than learning something new at this late stage. The biggest attraction for some of them was the chance to play solitaire on the screen. They loved that, and we even got to the point where we integrated the game into training in order to keep their attention. Apart from the training, the computerization of all the records was a huge job that took us the best part of two years.

Joining the education unit gave me the chance to focus on another aspect of prison life. Prior to the 1990s, education was at a very primitive stage in Irish prisons. In theory, education is supposed to be the element of imprisonment that involves rehabilitation. In practice, in my experience, behind closed doors rehabilitation is never given the status that it has in theory – although that has changed in small ways over the last thirty years.

When I was in Mountjoy, there was a workshop for training in woodwork, as well as some basic literacy classes. There was also a bakery where prisoners could learn the basics of that trade. There was nothing else by way of training for a useful qualification.

Things began to improve in the early 1990s, and the credit for trying to modernize things goes to one man, Sean Wynne. Sean, a thorough gentleman, was employed by the local Vocational Education Board (the VECs are known as Education and Training Boards today). From what I recall, his primary training was in career guidance and he started developing all sorts of education programmes in Portlaoise and in other prisons across the state. One characteristic he had – which came in handy, considering how many people he had to deal with – was that he never forgot somebody's name, no matter how brief an encounter he may have had with them.

The thirst among prisoners for learning, or bettering themselves, in Portlaoise was greater simply because it housed the subversives. Among themselves they were encouraged to take courses. The other thing about the subversives was that many of them were politically aware and eager to learn more about politics, economics and that kind of thing.

The location for classes was a group of prefab cabins that had been set down in the exercise yard and enclosed with a fence. Prisoners would be escorted to the cabins where classes of up to maybe eight were taught. Some of the classes were one to one. At first, there was basic stuff like literacy, and the teaching was done by nuns on a voluntary basis.

Sean Wynne oversaw the professionalization of the service with the employment of qualified teachers. More emphasis was put on the sitting of Inter Cert (now Junior Cert) and Leaving Cert exams. The exams were sat at the precise time they were taking place in schools all around the country. We might have had up to a dozen or more students for the Leaving. In most cases, they wouldn't be sitting the seven or eight subjects that the majority of students do, but these were baby steps. Remember, prisoners have among the lowest education attainment rates in the country.

One of my duties was to protect the teachers. This basically involved keeping an eye on things, making sure that none of the prisoners got out of hand. Once or twice, I saw a prisoner making a pass at a female teacher, nothing too serious or certainly not intimidating, but I would have stepped in and told him to cop himself on. As I said earlier, there was a strange honour among many prisoners towards women that belied what some of them had done or were capable of doing on the outside.

One important task I had while on the education unit was to take possession of the Leaving and Inter Cert exam papers when they were delivered to the prison a night or so before scheduled exams. Some of the prisoners who were due to sit an exam would often rib me and try to find out what was in the paper. That was one thing, but I also had officers coming up to me who would have had children sitting the exam, offering me a few bob to give them a sneak preview. I never did. You can imagine the scandal that would have ensued if it ever got out that the son or daughter of a prison officer had been given a sneak preview of the paper.

When the results of the state exams came out, we would have a little party for those who had sat them. The teachers, the officers who helped out, and the prisoners would all get together in one of the prefabs and break open the Coke and Fanta and hand out a few cakes. Now and then, it wryly occurred to me that a few of these lads might be more used to having parties on the outside with the kind of coke that isn't a soft drink.

As with most other prison matters, the subversives did their own thing. They had their own get-together on their landing rather than with us.

I know that victims of crime might feel anger at the thought of perpetrators, and particularly those who had been violent, celebrating a Leaving Cert result with a party. But these were small events in the big scheme of things. The everyday grind, the deprivations and indignities of imprisonment are huge by comparison.

*

Another duty that I sort of wandered into was that of censor. During my time in the education unit I was deployed to work in the office censoring the material that was sent into prisoners. Primarily this was letters (I'll explain the kinds of issues that arose in personal letters in Chapter 9: Love in a Cold Climate), but it also involved evidence being sent to a prisoner in advance of his trial. The material for court cases was, for the greater part, fairly mundane. Most of this would have been CCTV footage about a suspect's movements or what had occurred in the vicinity of a crime. Sifting through that kind of stuff for hours without end is no joke. Then there were the crime-scene photographs. Many of these were from scenes of violent death and could be really disturbing.

One case I always remember was that involving John Gilligan, who was tried – and ultimately found not guilty – for the murder of Veronica Guerin. The evidence gathered from the trial included video footage from a hotel in Spain in which Gilligan and his co-accused, Brian Meehan, and others were celebrating. The footage had shots of the gang in a jacuzzi on the balcony of their hotel room. I've never come across a jacuzzi on a balcony but I'm sure it is all the rage among the super-rich. And here were these fellas, toasting themselves with champagne, living it up in the lap of luxury, making gun gestures with their fingers a few days after Veronica Guerin had been shot dead. At one point during the footage, the group of them burst into a chant celebrating the fact that the journalist was now dead.

Other footage for that case involved the gang attending a concert in Spain in which they were ensconced in a cordoned-off VIP area. In attendance with them were women, some of whom were topless and unlikely to have been life partners, or any kind of partners, of the gang members. There was also another film in which there was nudity. Gilligan nominated me to view the footage because, I suspect, he didn't want the video circulating among officers who might enjoy viewing the footage of the topless or naked women with whom he'd been consorting. He obviously came to the conclusion that, if he had to trust anybody on the staff, he would trust me.

The other duty of the censor's office was viewing the material coming and going from the subversives. These lads weren't stupid – they were never going to be leaving themselves exposed with anything important to their campaign – but there were often small nuggets of information that we passed on to the gardaí in case it was of any use.

Frequently, we would photocopy letters to or from their fellow campaign members on the outside. This would then be passed on to detectives in Portlaoise as part of a standard arrangement. Much of it was mundane but there was stuff like, for instance, swapping agendas for an upcoming visit. News of this would alert the detectives to the time of the visit, and they would frequently be in situ outside the prison, monitoring and photographing the visitors who arrived. Those in Sinn Féin and IRA circles liked to characterize this as harassment. But from the law enforcement point of view it was intelligence gathering, and I had no problem in playing a minor role in that.

Deployment to the education unit also gave me the opportunity to work in the library. I was put forward to receive training as a librarian, but the only place that was available was in Belfast. Today, Belfast is another city a few hours up the road. Back then, when the Northern violence was raging, it presented a high-end risk to the life of anybody involved with the security forces, including prison officers.

The training involved regular trips to Belfast, where I attended the college over two days. Each time I was due to travel, I had to contact the RUC and let them know my dates. Once I was over the border, I was followed. I have to admit that I didn't always recognize my tail, but I am certain they were there.

The RUC organized the bed and breakfast accommodation for me, and it was never the same place twice. I was told the name under which I was booked in and was never asked to produce identification by the people running the houses. Secure off-street parking was always provided because car bombs were a weapon of choice at the time. Once parked, the car was to be left there for the length of my stay in the city. Each day, I went off to the college, attached to Queen's University, and all was grand there. In the evenings, I was told where I could eat and, if I wanted a few pints, where I could drink. Again, I was under the impression that I was being watched at all times for my safety.

At the end of the stay, I was again accompanied to the border, where sometimes my escort might flash headlights or wave as I crossed over back into the Republic. I never met or even spoke to the detectives who were guarding me during that period. It was surreal, and a bit weird, but fortunately it worked. I got through it, safe and sound.

The library in particular, but all of the other duties that I took on, brought me into greater personal contact with a whole range of prisoners. Despite working in close proximity to these men every day, there was not then, and to a large extent still isn't, much of a personal relationship between officers and prisoners. In some ways, this is understandable. We must be on our guard at all times, conscious of security, thinking of both the potential for escape or any threat to the safety or welfare of fellow officers. That's just the nature of the job. There is, however, room to form some kind of a working relationship. That cuts down on the stress and it also invites officers to come into contact with the human side of prisoners.

One figure in the service who deserves credit for promoting that kind of engagement is John Lonergan, who was for over twenty-five years the governor of Mountjoy. John wouldn't necessarily have been my favourite governor. Like some of my colleagues, I thought that at times his attitude maybe favoured the prisoners over staff, but I would give him huge credit for being the first senior figure in the service to emphasize the importance of proper engagement with the prisoners. This wasn't about being nice, or making them feel at home, but about making life easier for all of us. Before Lonergan introduced that kind of culture, talking to prisoners on any human level would have been considered weird, attracting questions as to why you'd be doing it. But it made a huge difference in how prisons were run.

One thing that I learned early on about any relationship with prisoners is the importance of trust. If you tell a prisoner that you'll call his girlfriend for him, if he needs something or whatever, then you better do it. You can tell him that you won't or can't do it, and that's grand. But if you say you will, you have to follow through, because otherwise you fracture trust. That is huge to the prisoner. He is locked up. You are one of his few routes to the real world, even if it's something small, like he asks you to pick up a sweatshirt and runners that have been left in the circle for him. You can say no. But if you say you'll get it, then you have to do that. Every slight takes on huge significance to the man who is locked up. You might simply forget, but that's not how he will see it.

I have seen officers promising something and not

following up, and the change of attitude in the prisoner is noticeable. Nothing may come of it, but just keeping your word means that you're not piling needless stress on him And if a prisoner is stressed or resentful, that may come to haunt you or one of your fellow officers down the line. Trust is absolutely massive in this respect.

The jobs that I got to do in Portlaoise during those years certainly exposed me to prisoners in ways that wouldn't otherwise have been the case. For instance, the subversives wouldn't so much as give us the time of day on the landings. They simply ignored us as much as possible, considering themselves to be prisoners of war; we were merely an irritant in their long-term project. Behind the closed door of the library, it was a different matter. Alone and removed from their comrades, they were willing to engage on the same kind of superficial level we all do when circumstance throws us into contact with other people. When I found myself dealing with some of these people on a one-to-one basis, they were perfectly approachable and friendly.

Then there were the interactions with some of the most notorious criminals in the state. Today, Christy Kinahan is a well-known figure because of the international crime cartel he heads up, or at least did. The Kinahan Cartel is reputed to be one of the biggest importers of drugs into the state, and gang members have been involved in dozens of killings. When I dealt with him, Kinahan was serving a sentence in Portlaoise for drugs offences. He must have been taken very seriously at the time, since he was housed in our prison rather than Mountjoy, but he was a model prisoner. He was never any trouble, always well turned out, his clothes impeccable. (I can see how, in later years, the tabloids would give him the moniker 'the Dapper Don'.) He was polite and straightforward and always trying to better himself through education. In particular, he had an interest in learning foreign languages.

A few times, he asked to have a word with me in his cell, to explain that he was doing a particular course and wanted to get a book on this or that from the library. As with any other prisoner, I assessed what he wanted and decided whether or not it could be provided. When it couldn't, he would simply ask why and then accept the outcome. I don't think I ever saw him angry – and most certainly never violent. He was a model prisoner.

Am I surprised by what he appears to have become, once he served his sentence? Not a bit of it. The way he handled himself in prison suggested a high intelligence, including emotional intelligence, an attribute that is rare among prisoners. He knew what he had to do, to get to where he wanted to go. And it would appear that he arrived there and became enormously wealthy and powerful as a result. At the time of writing, he has not been apprehended and is among one of the most wanted criminals in this state.

Another figure who looms large in Irish organized crime is John Gilligan. In the early 1990s, his gang was reputed to be the biggest importer of cannabis into the state. The gang operated for the greater part below the radar, until Veronica Guerin's investigative work in the *Sunday Independent* exposed their activity. At one point, Veronica confronted Gilligan at his home on a stud farm in Co. Kildare, where he assaulted her viciously. He was due to go on trial for that assault when Veronica was murdered. If found guilty, he would most likely have been back in prison for another stretch.

While he was found not guilty of her murder, his right-hand man, Brian Meehan, was convicted for the crime. Meehan was reputed to have driven the motorcycle used in shooting Veronica dead on the Naas Road, in June 1996. Another gang member, Paul Ward, was also found guilty, but ultimately that conviction was set aside.

Gilligan arrived in Portlaoise after being arrested in the UK. He was, from the word go, Mr Charlie Big Potatoes on E1. In the first instance, it was obvious that he had access to plenty of money – and if money talks in general society, then it sings like an angel in prison. He was, particularly in the early years, adept at splashing out to feed a good shower of the inmates on E1 with the odd steak.

He also had plenty of female admirers. They used to visit separately from his own wife, who was also a regular visitor. Often, Gilligan would ask that sums of money be taken from his account and given to one of the visiting women.

His status as top dog was enhanced by his physical power. He was a small man but, by God, was he powerful. I saw him in action, once or twice, and there is no doubt that in his prime he would have been difficult to get the better of in any sort of a fight.

When it suited, he could turn on the charm. At times, you couldn't shut him up. Whenever he was brought to Dublin for one of his court appearances, all he talked about in the back of the van was the horses. A little interaction is grand – it breaks the journey and eats into the boredom – but Gilligan just wouldn't give it up. It was as if he was trying to torture us with his knowledge of the runners and riders at some race-track in the heart of England one rainy day the previous September.

He could spend hours in the company of an officer and be his best pal, full of amiable chat. And then, that evening, if something blew up on the landing he could just as easily attack the same officer and be every bit as vicious as his reputation suggested. Violence was never far away with that man.

Once, thankfully, he used his power to my advantage. One day, I was on E1, at the bottom end of the landing, and something kicked off up the other end. Around nine or ten prisoners got violent and began throwing pool balls and generally lashing out. It was totally unexpected, but the way it unfolded left me effectively trapped with a gang of these men in the mood for trouble. I remember looking up the landing and thinking *I'm fucked*. For some reason, I wasn't afraid. I knew that if they turned on me, it could get very ugly, but I got ready for it.

Sure enough, I was spotted within seconds. The man who saw me looked, in that instant, as if all his Christmases had come at once. This was Paul Ward, a member of Gilligan's gang and one of the defaulters whom we had treated so badly over in D block. He and I had also had words at various points, even since he was put back on to E1.

He had a large chiv in his hand and he came towards me. I knew that if he got stuck in, four or five others were likely to join him. But then as he approached, Gilligan let out a roar at him. Ward said something back, but Gilligan became more adamant, telling him that I was not to be touched. John Gilligan actually saved my bacon. Ward backed off and, within minutes, the stairgate was opened, some officers poured in and things were brought under control.

Why did Gilligan do it? We certainly weren't buddies, but I'd had dealings with him over stuff like viewing the videos of his gang in Spain. I believe the real reason he brought Ward under control that day was just to demonstrate he had the power to do so. He was, in his own way, letting me know that he had the power, that he could decide who got a hiding and who didn't, that he ruled the roost on E1 landing. While he saved my bacon that time, I have no doubt that if I was standing at the gate of the prison, the only barrier to him escaping, and if he was armed, he wouldn't hesitate to shoot me.

For a long number of years, Gilligan ruled the roost on E1. But following a controversy over a prisoner phoning *Liveline* on Radio One, in 2007, a new governor was brought in who clipped his wings. Ned Whelan was a no-nonsense type of governor. He was known as 'Nike' after the company's advertising slogan 'Just Do It'. Before Ned came in, whenever Gilligan was meeting the governor there was a chair there for him to settle into for a conversation. Ned got rid of that chair. He told Gilligan that he would stand before him when they were interacting. That was just a small gesture, but it was one that came to typify Ned's dealings with the man who thought he was the real power on E1.

Brian Meehan never gave me any trouble. He was always polite, and always crafty. If he wanted something done – another prisoner assaulted or whatever – he got somebody else to do it for him. He was a flash character, too; he wore a Rolex watch that was valued at around €60,000.

I remember his partner bringing in their son as a baby, soon after he began his sentence. Years later, the same baby was visiting as a grown man. That's just an indication of how long some of these men are in prison, what they miss on the outside, and how the world merely carries on while they lead a kind of suspended life.

When I suffered a loss of my own, I saw a particularly human side of Meehan. In 1999, my brother, Matthew, was killed in a road accident. Matthew was a prison officer as well, based in Mountjoy. The accident happened one morning as he and some colleagues were on their way to Dublin from Portlaoise, where he lived.

I took the death badly. We were the only siblings in our house and had always been close. My mother had died some years before, which had tightened the bond between us and our dad. As with many of my generation, I didn't deal with the grief in any proper way and instead drank more than was healthy for a few months.

Soon after Matthew's death, I was out at the general office one day when Meehan was being escorted by two officers. I have no idea why he was there, but when he saw me he walked over and put his hand out, offering sympathy for my loss. I hesitated to accept his hand. We were in view of other officers, and I didn't know how it would be perceived – and frankly, I was a bit taken aback – but I did then shake hands with him.

'It's a stressful time for you,' he said. 'If you're on E1, believe me, you'll be as safe as houses.' He was letting me know that I wouldn't get any trouble on the landing. Nobody would be using the bereavement to have a go at me or anything like that.

The episode was unsettling. As with Gilligan, I believe that if I stood between Meehan and freedom, he wouldn't hesitate to kill me if he felt he had to. And yet, he was also able to show he had a human side.

The man who was believed to have actually shot Veronica Guerin was Patrick 'Dutchy' Holland, another member of Gilligan's gang. He was a career criminal and had associations with all kinds of subversive groups. He was arrested in 1997 and, on foot of statements from one of the gang who had turned state's witness, he was charged with the murder. The charge didn't stick, but Holland was also charged with drugs offences for which he was sentenced to twenty years, though this was reduced to twelve on appeal.

If you didn't know his true nature, you'd let Dutchy Holland mind your grandchildren. In prison, he came across as the nicest person imaginable, a grandfatherly type of figure.

You could have any kind of a conversation with him about any subject and he would engage fully. On a day away in court, you could talk to him about politics or football or foreign travel, and he was well versed in everything. There would be no pulling at the cuffs, as you'd have with some of them, or trying anything silly.

He was very mannerly, without being in any way over the top. Unlike many prisoners, you felt totally at ease in his company. He was never in any sort of trouble. If something kicked off on the landing, he would simply go back into his cell and have no part of it. He always dressed respectfully and always had a smile on his face – a genuine smile, not the kind of smirk some prisoners would flash, as if they knew more than they were letting on.

In fact, the biggest problem with Dutchy was that you had to keep reminding yourself he wasn't just a prisoner but probably the most dangerous criminal in the whole of The Bog. It was that easy to become friends with him.

This was also the man about whom John Gilligan is reputed to have said he was the only person he feared. Holland was a cold-blooded killer. Despite his amenable exterior, no prisoner would ever try it on with him. Despite his outward appearance, you never knew what he was like behind closed doors, where he would be organizing for other prisoners to do his dirty work for him. It was nearly unbelievable, yet all too real, that this man was some class of a sociopath who killed people for money.

He was released from Portlaoise in 2006, and resumed his former ways. A year later, he was arrested in England on suspicion of planning the kidnap of a businessman for a £10m ransom. In 2009, he was found dead in his cell in Parkhurst Prison on the Isle of Wight.

8. The Border Fox, the Cop Killers and the Garlic Man

Among those who were classed as subversives there were a few whom I got to know. The most fascinating of these was Dessie O'Hare, who was known as the Border Fox from the days when he was a notorious criminal operating under various flags of convenience. He had been responsible for some horrendous crimes and was lucky to still be alive.

O'Hare was from Keady, in Co. Armagh. He had grown up during the Troubles and joined the IRA while a teenager in the mid-1970s. Over a few short years, he gained a reputation as a ruthless gunman. He was wanted by the RUC in connection with a number of murders but was never charged. Over the course of his activities, he had been involved in shoot-outs with security forces. Twice he was in a car when another occupant ended up dead: the first occasion when the vehicle crashed, and the second when his accomplice was shot dead by the security forces.

His short career came to a juddering halt when he was arrested in Co. Monaghan, in 1979, in possession of a rifle and spent eight years in Portlaoise Prison. He was released in 1987. By then he had fallen out with the Provos and joined the INLA, and then fell out with that outfit and set himself up with a crowd he created himself, which he called the Irish Revolutionary Brigade. This consisted of himself and a few others he'd met in prison who were apparently unhappy with the strictures imposed by an organized outfit.

On 13 October 1987, he and three others kidnapped a

Dublin dentist, John O'Grady. Their target had been O'Grady's father-in-law, Austin Darragh, a prominent doctor and businessman. The gang were after money for whatever cause they claimed to be espousing. The kidnapping set off a big manhunt, and over the following weeks there were random sightings of the gang. Meanwhile, O'Hare was making phone calls to organize the ransom of £1.5m. At one point, frustrated at the lack of progress in getting a response to his demands, he ordered one of his men to cut off O'Grady's fingers. The tips of two of the dentist's fingers were duly chopped off.

After twenty-three days, during which time the kidnap victim was moved around the country, his ordeal came to an end in a house in Cabra, in Dublin, when gardaí were checking out a routine matter. One of the gardaí was shot in the confrontation, but not fatally. The rest of the gang were captured at the scene, but O'Hare wasn't present. The search went on, and as the details of what O'Grady had been subjected to gradually emerged, O'Hare's notoriety grew. At one point, he was spotted in Cavan with his wife. After an apparent argument, he fired shots at her from a shotgun.

Eventually, a tip-off suggested he was staying near Kilkenny city. A roadblock was set up. As the car approached, the gardaí and army opened fire. Most of the bullets were aimed at the driver, a man by the name of Martin Bryan, who was shot and killed instantly. It was never fully established whether Bryan was operating as a favour to the Border Fox or doing so out of fear for his own life. O'Hare had been thought to be driving but was in the passenger seat. For the third time in his short life, he was riding in a car where another occupant died violently. He survived, albeit with a bullet-riddled body. He was sentenced to forty years in prison.

In Portlaoise, O'Hare was kept in the basement under E block – the Base, as we called it. The Base was located under the South End. Just to explain the geography of the South End (because this becomes relevant later in this chapter), when you enter Portlaoise and go through the multiple security gates, you end up arriving in the circle. Even though it's called the circle, it doesn't follow the classical design of prisons, where you have blocks all radiating out from the centre, like the spokes of a wheel. It's simply a large area from where things are organized. To the left are the four E landings: 1, 2, 3 and 4. And to the right is the South End. This small landing was used for those subversive prisoners who were not accommodated on 2, 3 or 4 – either because they wanted to disassociate themselves from their former comrades, or because the commanding officers for the Provos or the INLA didn't want them on their landings.

The South End had about ten cells, with only five or so occupied. Garda killers Peter Rogers, Michael McHugh and Noel Callan were on the South End. All had originally been condemned to death for capital murder but had their sentences commuted to forty years in prison. Just off the landing there was the radio room, which was the centre of communications within the whole Portlaoise compound.

Beneath the South End there was the Base, which had four cells. This was where O'Hare was kept, initially on his own. Otherwise, the Base was used to house newly sentenced prisoners for brief periods. Once a subversive was sentenced by the Special Criminal Court, he would be brought to Portlaoise and kept in the Base until such time as the officer commanding of the IRA – or the INLA on E2 – decided whether or not he would qualify to be housed on their landing. This might involve waiting to hear from their own organization on the outside, and during that time the newly sentenced prisoner would await his fate.

O'Hare was in the Base, for the greater part, on his own. I got to know him through bringing him to the library on E4 landing. That was an ordeal in itself. He could only be brought there when everybody else was in their cells, usually during the teatime lockdown after 4.30 p.m. I'd have to check with the ACOs that there was nobody at all in sight – including cleaners – on the route from his cell up to the library. It was a two-way thing. O'Hare was deemed highly dangerous and volatile. If he encountered somebody against whom he held a grudge – usually going back to his days outside – he could attack. Equally, there were many among the regular subversives who had it in for him; this was often because of something he had done, or was suspected of doing, to someone close to them, during his brief reigns of terror. So, the coast had to be completely clear when Dessie and I made our way from his cell in the basement to the library on the fourth floor – or, at a later stage, across to the school. In fact, the most lasting memory of my interaction with O'Hare is the hassle we always had in moving him. Most times, it was quite an ordeal to ensure that he could have absolutely no interaction with anybody, on his way there or back.

When I first encountered him, he wasn't speaking to anybody. He communicated only through notes. He would pass a note if he wanted something, and usually keep a copy of the note himself. In the library, he would ask me to photocopy his notes if he was making a request to the governor for something, in order to keep the originals himself. As far as I know, he went through a period where he only communicated with his wife on visits through the written word.

Soon after I first got to know him, there was an incident in which he wrote to the class officer that he didn't like beans, yet he was given lashings of beans every day at tea-time. Whether or not it was the quality of O'Hare's handwriting, but the word went to the kitchen that he *did* like beans, so he got even more the following evening. Naturally, he went bananas when his food arrived, under the impression that he was being goaded over the beans.

He sent for me, because we had struck up a sort of rapport by then, and explained – in writing – what had happened. I was there, responding to him by talking, and him coming back with his scribbled notes. Anyway, I passed on the word as I understood it, and the following day there were no beans. I went down to see that everything was OK, and he passed me a note on which was written 'We sorted'. That was a kind of a rite of passage between us, and he trusted me on some level afterwards.

In the library, he would write down what books he wanted. At one point he was immersed in studying the Bible, and he often wrote to me to get him some informa-tion from the internet, to which I had restricted access. During those periods in the library there was just the pair of us there, and the door was locked. In the event of an emergency, I could press an alarm, assuming I could reach it, but it might be another twenty minutes before the key would be retrieved and help arrive. I never thought about it much at the time, but had things kicked off I might have been in trouble.

You could have the craic with him, up to a point. One time, while he was still in his silent mode, when we were returning from the library, we encountered an ACO who commented, 'Everything alright with the prisoner?' And I responded with, 'Perfect, sir, except this fucker has talked the hind legs off me for the last hour.' That brought a hint of a smile to Dessie's face.

His other interest was yoga. We organized that he could attend a yoga class on his own after everybody else was locked up. This took place in the school where classes were held during the day. I'd bring him over to the yoga instructor – who was a music teacher during the day – and sit there and tell him he was great as he went through the motions. That all might sound a little daft, but I had to be there. O'Hare was into yoga long before it was fashionable, and he was also a very early proponent of mindfulness, but he was also a highly dangerous individual. You just couldn't allow him to be in that room on his own with a civilian.

On one occasion he showed me his bullet wounds, some of which went right through his arm. He was certainly lucky to be alive.

There was only one time when things got heated between us. The day after the journalist Veronica Guerin was shot dead, in June 1996, we were in the library and I remarked that what had happened was shocking. 'She deserved it,' O'Hare replied. That got my blood up. The whole country was outraged at the murder of a young mother who was just doing her job, and I was no different. I challenged him and told him he was out of order, but he came back at me with more of it. I had a choice then. Do I keep ramping it up – as might be the case if, for example, I had got into a heated row with somebody in the pub or a gym or wherever. Or was it worth it? Where could it lead with this unstable individual, who was considered so dangerous that he had to be removed from the whole prison population? I backed down. What was there to gain by trying to argue about basic morals with this man?

Things never got worse than that with him. He never

threatened me, and he trusted me. Despite that, not once did he ever talk about the things he'd done, nor did he ever broach the possibility of regret.

O'Hare was released in 2006, under the terms of The Good Friday Agreement, having served eighteen years of his forty-year sentence. In 2019, he pleaded guilty to false imprisonment of a family in their home and to leading what the court heard was a 'disturbingly violent' attack on another man. By then aged sixty-three, O'Hare was sentenced at the Special Criminal Court to ten years in prison with the final three suspended. Passing sentence, Judge Tony Hunt said that the violent side of O'Hare's personality was not in remission and that the threat to society had 'not completely abated'. The judge added that the court did not accept that the offending was 'isolated', even though O'Hare had applied himself positively to some aspects of his life over the previous thirteen years.

In 2020, when I was retiring, I did my last hurrah in Portlaoise and the Midlands, just going around to say good-bye. O'Hare was the last prisoner I visited. He was an ordinary criminal by then, on E1 landing with the heavies, no longer part of the subversive set-up, which had been totally transformed over the previous twenty years. I had worked with him for so long, and when he came back in the previous year, I'd met him again. So now it was time to say goodbye.

He met me on the landing and invited me into his cell. He offered me a cup of tea, but I declined. 'I'm out the gap,' I told him. We chatted for a while – his silent phase was a distant memory by then – we shook hands and I left.

A prisoner who was also considered to be highly dangerous was the man who eventually shared the basement with

O'Hare, Peter Rogers. He got involved in the Troubles in the North as a teenager and was picked up when the British government introduced internment. He was held on the *Maidstone* – a ship in Belfast Bay – from which he escaped, in 1972. He left the North then, resettling in Wexford, but he continued with his IRA activity. Locally, he was known to the gardaí.

On 13 October 1980, a bank robbery took place in Callan, Co. Kilkenny. Immediately, it was suspected that this was the work of the Provos, and gardaí were alerted to keep tabs on known activists. In Wexford, Gardaí Seamus Quaid and Donal Lyttleton were given the task of tracking the movements of Peter Rogers. They spent most of the day looking for him, but with no success. Then, that evening, as they were returning to Wexford Garda Station, they came across his van, which they knew by sight, parked near a quarry. Donal Lyttleton told the *Irish Independent* in 2020 what happened then.

> I asked Peter Rogers, who was personally known to me and Seamus, to account for his movements earlier that day. He told us that he had been up hunting in the mountain. Seamus opened the back door of the van and we saw a number of sacks that appeared to contain potatoes. Seamus and I got in to search the van. I saw some holdalls hidden behind the sacks. It was later established that the holdall bags contained explosives and guns. As we were about to open the holdalls, Peter Rogers ordered us out. He was standing at the back of the van, holding a gun.
>
> I went towards Peter Rogers with arms outstretched and I asked him to put the gun down.

What then occurred is recalled in the citation for the

Scott Medal for bravery, which was awarded to Donal Lyttleton and posthumously to Seamus Quaid. The citation reads:

> In his [Rogers'] efforts to get them to the quarry, Det Garda Lyttleton was kicked twice by the driver, who was later to state in evidence that 'Lyttleton wouldn't move – he was coming towards me and I fired'.
>
> Det Garda Quaid drew his gun and there was an exchange of shots, during which the driver [Rogers] was wounded. Det Garda Lyttleton escaped but Det Garda Quaid was mortally wounded.

Donal Lyttleton managed to contact Wexford station for assistance. Rogers, who had been shot during the exchange, was arrested soon after. He was sentenced to death for capital murder, but this was commuted to life imprisonment.

When I arrived in Portlaoise, Rogers was housed on the South End. He would have started out there, as he was initially condemned to death and so removed from the general population. But I don't know why he stayed there once the sentence was commuted. Either he decided he wanted to disassociate himself from his fellow Provos or else they wanted shot of him. Either way, he was on the South End in the company of a few others, including Michael McHugh and Noel Callan, two men who had also killed a guard.

Michael McHugh was from Crossmaglen, Co. Armagh. In June 1985, he and Callan robbed the labour exchange in Moore Hall, Co. Louth. They were making their escape on a motorcycle when it crashed and garda sergeant Patrick Morrissey gave chase. The garda was unarmed and McHugh fired at him, wounding him in the leg. McHugh then went back, leaned over the garda and shot him in the face.

Both men were sentenced to death but this was then commuted. I got to know McHugh, but he was not somebody to whom you could warm. At one stage of his case, I had to censor some of the evidence that was sent in to him, which included crime scene photos. The images were particularly distressing, with a lot of blood around the dead garda's face. When I handed McHugh the photos, he grabbed them from my hands with a sense of glee, as if these were personal items he would treasure. I found that disturbing.

He wasn't too bright and didn't engage much with anybody. A few years back, there was a piece in the newspaper about state papers from the time when he was convicted and sentenced to death. There was a line that included the following: 'McHugh is regarded as being highly intelligent and reckless in the extreme when committing crime.' The latter part I could well believe. But if he was really bright, he was good at hiding it in The Bog.

In any event, circumstances threw McHugh and Rogers together in the South End. From what I could see, they had some form of a friendship, or at least an understanding, both having killed gardaí in separate incidents, both associated in one form or another with the Troubles, yet both removed from the subversives in prison.

However deep or shallow their friendship, it eventually ran into big trouble, because Rogers hatched a plan to kill McHugh. Rogers was big into gardening and spent a fair bit of time in the prison garden, which gave him access to fertilizer. He used that to make an incendiary device, a task which would have been no bother to him from his background in the Provos. This he set up in McHugh's cell, connecting it to the light switch, such that when McHugh came in and turned on his light the device would explode and cause a fire. Once the device exploded, Rogers planned to throw a heap of rubbish into the cell to ensure that the fire caught hold quickly and spread. Rogers would then shut the cell door, trapping his former pal inside and condemning him to death.

The first part of the plan worked out. McHugh entered his cell, turned on the light, and . . . *bang!* He did manage to get back out of the cell, but Rogers was waiting for him and a fight broke out between them. While that was going on, the fire spread out on to the landing and the smoke in such a confined space engulfed everything within minutes. Immediately, the alarm went off and an operation to evacuate everybody from the whole block got under way.

I was on duty on the roof at the time, in the company of three soldiers. The alarm was going like the clappers, smoke was pouring out of the windows, and all the prisoners were being herded out into the exercise yard. The smoke was so thick from where we were that we thought the fire must be on E4 rather than down at ground level. The soldiers had their guns cocked. For all we knew, this could be a diversion in advance of a big breakout. The prison had this huge machine gun installed on the roof, which was capable of taking down a helicopter. There was complete confusion and tension for several minutes. To make matters worse, communication was completely down because the radio room in the South End was engulfed by smoke and had to be abandoned.

Prisoners and staff on the South End all made their way to the emergency exit at the far end of the landing. This led out into a small exercise yard, but the military were reluctant to allow the door to be opened. In Portlaoise, any kind of movement – an officer going up on the roof, a prisoner being brought across to the school – could only be done after informing the military. Now, with communications down and everybody coming out of the buildings, they didn't know what was going on. In the end, the military relented and everybody trooped out the door, hands held high.

There was one person left inside, however, whose life was now in extreme danger. Officer Tom McQuinn was that day detailed to occupy the stairgate, which was effectively a cage from which the occupant controlled the gates leading to the landings on E block. Every shift, the officer was locked in by the ACO as a security measure: to protect him from prisoners but also to ensure that, in the event of an escape attempt, the prisoners wouldn't have access to the gates. The only person with a key to the stairgate was the ACO who locked it. And now that ACO was out in the yard, having left his post in panic over the smoke. Inside, right across the landing from the emergency exit, McQuinn was facing into a horrible death.

At some point, another officer out in the yard, Derek Brennan, grabbed the keys from the ACO, wrapped a towel around his head and plunged back into the South End. He crawled across the landing, staying low in an attempt to avoid the worst of the smoke, and made it to the stairgate. He opened the locks, and then he and McQuinn turned around and crawled back out, sharing the towel to keep the smoke at bay. There is no question but that Brennan's bravery saved McQuinn's life. Both men were taken to hospital suffering from smoke inhalation. (The joke afterwards was that Tom got a £20,000 work-related injury award while Derek got a medal worth a fiver.)

There was a delay in getting the fire engines into the prison, despite the fire station being just across the Dublin Road. It was strict protocol with the army that any time the alarm went off, there was complete lockdown – nobody in or out of the main gates. This was the army's brief, and they stuck to it rigidly. So, it took a few vital minutes before the firemen were allowed in to tackle the blaze. Eventually, they were admitted, and things brought under control, albeit after a fair bit of damage to the landing. It was down to nothing but sheer luck that somebody didn't die that day.

The post-mortem after the event was swift. The obvious thing might have been to charge Peter Rogers with attempted murder and criminal damage, but where would that have led? It would have involved an investigation and subsequent trial in the Special Criminal Court, with all the security and upheaval. And what would the outcome have been? The prisoner was already serving forty years. What more could be added to his sentence, and would it make any difference to how long he would be spending behind bars?

Instead, a decision was taken to just put him down in the Base with Dessie O'Hare. I got to know Rogers, mainly through escorting him and guarding him in the garden, where he spent much of his out-of-cell time. He was good at gardening, and I've still got some trees that he planted, which I was allowed to buy for a nominal sum at the time.

One night, I spent the best part of four hours at the door of his cell as he went through the events of the evening he shot and killed Garda Seamus Quaid. He didn't admit it explicitly but went through the details in a way that was conveying exactly what happened without actually saying he did it. He talked about how the two gardaí had stopped him, and everybody knew each other and had the craic initially, with him offering the gardaí an apple. Then the shooting occurred and Rogers himself was injured. I can still remember the way he described the burning pain of the bullet wound he felt as he was trying to escape. He also spoke of how he should have masked the Semtex in the van, to ensure that it wouldn't have been discovered in the search.

I got the impression that he really wanted to get the whole thing off his chest. Here he was, effectively removed from the general population for trying to kill another prisoner, about which he didn't appear to have any regrets, yet going into the details of how he had killed a garda, and he appeared to certainly regret it and feel for the victim's family.

Peter Rogers was released in 2011. He was reported to have sent an apology to the family of Seamus Quaid which, understandably, was rejected. He later stated that he purposely did not return to Wexford in order to ensure that Seamus Quaid's family would never have to come across him in any casual encounter.

Three other men who were condemned to death for capital murder were Peter Pringle, Pat McCann and Colm O'Shea. On 7 July 1980, following a bank robbery in Ballaghaderreen, Co. Roscommon, the getaway car was intercepted by gardaí who had been alerted. Detective Garda John Morley and Garda Henry Byrne were both shot dead in the incident. Two men, Pat McCann and Colm O'Shea, were arrested at the scene. A third man had been present and a manhunt was launched to apprehend him. Some weeks later, Peter Pringle was arrested in Galway and charged with the murder.

All were convicted in the Special Criminal Court. After their death sentences were commuted to forty years, they settled into life in Portlaoise, initially at least, removed from the general population of subversive prisoners. McCann and O'Shea were both strange individuals with whom it was very difficult to make a connection. Neither was a difficult prisoner, but they just didn't seem to be operating on the same level as most of the others.

Pringle was a different kettle of fish. He was obviously intelligent and he read up on the law to organize an appeal in his case. The most notable feature about him was that he ate a lot of garlic. Whether or not it was for a condition, I don't know, but you'd smell him long before you'd see him. He kept his head down for the most part, was interested in books, and, from what I could see, had a very high opinion of himself. He had one particular female visitor who used to come in regularly. The pair of them would often sit for long stretches and just hold hands, saying very little.

Eventually, Pringle's legal journey brought him to an appeal court, which resulted in his conviction being set aside. This was done because there had been an issue between two gardaí during his interrogation, which had not been made known at his trial.

When he was released, it was a quiet affair. He had always been a loner, as far as I could see, and there was no real hoopla for his release. That was in contrast to the usual routine – prisoners would often applaud when somebody was getting out.

After his release, his lawyer immediately demanded an interim payment of £50,000 as part of a large compensation settlement sought on the basis of Pringle having spent fifteen years in prison.

It was open to the state to retry him for the crime, but there was a problem: one of the gardaí who had been involved in his original interrogation had since died. For years after his release, Pringle claimed he was being prevented from bringing an action to have his case declared a miscarriage of justice. But one way or the other, such a hearing never took place, and he never received the compensation to which he said he was entitled.

Pringle met and married an American woman, Sunny Jacobs, who had been on death row in the USA but was eventually exonerated. The two of them have campaigned far and wide against the death penalty. They have told their story together on stage and have both written books.

McCann and O'Shea were released in 2013, following a court ruling that they were entitled to remission on their forty-year sentences.

9. Love in a Cold Climate

Let's talk about sex, because we have to at some point or other. When a convicted man – or woman – enters prison, they become officially celibate. In Chapter 5 (Back Home in 'The Bog'), I recalled the unofficial conjugal rights that the subversives enjoyed, in which the officer in the visitor box picked up his copy of the *Star* and tried to concentrate on the sports results while on the other side of the newsprint a man and woman engaged in sex, albeit in circumstances that were rushed and hardly conducive to real intimacy. Still, needs must. The subversives were granted that privilege because of their status as so-called political prisoners; they knew that the ordinary criminal would be entitled to nothing of the sort.

Another arrangement with the subversives was an agreement that their wives and partners would not be searched during visits. They didn't want prison officers physically touching their wives and girlfriends, which was perfectly understandable. In return, the subversives agreed to be strip-searched themselves after every visit, in order to ensure that nothing was passed over. They knew that if they attempted to smuggle anything in, their visitors would have to be searched from then on. As with the arrangements for temporary release for family bereavements, an element of trust was required. The prison authorities knew that each man could be trusted because if one stepped out of line, it destroyed everything for the others – and they wouldn't have that.

Sometimes the enormity of imprisonment is lost on the general public. Among the rights forfeited is the right to experience physical intimacy with another consenting adult. This isn't just about sex, but merely being in the company of a loved one, whether that is lying in bed, sharing a meal, or engaging in any of the activities that a couple enjoys, and which bring them closer. Simple acts like hugging and kissing are no longer available. The only connection retained is through phone calls and the weekly visit, which by its nature is a stilted affair.

For many men, a poor replacement for the absence of physical female company is a poster on the wall of their cell, to excite the imagination. The most common poster in the 1970s was Athena's 'Tennis Girl' – a shot of a female tennis player without underwear. The photograph is taken from behind as she stands in the tennis court with her left hand on her buttocks. If the woman in the photo – who was only eighteen when the shot was taken – had received royalties for every copy of the poster that was on display in prison cells in this country, and I presume many others, she'd have been on a nice little extra earner for all her adult life.

Separation from the world outside takes a toll on the prisoner, but what is often forgotten is that it also takes a toll on the partner. If the sentence to be served is relatively short, couples can manage it. The real problems arise when there is no prospect of the prisoner being released for years. And, more often than not, these are prisoners who are the most volatile and unstable to begin with. How the partner on the outside reacts to the situation is crucial. There may be loyalty and genuine love, rooted in a long-term relationship. Or, in the case of serious criminals, maybe the partner had grown accustomed to a high-end lifestyle that has now come to an end. Does she move on to someone else, who will provide her with the kind of lifestyle to which she had grown accustomed?

I saw a couple of examples of these situations later in my career, when I was working in the Operational Support Group.

The wife of one of the Limerick gang criminals showed up for her regular visit, one day. Her husband was, and still is, serving a life sentence. She was quite obviously pregnant.

'Have we a problem?' I said to her.

'I don't know about you,' she replied, her hand going instinctively to her bump. 'But maybe I do.'

'Are you going to tell him?' I asked.

'I think I have to,' she said.

Immediately, I could feel the tension. What was supposed to be a routine visit had suddenly become an operation in which our priority was to get this woman in and out of the visitor box safely, and to get her husband back to his cell with the minimum of fuss.

I phoned down to the visitor area and told them to have two officers in the box for this visit, and another two outside waiting for this prisoner once it was over. As I feared, he did go absolutely apeshit. On a human level, you can understand it. Later, that man put out a contract on his wife – not to have her killed but beaten up. We came across this through intelligence and passed it on to the gardaí, who gave her a warning. To the best of my knowledge, the contract was never fulfilled.

By contrast, another Limerick prisoner from the same scene, who has by now been locked up for over two decades, received a weekly visit from his girlfriend through nearly all of that time. Her loyalty was quite astounding and, in different circumstances, you might say touching. Whatever arrangement they came to, in terms of her physical needs, was their own business. But I suspect that it was probably left unsaid between them, and that suited both.

Their significance to each other meant that, at one point, a rival gang was targeting her in order to get at her man in prison. He organized for her to be put up at a Traveller encampment where it was felt that she would be safe. Again, to the best of my knowledge, no harm came to her. Quite obviously, their relationship was a significant affair for both of them.

In Portlaoise I had a unique insight into affairs of the heart – and the body – through my role in the censor's office. One aspect of the job was to read letters, and this included the intimate ones sent in to prisoners.

With the subversives, the only issue that generally arose was a wife or partner complaining to her imprisoned other half that another man had designs on her or was hassling her in some way. Alarm bells go off at the sight of such material. For the man in question it could be a death sentence or, at the very least, he might end up getting a severe hiding. In those instances, I passed it on to the gardaí, who would tell the man in question that he was playing with fire and he'd want to cop on to himself. By and large, the partners of subversives stuck in there while their partner was serving his sentence.

For the ordinary criminal, the contents of a letter could easily spark off major mood swings that might bring trouble. For instance, she writes that she is going on holiday to Spain for a week. He reads this and his imagination immediately rewinds to the holidays they had together, and now she is going without him. But who is she going with? He reads and rereads the letter, and maybe previous ones too, looking for clues. Is somebody else on the scene? What is she holding back?

Small things like that can easily get into the prisoner's head and he can react accordingly, either sinking into a depressive mood or lashing out. Sometimes, there can be a cumulative effect, with that kind of resentment carrying over into a visit, and suddenly there may be an issue between them. Sorting out a domestic row, as we all know, can be no small thing. But try doing it when one half of the couple is locked up.

Of course, what really used to set things off were the 'Dear John' letters. It was routine for partners or wives of prisoners destined to be behind bars for years, or possibly decades, to decide they had to move on. Put yourself for a minute in the prisoner's shoes. Rejection is never easy, whether it comes during the teenage years or in the course of a relationship that has developed over a long term. Most of us know at least one friend or colleague who has gone through a divorce, and we understand the mental toll that takes on people.

Now imagine going through all those feelings in a confined space: where there will be no moving on for you, where you will be locked up in your cell at night with thoughts of your ex getting on with her life in the company of another man. Imagine all that in the context of many prisoners who would have very little or no emotional intelligence to begin with, and who very often came from unstable backgrounds.

After a while in the censor's office, I got the hang of how to handle the 'Dear John' letters. First off, I would contact the class officer on the prisoner's landing, letting him know, just so he could keep an eye on the man. The class officer would pass that information on to the night guard, and the prisoner might be put on special observation on the basis that he could be a suicide risk at the moment.

Sometimes, I might hold back the letter for a few days just to ensure that any staff on the landing were aware it was on the way, giving them time to prepare. That might seem over the top, or even an infringement of the man's rights by delaying passing on an intimate letter. But it was being done for no other reason than attempting to manage what was going to be a tough situation in human terms, and possibly a risk to security.

Another tactic I developed over time was to contact a mate of the prisoner in question. That wasn't always possible, depending on the people involved, but if it was, I might pull a friend of his aside and have a quiet word, tell him that the bad news was on the way and he might want to keep an eye on the man in question.

None of it was easy. But this is all part of life within prison walls to which most people don't ever have to give much thought.

For some prisoners, their relationships developed in a different way, at least for a while. In the 1990s, the video recorder was all the rage. There were a few recorders on E1; these were passed around, and a system was in place where one of us would go out to Xtravision (for those of you who remember video shops!) on a Friday to get a couple of movies for the landing.

The recorders also came in handy for the few prisoners who were the recipients of what you might call home-made blue movies. Again, I had access to this stuff through my role as censor. Basically, some partners or wives performed sexual and provocative acts with themselves – often using sex toys – for the camera and posted the result off to their loved one. Some of these were pretty explicit. One I remember involved a partner and her own sister doing their stuff in order to provide some satisfaction for her man who was locked up.

There was no reason to deny the video treat to the prisoner. Typically, after viewing it to ensure there was nothing of a security interest, I would bring it to the landing and hand it over to the prisoner. Both of us would know what the content was but the exchange would be conducted with straight faces, as if I was passing on an innocuous piece of court evidence.

The other surreal aspect to the home-made blue movies occurred when the partner in question would visit. If I came across her, I might have to do a double take to remember where I had seen her before. Here is this woman, fully clothed and suitably sombre on her visit, and the last time I saw her she had a very different expression on her face, was all eyes for the camera and wearing no clothes. When such a situation did occur, I had to stop myself offering her a familiar smile as if we had met before.

Of course, the other aspect to sex in prison is when it occurs between prisoners. This, in my experience, is not as common as is often portrayed in movies – certainly not in this country. When it does happen, it tends to be between prisoners who are doing a very long stretch. Down through the years, there were times when I walked in on a pair of them at it in a cell. Usually on a landing, or maybe a block, there are one or two who are 'bum buddies', willing to have sex with other prisoners, often for a consideration of some sort.

Two individuals come to mind in that respect. One was part of a gang who had all received long prison sentences, and this man made himself available to the other members if they were of a mind to have sex. The other was a prisoner who was locked up for decades and was equally indiscriminate about who he partnered. The latter individual was somebody who, I believe, had lost full command of his senses a good while back. But whether that had anything to do with his lifestyle, or whether his lifestyle was the result of his mental state, I simply don't know.

Another aspect of prison life that is sometimes portrayed in the movies is rape. During my career I never came across, nor did I ever hear of, a situation where it was known to have taken place or even suspected of occurring.

Occasionally, a relationship develops between a prisoner and member of staff. Among male prisoners, respect for a female officer can sometimes grow into feelings of affection. I have seen, for instance, some of the most dangerous criminals in the country react with immediate obedience to a female officer, whereas it might take three or four males to physically restrain a prisoner in order to get him to do the same thing.

Apart from this 'mammy syndrome', the proximity of a woman in a man's world can give rise to feelings of attraction. Often, women officers – who tend, on the whole, to be fairly intuitive – will spot this and remain professional, being friendly but keeping things entirely platonic. Sometimes, a woman officer will find that she is responding with feelings of her own.

I knew of one case where a female officer definitely developed some kind of a relationship with a high-profile criminal in the Midlands Prison. They were never actually caught having sex, but the general consensus was that it was going on. In situations like that, no governor is going to want to make a big deal of it and have a light shone on his or her prison by the service or the department. The usual reaction, as occurred in this case, is to move the officer to another block and ensure there is no further opportunity for contact between them.

I recall that, in this particular case, the female officer often tried to get back on to the block where the prisoner was housed. Eventually, the ACO made a point of accompanying her any time she showed up on the block. That was one of the very few cases that I personally came across of that kind of relationship.

In February 2022, a few years after I had retired, an incident arose that was unusual in that it made it into the public domain. Two female prison officers working in Dublin were on a sun holiday when one noticed the other FaceTiming someone. She was shocked to realize that her friend was interacting with a prisoner currently locked up in the jail where they both worked. The officer (let's call her 'Anne') couldn't believe what she was seeing. Former colleagues told me she confronted her friend (we'll call her 'Breda'). Shortly afterwards, Anne got a text message from the prisoner who had been on the FaceTime call. Now, I don't know how that man got her number, but you would have to guess that maybe Breda gave it to him. He threatened Anne that if she breathed a word about his relationship with Breda, he would make sure that she came to some harm.

Anne contacted the prison she worked in, and management there advised her to leave her friend and get back home. The management then contacted the gardaí about the whole affair, and they conducted an investigation. Meanwhile, in the prison, the OSG did a thorough search of the prisoner's cell and found the mobile phone he had used. From what former colleagues told me, Breda was suspended immediately on return from her holiday and left the service soon after that. Again, this kind of relationship was rare; what was extraordinary was the way that it came to the prison authorities' attention.

It is more common, and well known within the service, for relationships to develop between male officers and female prisoners. Whether it is a reflection on male impulses or on the character of men – as opposed to women – in the service, I don't know. But I have known of cases where this has happened. Again, a governor won't want to put it up there in lights if something is discovered, but one case I'm aware of in recent years involved the suspension of a male officer in a female prison. He had been having a relation-ship with a prisoner, although they were never actually found having sex. He had moved into the prisoner's family home, where the prisoner had a child to be cared for. He was quietly suspended rather than sacked. I believe he left the service sometime after that.

10. The Night They Drove Old Dixie Down

Incidents, usually involving violence, happen all the time in prison, but there is one occasion that stands out for me. And it's not just me. I know it still lives in the minds of many who were there that evening – and many more who were not. It was a major event because of the psychological impact it had on a whole generation of officers in Portlaoise. In terms of the lingering fallout, it left one overriding emotion – shame.

By the late 1990s, there was a whole platoon of officers who had been working in The Bog for over two decades. I was one of the youngest in the prison, still in my early thirties. They called me 'the Garsún'. These older lads had seen it all. They had been there in the early days when the authorities in the prison and in government were constantly petrified at the prospect of mass breakouts by the Provos. They had witnessed, and many had taken part in, the regime which was aggressive towards the subversives, and which culminated in the murder of Brian Stack and its aftermath. And they had seen on E1 landing the changing nature of the heavies, the most dangerous criminals in the state.

Many of these officers were in service in the 1970s, when the Dunnes, the notorious drug-dealing family from Dublin's inner city, had been the main threat. And they would all have agreed with Larry Dunne's famous warning: 'If you think we're bad, wait till you see what's coming after us.'

The Dunnes had since been replaced by the likes of John Gilligan and his gang, and others of a similar calibre. This newer crowd had also formed themselves into gangs in a way that was new to the system. These prisoners saw the kind of privileges that were available to the subversives on the landings above them and reckoned that, if they banded together, they might get a bit of that.

One of the big issues about working in Portlaoise during those years was the boredom. Rank and file officers – known as buckets – had absolutely no opportunity to show any initiative. The security apparatus ensured that everything was done on a military-style basis, with no deviation allowed. For instance, if you were on duty on the stairgate, you sat inside a cage for the shift and did absolutely nothing. More often than not, the officer in question would bring a newspaper with him, hidden in the pouch in his uniform designed for a baton, in order to while away some of the time. (Officers were only allowed to read newspapers on the job when supervising visits.)

In other prisons, there was always some chance to show initiative, if you were that way disposed, whereas the routine in Portlaoise was mind-numbingly boring. The prevailing culture at the time also meant that officers could work as many hours as they wanted. Most took the opportunity of overtime; there were few among them who didn't, for long stretches of their careers, work up to one hundred hours a week. The combination of the constant threat of violence, the mind-numbing boredom and the long hours takes a toll over the years. It doesn't take a professional in mental health to know that the accumulation of those factors can have a toxic impact on well-being.

By the late 1990s, many of these men were in their late fifties or sixties. I had gone to school in the local CBS with their sons. Back in those years, they had the reputation of being hard men. Whenever it was deemed necessary to meet force with force in interactions with the subversive prisoners during the 1970s, these men did not shy away. But they were older now. They had not moved on, had not moved around in the service. They were classic examples of burnout.

That became evident on the evening in question. This was in early 1998. Nobody I have spoken to can remember now the specifics of what kicked off the violence that evening. One former colleague remembers it as having something to do with visits at the time – there was always resentment on E1 about the privileges and liberties afforded to the subversives. Maybe some small incident led that issue to mushroom in the minds of a few of the heavies, and they lashed out.

E1 landing is about 100 metres long, with 25 cells on either side. At the end there is a few steps down to the sluice room, where prisoners bring their waste, or slop out. Another door leads to the recreation room. At the rear of the landing a gate opens out into the exercise yard. There is also a backstairs up to E2, where the non-IRA subversives were housed (the IRA were on E3 and E4). At the top of the stairs another gate is manned by an officer 24/7.

It was down at the rear of E1 that things kicked off, around 5.30 p.m. There were eight officers present at the time, moving the prisoners from their cells to the recreation room or possibly the yard. In a split second, as is often the way with violence in prisons, punches were thrown, officers were grabbed and flung to the ground and kicked viciously.

At least thirty of the forty or so prisoners on the landing were involved. They got their hands on weapons – pool balls, chivs, the steel legs ripped from chairs – and they proceeded to give the officers the mother and father of all hidings.

The alarm went off, as it always does when something like this arises. On hearing the alarm, practically everybody rushes to the point of the trouble. All in, that's the way it has always been – and rightly so. In prison, in those instances, your colleagues are your comrades, your brothers and sisters, thrust on to a battlefield where you must go and rescue them, just as you would expect them to do the same if you were the one in trouble.

That's our response as prison officers. The response of the military, manning the walls and gates outside, is to go straight into lockdown mode. None of the rioting prisoners were going to come barrelling out the door on to the yard. They knew that guns would be trained on them immediately, and it wouldn't take much for the shooting to start. After that, you wouldn't be going down to the bookies to lay odds on the prisoner's survival.

All available officers came running from the other landings on E block, across from D block, in from the yard, pouring down into the circle which led to the entrance to E1, everybody ready to do battle. At the time, there was no official issue of batons, as there was always the security fear that a baton could be taken off an officer in a violent situation. Some officers, though, carried their own batons. And right then, hands reached down into the pouch on their trousers and pulled their weapon out. Most officers had been through this type of situation over the preceding years and decades. They knew the routine. You go in and quell. You do what is required to restore order. The prisoners are dangerous individuals, some of them unstable, and there should be no pussy-footing about.

The circle began to fill up with the officers from across the prison, arriving to save their colleagues and mates, their comrades. Meanwhile, at the far end of E1 the beatings continued. The only real hope of escape for the officers was up the stairs on to E2. Some of them managed to get to their feet and stumble towards the steps and climb for their lives. They knew that if they got through the gate at the top of the stairs, the prisoners wouldn't follow them.

The rioting prisoners might be heavies, some of the most dangerous criminals in the state, but they were never going to mess with the subversives – not even to the extent of showing up on the subversives' landing. That would not be tolerated and retribution would, in all likelihood, be dealt swiftly, not just within the prison but outside it.

At the top of the stairs the problem arose. The officer manning the stairgate, a decent man who had been on the job just too long, froze. He was programmed to never, under any circumstances, open the gate for anyone, as that might lead to some of the heavies entering E2. That was just written in stone. And here he was, seeing his battered colleagues, injured and fleeing, being pursued by prisoners who had gone completely apeshit, pleading with him to open the gate. And he couldn't. He was afraid.

Meanwhile, something in the same vein was happening at the entrance to E1. All of those who had come running suddenly froze. They knew what they had to do. They had done it many times over the years, but there hadn't been violence on this level for some time. As young men, these officers had answered the call, rushed in and flaked all before them, let the prisoners know who was boss, and what the consequences would be if any of their colleagues were messed with in any way.

But now the accumulation of years was catching up with them. A good share of them simply froze. To burst on to the landing would be to confront these criminals, younger men in the physical prime of their lives, who were worse than the likes of Larry Dunne who had gone before. Now, the prison officers with so many years of long service, who could see their pensions waiting for them across nearby hills, weren't up for it any more. They were afraid of all they now had to lose, of the fact that they would have to face up to the reality of their advanced years.

For a crucial few minutes, the eight officers on E1 continued to get the lard beaten out of them. Two interventions saved them from far more severe beatings – if not an even worse fate. Up at the stairgate on E2, one of the subversive prisoners took the initiative that was sadly lacking in the officer on duty. A former garda, who had been jailed for assisting some subversive outfit, grabbed the keys off the officer and opened the gate. The stricken officers began to pour through to freedom. Whatever motivated that prisoner to act as he did, it was certainly the saving of these men.

Down at the entrance to E1, one of the young officers stepped forward to take the initiative. Danny Robbins, who was, like me, a relative garsún among the old-timers, went to the front of the crowd, got the key and led the men on to the landing. By that time, the prisoners were largely spent. They had done their worst. They offered some resistance, but it wasn't an all-out battle or anything. Within a short time, we had them all back into their cells.

If it had been another prison, the leaders would have been identified and taken off to a strip cell, where they would have been left dressed in nothing but their jocks for two days. But The Bog didn't have a strip cell. There was no punishment block, so the only option was to leave them be in their own cells.

Nine officers were treated in Portlaoise General Hospital

that night. The injuries weren't serious but the admittance of that many injured officers was a notable occurrence in the prison service. Most of the staff were told to be in for work at 6.45 a.m. the following morning, rather than the usual start time of 8 a.m.

The early start was to organize for E1 to be searched. The previous night, the urgency to get all the prisoners back into their cells meant that they would still have had possession of weapons, and we needed to remove them.

There was a sombre feeling at the gathering that morning. Riots happen, violence occurs, but everybody present knew that the previous night had been something completely new. I can only speak for myself, but in my opinion one of the worst insults that could be hurled at you in the service was that you were a coward. You could be called lazy, useless, stupid, a bully even, but never a coward. The job, certainly at that time, required physical courage, particularly when it came to backing up colleagues. A failure to do that led only to shame. And that was the feeling that permeated the gathering, the morning after – shame. Our fellow officers had been let down.

There were well over a hundred officers at the meeting, that morning. The chief officer gave a speech, basically saying what happened the previous evening had happened, and now we had to go in and do a proper and professional job. He didn't spell it out, but the message was that there was to be no afters. In any event, we would be accompanied on the searches by the gardaí, as was standard. If any officer thought he was going to lash out because of what had occurred the previous night, he could well find himself in bigger trouble. We were not there to get revenge, but to search and confiscate weapons.

There were no incidents in the searches that followed. Here and there, you could detect a smirk from one of the prisoners. They knew, on one level, what had gone down, but I doubt they had any idea of the enormity of it. The sense of shame hung in the air for some time afterwards.

Anybody I have spoken to in recent years about that night has agreed that it was a major event in the modern history of Portlaoise. A good share of the older officers retired a relatively short time after it. Others were put on duties that meant they would have minimal or no interaction with the prisoners.

In one way, it was the end of an era. The Bog, as it had evolved after the subversives were sent there in the mid-1970s, had its own character. The threat that was perceived to come from the IRA and their fellow travellers was conveyed down through the system to those who worked on the floor. The regime was pretty brutal, but the officers were schooled in the view that the prisoners were capable of, and many had been involved in, cold-blooded murder for political ends. Just as other elements of the security forces were aggressive in confronting the Provos and their political wing on the outside, so also it was seen as necessary to ensure that those locked up would not pose any further threat, particularly through attempts to escape.

Then there was the experience of dealing with the heavies down through the years. These were the most dangerous criminals in the state and, at times, there was a need to confront them, which took a good deal of physical courage. As a teenager working in The Hare and Hound, I had seen these men in their prime, seen the hard drinking and camaraderie that fuelled them.

Now, two decades later, I was there on the night when something of what existed between them died. The era when the officers in Portlaoise were considered the hardest and the toughest was coming to an end. A few months after the events of that evening, The Good Friday Agreement was signed in Belfast. That, of itself, was going to change the whole nature of Portlaoise Prison, with the mass release of subversive prisoners over the following years.

11. Moving On, Moving In Next Door

By the year 2000, I was itching for change. I was coming up to nearly ten years in Portlaoise, and my time there had been fruitful as far as my career was concerned. I had learned truckloads about all aspects of the job, including in the education unit, and was becoming aware of the growing importance of computers. The job, however, was confining. And because of the emphasis on security, particularly in dealing with the subversives, the work could be boring.

It was a good time to be seeking a change. At around the time, most of the subversive prisoners were getting released, thereby changing the character of Portlaoise Prison. The prison service itself was also going through a major change: for the first time in decades, in order to deal with chronic overcrowding, a new facility was being added to the system.

The Midlands Prison was built literally next door to Portlaoise and was officially opened on 9 November 2000. It was a big project, costing £43m, and it represented the bright, shining future of incarceration in the state. The prison had the traditional circle and blocks structure – the spokes in the bicycle wheel – with four blocks, each three storeys high. There was in-cell sanitation and mainly single-occupancy cells. Recreation rooms were located at the end of each landing and there was an education block, which had science labs, metalwork facilities and an art room. There was also a gym, chapel, medical unit and counselling rooms.

The technology really stood out, with an advanced locking

system and CCTV cameras everywhere. All of this was standard fare in most developed countries, but it was new to the Irish prison system.

Across the way, in The Bog, we had watched with curiosity as the new building took shape. This new prison would require a good share of staff, and it was also opening at a time when there was a shortage of middle management in the prison service at assistant chief officer (ACO) level.

A competition to recruit new ACOs was initiated. Successful candidates would be put on to a panel from which they would then be assigned to prisons whenever a vacancy arose. The competition consisted of an aptitude test and an interview, with the latter being the main component. The interview took place in front of the governor of the prison in which you were currently serving, plus an official from the Department of Justice along with a psychologist. A total of 296 officers were selected for the panel from the competition. I found out that I had come out of it very well, as I was near the top. As a result, I wouldn't have to wait for a vacancy but was going to be promoted immediately in the first batch of appointments.

I had the Midlands as my first choice, and my seniority on the list meant that I was practically guaranteed it. Had I been assigned somewhere else – to Limerick, or Cork or one of the Dublin prisons – I would have commuted until such time as I could get back to one of the Portlaoise prisons, hopefully within a few years. There was no vacancy in Portlaoise itself, but that was no bad thing. If you're being promoted, it is definitely a good idea that you change prisons. As an officer you've obviously made friends and worked shoulder to shoulder with colleagues, but being promoted means you can't be a friend at work in the same way.

In any event, I got the Midlands where about twenty

ACOs would be needed from the start. My promotion and transfer out of Portlaoise all happened in jig time. I was informed that I was heading across what was now a campus to the Midlands, told to turn up at the uniform stores for my new uniform, and report to the training centre in Stack House the following day.

There was no big leaving do. I was just out of the door with the minimum of fuss. I did get to shake a few hands and say goodbye to some fellas who wished me well. Inevitably, there was also the odd begrudger who was waving me off with the least amount of enthusiasm they could muster.

The training took place over a very intense five days. Normally, this would have been spread over a few weeks, but there was great urgency to get people in place in the Midlands as the prisoner numbers there began to build up. So, within a week of first being informed of my new job, I was walking through the doors of this spanking new prison.

First impressions of a new place often stay with you, and I can still recall the sense of awe I felt on entering the Midlands. Everything was spick and span, clean and airy. Coming from The Bog, this was like walking into the light. And the first thing to strike me was how bright the whole place was. The landings were covered over with skylights that could be opened. The light was let in, and the smells were allowed to drift out: the stench of old paint, the sweat, the waft of rotten food, all the smells that literally polluted the air in Portlaoise, were absent. Compared to all that, the smell of fresh concrete that lingered was like perfume.

The place had literally only opened its doors about a fortnight before I arrived. There were fifty prisoners already being housed there, most of them trustees who were helping to get the place shipshape. The construction crews had only recently departed; there were screwdrivers and nails and what have you lying around, just as on any near-finished building site.

The technology was a pure joy to operate. The automatic gate-locking system meant that every employee had their own key, which gave them the individual level of access that their job required. For instance, as ACO my key allowed me access to practically all areas. But a teacher's key was designed to access just the education unit.

I'm only touching here on the enormity of the difference between my new place of work and where I had come from. It was, in one way, like moving from a thatched cottage with no running water or central heating to a pristine, modern high-tech new home.

That was the new environment I would be working in. The new job was daunting in its own way, also. Assistant chief officer is quite a step up. In the service in Ireland there are about 4,000 officers but only 140 ACOs. The next step above ACO is chief officer, a level which is graded from two-bar chief to three-bar chief. Each prison will only have one three-bar chief, which is the highest-ranking officer in uniform. (Assistant governors and governors wear civilian clothes.)

The strange thing is that an ACO would very often be earning more than a three-bar chief, as the ACO was on the roster and so eligible for overtime. All of this was hugely important to me at the time, having a mortgage and two young children.

The job is one of direct middle management. For instance, each landing in most prisons is overseen by a class officer, and each division or block – usually including three landings – is managed by an ACO. The only exception to that was Portlaoise, which was top heavy with staff. In The Bog, there was an ACO for every landing. He or she was the person who dealt directly with the prisoners' commanding officer (on the landings for the subversive groups). In fact, communicating with the heads of the subversives on the landings was really the only authority that an ACO had in Portlaoise.

In the Midlands, as in any other prison, the ACO had to be on top of everything that was going on. Central to this was knowing the prisoners: what they were in for, checking warrants on the information system, getting a handle on their backgrounds and personalities.

In the newly opened prison, we were getting the whole range of prisoners, from drug dealers to counter jumpers, paedophiles to violent sex offenders. The ordinary officer often wouldn't know what the prisoner was in for, but as ACO it was your job to be across it. Then you had to deal with these people, some of whom had committed horrendous crimes. Two of the early prisoners I had to deal with were in there for a series of robberies in which they broke into the homes of elderly couples and put the woman sitting on the hot range until the man told them where the money was being kept. Another fella on the landing had raped a number of his daughters. It takes a bit of compartmentalization to treat people like that the same as you would some poor fella who was in there for being more stupid than bad in getting involved in low-level crime. But that's the job.

At the outset, as ACOs we all had to take on secondary roles, as well as looking after a division. Sean Wynne, whom I knew from Portlaoise, asked me to help him set up the education unit, and I was delighted to do so.

*

A prison is not unlike a school where the principal sets the tone. In a prison, the governor is the person to do that. And the man appointed to steer the ship of the bright new specimen in Irish penal history was John L. O'Sullivan – 'Sully' – one of the two most senior governors in the prison service at the time.

I got on well with John L, as he was known, from the off. Some may have found him blunt, but for me he was just straight up. He also made it plain, early on, that there would be a serious regime in the Midlands. Word had gone around that things next door in Portlaoise had got a bit slack, and John L was going to have none of that.

To be fair to those in charge at Portlaoise, if things were loose there, it was within a particular context. The Good Friday Agreement had changed the nature of the engagement with the subversive prisoners as they all prepared to soon be released. The old days of confrontation and a harsh regime were long gone – and rightly so, too. One aspect of prison life in Portlaoise was that the heavies managed, to some extent, to piggyback on the lighter regime. They therefore had it easier than would ordinarily be the case in what was effectively a maximum-security prison.

John L made it plain there would be nothing slack about the Midlands. He was from south Kerry, and a countryman to his heart. He was a great man for lifting the morale of the troops with the kind of attitude that we were all in the one boat – just as long as everybody knew he was doing the rowing. He got very animated. Whereas some governors would talk quietly to you, John L might roar. It wouldn't necessarily be a roar to have a go at you. If he wanted you to do a job – escort a high-profile prisoner, for instance – he would grab you and tell you that you were the only man for the job, that the prison was relying on you to put your best foot forward. You could imagine him in a dressing room, geeing up a team to go out and die for the county, and working them into such a lather that they would literally lift the hinges off the dressing-room door on the way out. That was John L: full of beans, mad for the job, and always reaching out to take others with him. And many among us, including myself, responded in kind. We were Sully's men and willing to go the extra mile for him, which I suppose is a sign of a great leader. Not everybody's cup of tea, to be sure, but I built up a good relationship with him.

John L did a tour of the prison every day, and the prisoners respected him for that. But not everything he did was a big success. At the outset, he brought in a smoking ban in the punishment block, which I oversaw. The prisoners went ballistic. I remember one or two begging me to allow them to smoke. There had never been any ban on smoking in prisons. When the smoking ban was introduced in the country as a whole, in 2004, prisons were allowed an exemption.

But John L decided that part of a punishment regime would be a ban on smoking. It was not a success – and to be fair to him, he reversed it not long afterwards.

Apart from that, though, he did insist on high standards. If a prisoner came out of his cell heading to the servery for breakfast in flip-flops and shorts, he was sent back. There was going to be a basic dress code. And if the prisoner wasn't out and heading for the servery by 9.15 a.m., he'd be locked up for the day.

Some of that might sound harsh, but we weren't running a playgroup. John L had been around for a while, and he knew this was a major gig, opening the biggest prison in the state at a time when the crime world was producing some dangerous individuals. If you allow things to slack off in such a big institution, it can quickly lead all the way to chaos. He had seen that happen before – as had some of the rest of us – and I was certainly glad that a marker was being put down, early on.

All of that was exciting for me at this stage in my career. It was flat-out – I was regularly working twelve and more hours a day – but I was loving it, getting to learn the ropes of management, and being part of a new set-up. I was also getting my first experience in dealing with a category of prisoner that is, in many ways, a pariah in large parts of society, both inside and outside prison – the sex offender.

During my first month in the Midlands, I had to perform one of the more difficult tasks of the job. A call came through to me at work one day, conveying that a prisoner's brother had passed away. The chaplain wasn't available, so it fell to me to break the news to the prisoner.

This man was serving a long sentence for raping a sixteen-year-old girl when he was about twenty-two himself. He was considered dangerous. I got a hold of three officers I wanted to accompany me to the cell. There was no knowing how this man would react to the news. With three others present, if things turned ugly, maybe we could restrain him with as little fuss as possible.

I told the three to wait outside the cell and if I let out a shout, they were to come in immediately. I went and broke the bad news. The prisoner reacted as I'd expected, going apeshit, thrashing about. To be handed that kind of news when you are confined in a prison cell is a hell of a lot to deal with in any circumstances. As with many others who end up behind bars, this man hadn't much in the way of control when it came to his emotions, especially at a time like this. I just sat on his bed as he was throwing things and allowed him to let off a bit of steam. Then he sat down beside me. He leaned forward and dropped his head down into his lap. Beside him, I patted him on the back, as anybody would do in a situation like this.

That wasn't how the three lads looking in through the flap in the door saw it. From their vantage point, or so they claimed, it looked as if the prisoner was giving me oral sex and I was tapping him on the head. When I got up and went outside, they were falling around the place. The man inside had just received the worst news imaginable for somebody in his situation, and these three were laughing as if the whole thing was a bit of a gas.

I let it go. It was new to me, this level of responsibility, both in terms of engaging with the prisoners and having officers directly answerable to me. It was an example of the black humour of some aspects of prison life that wouldn't be easily explainable to those not accustomed to it.

That prisoner was one of the sex offenders who were housed on C block, where I was in charge. This was also a whole new ball game – as far removed from dealing with the subversives and the heavies as you could imagine. The sex offenders were not only relatively new to me but also, for the greater part, to the country as a whole. It might be difficult for younger people to believe now, but it was only in the 1990s that a whole explosion of sex offences was dealt with by the courts. Before that, as with other seamier sides to Irish life, much of it was brushed under the carpet, and victims were left to suffer in silence.

In what would be totally unacceptable in public parlance, we privately referred to the offenders as 'jockeys'. We wouldn't use the term openly, only between staff. As far as guarding the sex offenders was concerned, a sheepdog could do it. They are no trouble at all, most likely because they are not constitutionally violent. Don't get me wrong, the crimes for which they are convicted are horrible and demeaning. But while a man can be physically capable of inflicting terrible violence on a woman or child, he may be the biggest coward when incarcerated alongside other men. By and large, these men didn't get involved in any violence inside prison, which is usually the biggest issue in controlling prisoners.

Within their group they had their own hierarchy. Some of those who were convicted of rape would consider paedophiles to be subhuman. Unlike the general prison population, which tended to be overwhelmingly made up of young men, the sex offenders were all ages, including some who were obviously infirm, and more than one who required a wheelchair. Among those were a few priests and Christian Brothers.

The sex offenders were one of the two special categories of prisoner I had on C Block. The other was those on protection. At any one time, there are a considerable number of prisoners on protection. Most of this has to do with gangs, debts or personal animosities that arise in prison.

When a prisoner is first brought in, he is interviewed and asked whether he has any concerns. The existence of connections between those on the inside and outside often means that these new arrivals know exactly who is on which landing. For instance, a fella might say, 'I'll be grand on B block but don't put me anywhere near D.' He knows that life on D will be hell. He will be looking over his shoulder until somebody finds an opportune time to cut him up and assault him.

That's all grand, if he can be accommodated with his buddies on B block. But if not, he has to come to me in C, the protection block.

When anybody arrived on C, I'd just have a chat with him, tell him to keep his head down. Despite that, there was no end of trouble on the block. These men would be constantly getting into some form of bother – with each other and also with the staff.

At any one time, up to a quarter of the 110 prisoners on C2 and C3 – which were the landings for protected prisoners – would be locked up for most of the day, as a form of punishment.

The other source of trouble was if anybody managed to get moved on to the block, intending to slice somebody up. All of those on protection were there because somebody wanted to do damage to them. Sometimes, a prisoner will pretend that he needs protection, just to get on to C and attack his target. This prisoner might be on a long sentence and have nothing to lose, and he could be doing it for money. He will go to the governor and say he has fallen out with some fellas on his landing and his life is in danger. In order to boost his story, he may organize to get somebody to give him a few thumps. Then when he's on the protection block, he seeks out and cuts up his target. If he succeeds, or even attempts it, he will get a long stretch locked up in punishment, but he will have factored that in before he took on the job.

Between all these demands, running the C division in the Midlands was full on. I was working long days, with little time off, learning all sorts of new aspects to the job. It was hectic, but I was in my element.

12. Here Comes the Night

One of the major duties of an ACO is to take control of the prison at night. The governors and chief officers are not on the roster, so they go home in the evening. The ACO is in charge, elevated for the night shift to the role of de facto governor. A second ACO will be on duty in the control room, overseeing all the cameras and security there, but it is the first ACO who is effectively in charge.

The sense of responsibility totally dwarfs any notion of power. The volume of work ensures that it can be both exhilarating and exhausting. If, for instance, you had a smartphone or Fitbit, I can guarantee that you would regularly hit 50,000 steps during a night in charge of the prison.

The biggest difference in the prison at night is the noise. During the day, there is no getting away from it. At night, silence reigns. You could hear a pin drop, or the footsteps of an officer on the landing, but more obviously the odd shout from a prisoner in the grips of a nightmare behind one of the closed cell doors.

Despite that, there is never a dull moment. A prisoner might suffer a heart attack. Frequently, somebody will have an epileptic fit. It's not uncommon for somebody to overdose on hard drugs at night. And then there is the tragic spectre of a suicide, which most often occurs in the wee small hours. There is always something happening in the silence. Just as the clock crawls when you're detailed for a boring job – such as sitting in the stairgate in Portlaoise – so it speeds wildly ahead when you're running a prison through the night.

One reason for the increased workload is that a skeleton staff operates at night. Usually, there is one officer for every two landings, which might mean – and certainly did, at that time – overseeing ninety prisoners. Each cell has to be checked on every half-hour. There has been controversy, particularly after deaths in custody, over prisoners not being checked as frequently as policy dictates, and there are some officers who will take short cuts. All of the landings in a modern prison like the Midlands are covered with cameras, so it's possible to see whether the officer is doing his rounds. Occasionally, you will spot somebody who zips down the landing for the sake of being seen on camera but is not actually checking in on every prisoner.

The cells have two sets of lights: the normal bulb and a blue one. During the night checks, the officers turn on the blue light to see whether the prisoner is alright, without disturbing his sleep. If anything appears not to be as it should, the full light will be turned on. At the end of each landing there is a button which must be pressed, in order to confirm and record that a check has been done.

My first night was full of the kind of drama that was to become routine. I arrived at the circle to take over from the chief officer. The handover involved the CO giving the rundown on any problems that had arisen, and what they might mean for that night. He told me we had a problem with a prisoner called Michael Murray, a man whom I and the whole prison service would subsequently come to know well. Murray was doing a stretch for some form of robbery, but his crimes would turn really nasty afterwards.

Anyway, the chief, J. J. Carey, told me that Murray had cut himself up with razor blades and had been brought to the strip cell. This is the punishment cell, although it serves other purposes when needed, such as keeping an eye on a prisoner thought to be suicidal, or removing a prisoner from the general population in an emergency. The cell is bare but for a concrete bench, acting as a bed, and a flame-retardant mattress. The prisoner is left in his white jail jocks and a prison poncho made of flame-retardant wool. These days, the strip cell is known as the Special Observation Cell.

The chief told me that Murray also claimed to have swallowed some blades. This had all happened just ten minutes before I came on duty. My timing was perfect.

The cell was a mess. There was blood everywhere and a nurse was attempting to bandage him up. Absorbent powder, which is used any time there is blood, was scattered around the floor and walls.

'You'll probably have to get him to hospital,' the chief told me, and with that he headed for the hills himself.

Despite it being my first night, I couldn't have expected anything else. The man was just coming off a twelve-hour shift – and if it wasn't going to be this emergency, it might well be another one in the course of the night. So, he left me to sink or swim.

The first thing required to take a prisoner to Portlaoise Hospital is bodies. I needed three officers. In time, I would come to know a few whom I could ring up and ask to come in when this kind of emergency blew up. Every ACO has a few people he can rely on: people who are willing to do what's needed for the extra few bob, even if that means getting a call at 2 a.m. or 3 a.m.

Ideally, somebody going off duty is asked to stay on to deal with the problem, but you won't always get that. Anybody who does agree to stay on gets overtime. And if they are required for more than five hours, then they don't have to come to work the following day either.

On this night, I only managed to get one lad who was

going off duty. That left me needing to juggle staff in order to get two others to accompany Murray to hospital. I had to take two officers off the landing that night, leaving two others covering four landings each – which was no joke, as it involved caring for around 180 prisoners each while their colleagues were diverted.

I had to email the Irish Prison Service (IPS) headquarters in Longford to officially record that a prisoner was to be taken to hospital. Then I checked the Prison Information Records System (PIRS) to find out the status of the prisoner in question. If the individual is deemed dangerous, an armed escort is required, so the local gardaí will be contacted and asked to supply two detectives to accompany the officers.

Over in Portlaoise Prison, an armed escort to hospital for one of the subversives also involved the military. In that case, the convoy leaving the prison for the very short journey to the hospital would include the prison vehicle, a patrol car, an unmarked garda car and at least one army jeep. Portlaoise Hospital staff are used to this kind of convoy turning up in the dead of night, but it would be a strange sight even in a city, never mind a provincial town.

On this occasion, the three officers – one driving, the other two accompanying the cuffed Murray – went over to the hospital, and the prisoner got treatment for his injuries. He was X-rayed and this showed up the razors he said he had swallowed. However, the razors weren't in his stomach but Sellotaped to his back inside his shirt. This is a trick that some prisoners try on, in order to spend a night in hospital. It must have worked at some point, because they persist in doing it, but any time I've come across it the ruse has always been detected.

Following that, Murray was returned to prison and placed

back in the strip cell, as per regulations. The whole thing took up three hours, during which time I was up the walls, but it all went off smoothly.

I got to know Murray over the years as he came back, initially on another conviction, and eventually for a vicious rape. I can't say that we ever connected on the human level that was possible with some other prisoners. He may have possessed redeeming features, but I didn't get sight of any.

The night is also the time when suicides occur, so it was unusual that the first one I encountered was during reserve period, after dinner but before lockdown, which runs from around 5.15 p.m. to 7.30 p.m. At this time, most prisoners are out, usually in the recreation rooms. Those who are still in their cells tend to be 'behind the door', as we call it. This means they are confined to the cell because maybe they didn't get up in time that morning, and therefore have had to forego all the privileges of the day, or maybe they've been kept in the cell for some punishment. Others might stay in their cell during this period if, for instance, they have worked in the kitchens all day and want to watch something on TV in a little peace and quiet. At any one time, there could be up to a quarter of prisoners on a landing behind the door.

At around 7.20 p.m., the class officers will open all the doors in preparation for lockdown for the night. The cells where prisoners have stayed behind during reserve period are also opened up at this time. That was when the class officer found this man, who happened to be a Traveller. The class officer couldn't open the door, as it was jammed. He rang for help and for the nurse; he knew from experience what was most likely on the other side of the door.

The man had tied a wet towel around his neck and hung

himself from the door handle. On the floor there was another wet towel, which had allowed him to slip forward when he sat down. Once that's done, it is very difficult to retrieve the situation, even if the prisoner gets second thoughts.

The class officer rang for help. A Hoffman knife, a specialized rescue tool, is kept secure on every landing for situations like this. The class officer cut the prisoner down and laid him out on the floor. Because we hadn't yet switched to the night schedule, there were four nurses on duty, and they arrived in a hurry. They tried to pump his chest, checked his pulse. I was in the cell by then. At such a time there is nothing you can do but stand back and let them at it. There is also a duty to ensure that the cell remains as it was before the incident, which can be difficult, unless you stop the flow of officers coming in, some of them just to rubberneck what's going on.

In this case, because the prisoners weren't yet locked up, everybody was crowding around on the landing outside the cell in question. But there was no trouble. Even among some of the most dangerous or violent inmates, there is a certain etiquette at times like this. Suicides heighten the camaraderie that exists between prisoners. These men live in close proximity to each other. They spend 90 per cent of their time out of cell with the same people, confined to a relatively small area. They see the same faces day in, day out. They mightn't necessarily get on, but they are all, to some extent, in the same boat, travelling in the one direction towards the far shore and release. In that sense, a suicide is like losing a man overboard, somebody who just didn't have what it took to make it through. Things like that can't help but impact on everybody who remains and provide them with a little food for thought.

This applies even to those who are locked up for killing other human beings. In a strange way, in the aftermath of a suicide, they can – for a short while, at least – feel a sense of loss for somebody whom they might have been perfectly willing to murder, in different circumstances on the outside.

(The prisoners' sense of camaraderie comes out in other ways, too. I have seen a prisoner coming to the end of a long sentence and he does something wrong, but rather than see his stretch extended, others will step in and take responsibility for it. I've seen the lowest of the low getting released, and most of those on his landing will come and shake hands with him, wish him well.)

Following a suicide, everything must be left as found, until the investigation takes place. Later in my career, I developed a huge interest in this area, and particularly in how suicides were investigated, but in my early years as ACO I just followed procedure. When I handed over to the chief officer on the following morning, the numbers – it's all about numbers, remember – recorded that we were down one prisoner.

An ambulance would be called in these situations, but if we were dealing with a dead body they wouldn't take it away. The body would remain in the cell until the undertaker arrived. Afterwards, all the prisoner's personal effects were taken from the cell and put in bags for his family. If there was a nude poster, we might just give it to a neighbouring inmate as it's the last thing the family would want to contemplate.

Thankfully – and this is something the public doesn't realize – many, if not most, attempts at suicide are caught in time. A few weeks before the above incident, I came across an attempted suicide. This was the first of its kind I had encountered. This man was hanging from the window in his cell. The windows have metal bars inside heavy casing, with small strips of perspex. The bars spin, which makes it more difficult to cut into them, and under the windows there is a vent to let the air in. This man had cut a hole in the perspex, through which he had fed the sheet.

We got to him in time. The nurse, who was a former prison officer, saved the man's life. A mask was put on his face and oxygen pumped in from a canister the nurse had brought with him. There was no response for a few minutes, and I thought the prisoner was gone, but then his chest jumped as if it was about to explode. That man went on to complete his sentence, and to the best of my knowledge had a decent life afterwards. His problem was that he simply couldn't hack prison at the time, but fortunately he made it through in the end.

There are, and always will be, suicide risks in prison. Some will be under observation, which means they should be checked every fifteen minutes through the night. Others are brought to strip cells for their own safety, because they can't do themselves any harm in the strip cell. Sometimes, a class officer will spot somebody who may be a suicide risk. Whenever that happened when I was in the service, I might go and sit down in the prisoner's cell and have a chat with him, suss out what the story was. If the prisoner broke down and said he wanted to end it all, or gave any kind of a strong indication that he might be a risk to himself, I would have to act.

The only course of action would be to remove him to a strip cell. A case could certainly be made that dealing this way with a man who is in danger of taking his own life is cruel. Instead of getting due attention, he is just removed to uncomfortable surroundings in which he can't do himself any harm. Needs must, however. With hundreds of prisoners to watch over, it simply wouldn't be possible to do anything else. All you can do in the short term is hope that his suicidal impulses are a passing thing, and that he will come to terms with prison life, in time.

Suicides are not the only form of death that mainly occurs during the night. The drug overdose is also not unknown. This will only be discovered during rounds if an officer looks in and sees that the prisoner does not appear to be sleeping as normal. The blue light might show that he is slumped out of his bed, or maybe there's a pool of vomit beneath him. Retrieving a prisoner from that situation is down to timing and luck.

Similarly, a prisoner may be in danger of choking on his own vomit after drinking hooch, the home brew that is made in prisons. This stuff is manufactured from fruit, sugar and yeast, usually carefully assembled over a period of time among a group of prisoners, using items taken from the servery. Prisoners are given plenty of fruit because they eat so much grease, and it provides some balance in their diet. But between that and the availability of bread and sugar, they can easily pull together the ingredients and brew the stuff in their cells.

Hooch drives some of the men around the bend. The most placid fella can turn into a lunatic overnight, ready to fight anybody who so much as says boo to him. All of that gives rise to plenty of grief, but then there is also the possibility of getting sick in their cells while half comatose from the stuff.

Between it all, the night is a time of danger and high drama.

13. John Daly Talks to Joe

On 1 May 2007, a telephone call was made from a cell in Portlaoise Prison to the RTÉ radio programme *Liveline*. The call was to have a transformative effect on the Irish Prison Service – and on my career.

John Daly was coming towards the end of a nine-year sentence when he made the call on a mobile phone. Daly had been arrested in 1999 and charged with armed robbery and firearm offences. He and another man had robbed a service station on the Finglas Road in Dublin using a sawn-off shotgun. A week later, they robbed the same service station again. When Daly was arrested, he was in possession of around €4,000. He received a sentence of six years for armed robbery and firearm offences, and another three years for handling stolen property, with the sentences to be served consecutively. Daly was considered a dangerous criminal and served most of his sentence on E1 landing in Portlaoise.

On the day in question, he was listening to the *Liveline* programme in his cell when an item about criminality was introduced. The presenter, Joe Duffy, had two contributors on the line: Christy Burke, a Sinn Féin councillor from Dublin's north inner city, and high-profile crime reporter Paul Williams. Burke had taken exception to a piece Williams had written in the *Sunday World* linking criminality to the Republican movement.

The two men engaged, arguing back and forth on their opposing views, with the conversation moderated by Duffy.

After a while, members of the public entered the conversation, and then a man introduced by Joe as Alan Bradley came on the line. He was a native of Dublin who was suspected of involvement in organized crime. (Bradley was subsequently sentenced to nine years in prison for the attempted robbery of a security van.) He attacked Williams for how the reporter had portrayed him in some articles. One of the issues that Bradley had with the newspaper reports was a suggestion that he had left the country because John Daly had threatened to have him killed. After some heated exchanges between Paul Williams and Bradley, Joe Duffy intervened. This is how the call went from there on.

JOE DUFFY: John Daly's on the line. John, good afternoon to you.

JOHN DALY: How's it going? Alright?

JOE DUFFY: You're in Portlaoise Prison at the moment?

JOHN DALY: I'm in Portlaoise right now, yeah, there's only one place I can be. Paul Williams knows that very well.

JOE DUFFY: Take your time now, John.

JOHN DALY: I will do. How's it going, Alan, alright?

ALAN BRADLEY: Not too bad. Yourself?

JOHN DALY: Yeah. Thanks for the postcard while you were away. Now, Mr Williams. How many thousands of people would you say read your newspaper every Sunday?

PAUL WILLIAMS: Almost a million.

JOHN DALY: About a million? Do you know how much lies you tell every week? Do you know I sent a registered posted letter today with an article from that newspaper that you just wrote saying that I carried out armed

141

robbery when I got out on my review. I did not get arrested for any armed robberies.

PAUL WILLIAMS: You're in prison serving how many years?

JOHN DALY: It doesn't matter how many years I'm serving.

PAUL WILLIAMS: Actually, where did you get the mobile phone to ring out?

JOHN DALY: (*Getting agitated*) Who told you I had a spat against Alan Bradley who was a friend of mine who I grew up with? I have a complaint in against you, because if I didn't know Alan Bradley and Alan Bradley did not know me, you are kicking off a fucking gangland war.

JOE DUFFY: John, the language, the language.

JOHN DALY: OK, but that's what his intention is, to kick off war.

JOE DUFFY: John, you're in prison at the moment for armed robbery for an Esso station. Isn't that correct?

JOHN DALY: Yeah, back in 1999. I was eighteen years of age.

JOE DUFFY: And how many years are you serving in Portlaoise?

JOHN DALY: Nine years. Finishing off nine years.

PAUL WILLIAMS: You were let out of prison, then it was re-activated.

JOHN DALY: I'm going on holiday with Alan when I get out.

JOE DUFFY: So, you're denying you threatened to kill Alan Bradley?

JOHN DALY: Denied? The date, it was all in the *Herald* a week before Williams over in the *Sunday World*. You check that date in the *Herald*. And you check when Alan Bradley sent me a postcard, that very same day.

ALAN BRADLEY: (*Chuckling*) And that's someone I left the country over.

JOE DUFFY: John Daly, are you still on the phone there?

JOHN DALY: I can't stay long. I can't stay long. I'm in a cell. Paul Williams, you are a liar. You make up lies to start war. If I didn't know Alan Bradley and Alan Bradley did not know me, you would have kicked off a war there. People would be wanting to get one person before the other person got the other. Now, I'm going. Get off the phone, you fucking liar.

With that, the line to John Daly went dead. A prison officer entered his cell and seized the mobile phone. Within political circles, the brief call kicked off a storm. The Minister for Justice, Michael McDowell, ordered an inquiry into how a prisoner could have possession of a mobile phone and feel comfortable enough to use it to speak on the national airwaves.

McDowell said he wanted a quick outcome from the inquiry. 'There better be a very good explanation for what happened,' he said.

The Opposition Justice Spokesperson, Jim O'Keeffe, didn't hold back in getting stuck in. He said the incident was 'absurd' and 'highly embarrassing' for McDowell.

'Under this minister, many prisons have turned into operation centres for some of Ireland's most dangerous criminals,' he said. 'Drugs and mobile phones are routinely smuggled inside, with criminals finding ever more inventive ways to breach security.'

By pure coincidence, on the very same day, May 1, a new law came into effect which made it illegal to have a mobile phone in prison. The penalty for breaking the new law was twelve months in prison and a fine of up to €5,000.

The day after the *Liveline* conversation, a second prisoner rang in to a radio station. This time, an unidentified individual spoke on the Dublin station FM104 from, he claimed, Mountjoy Prison.

In a further coincidence, that very week the Prison Officers' Association (POA) was holding its annual conference. Just before the conference kicked off, the president of the POA, Gabriel Keaveney, said that his members were regularly spat at, assaulted, bitten and threatened when they seized contraband material.

'How many people have you seen brought before the courts for smuggling contraband material into prisons, despite the thousands of seizures every year?' he asked. 'I don't know of any.' He mentioned that there had been an announcement the previous year about the introduction of dogs into the prison service. 'We still only have one dog for the entire prison system,' he said.

At the POA conference, McDowell said that it should be more difficult to get a phone into an Irish prison than on to an aircraft. He rejected any suggestion that there was a lax regime for allowing phones or drugs into prisons. He also mentioned that it would be remiss of him not to note the trafficking by a small minority of staff who, he said, were letting down the overwhelming majority of honest prison officers.

The following week, a thorough search was conducted on E1 landing in Portlaoise. At least eight phones were discovered, three SIM cards, around 150 tablets, thirty syringes and a large amount of hooch (the home-brewed alcohol). A budgie, believed to have been smuggled into the prison by a female visitor who concealed the bird internally, was also found.

Between it all, the controversy was a public relations disaster for the minister, his department and the prison service. It highlighted what everybody in the service knew was going on. Prisons were awash with contraband, and the methods used to detect and stop smuggling were primitive. By May 2007, the plans to bring this element of security up to speed were way behind schedule. Now, though, something had to be done. Over the years, I've noticed how things that require any kind of upheaval in the service only get done with any urgency when there is a public controversy. It's as if the prisons inhabit some dark corner of the state, where they are expected to stay quiet. Only when major noise breaks out are they given the proper attention.

Following the Daly call, and all that flowed from it, there was finally a sense of urgency about putting a proper security regime in place. Plans got under way for the establishment of a new unit which would have overall responsibility for security. It was to be called the Operational Support Group (OSG), and it would be my home for the remainder of my career in the service.

John Daly was released from prison in August 2007. Just over two months later, in the early hours of 22 October, he and a group of friends were returning to his home in Finglas in a taxi after a night out drinking. As the car pulled up, a man approached the front passenger side of the car where Daly was sitting and fired five shots into his head. He died instantly. He had been warned by the gardaí that his life was in danger and was advised to stay indoors.

Nobody was ever convicted of his murder but reports at the time suggested he was attempting to set up a drug-dealing gang, and this may have prompted rivals to move against him. Other reports pointed to the fact that he was deeply unpopular among some elements of organized crime, as his phone call the previous May had severely disrupted the capacity of those in prison to continue engaging in criminal activity.

14. Three Heads of the New System

The Operational Support Group (OSG) was up and running within twelve months of John Daly's call to RTÉ. John L, the governor in the Midlands, was put in charge of it. Once I heard that John L was the boss, I was confident he might want me on board. We had always got on well, I respected him, and I sensed that respect was mutual. So it was that he approached me one day, in April 2008, and asked me would I join him. I had to think about it for all of ten seconds flat. This was something new, and it looked like it could be exciting.

Within a week, I was in the new job. Technically, the move required a transfer; the OSG was a separate entity to the prisons, answerable to our own governor and not to the prison governor. All of the staff were hand-picked, including ten three-bar chiefs, who had been promoted specifically to take up roles in the OSG. Each prison normally has one three-bar chief, so having ten across the unit nationwide was a sign that the OSG was going to be a full-on outfit.

The other reason it was top heavy with senior people was the acknowledgment that the OSG would get grief because of our autonomy in not having to answer to line management within the prison. For instance, as the ACO for the OSG in the Midlands, I would now attend the prison's daily management meeting. That meeting usually consisted solely of chief officers and governors, but I was there to represent our separate entity and feed into the management discussions from a security point of view. That indicated the kind of clout we were to have in the prison.

Sometimes during those meetings, I might say to the governor, 'Could I have a word with you afterwards?' This would be to brief him on a particular security issue which, by its very nature, would have to be kept confidential. But me saying that in the meeting used to drive some of the other senior management crazy, as I was effectively claiming that I – a mere assistant chief officer! – had information that would only be shared with the top man.

There were times afterwards when I'd get a call from the chief officer, or even an assistant governor, who'd ask, 'What's going on? What were you talking to the top man about?'

I might reply with a little ball hop, saying something like, 'Sorry, but it's confidential. If I told you, I'd have to kill you.'

I knew I was being provocative, having a bit of craic to wind some of them up. Behind it all, though, those of us in the OSG took the confidentiality of our work regarding prison security deadly seriously. It had to be that way.

There were other occasions when we got up the noses of management entirely unintentionally. Early on, there was one incident where a chief told me he had to take two of my staff to cover a shortfall. I had to tell him that he wasn't taking any staff, that they were not his to take. In some quarters resentment against the OSG never really died down, but once we got over the initial bumps in the road, it stayed beneath the surface.

Despite what was the establishment of a completely new unit in the service, there was no training. For the greater part, we learned on the job. There were similar security units in prisons in the UK and Europe, and management of the OSG borrowed ideas and systems from reading about and observing those units in operation elsewhere.

The first gathering of the new unit involved a meeting in Stack House. There were about 140 of us there, from prisons all over the state. John L gave his signature speech to gee us all up, and then he went through the challenges that we would face in the early days.

The security brief was to be broken down into three elements: the Security Screening Unit, which would search everybody on entry to the prison using new airport-style machines; the Operational Support Unit, which would oversee the searching of cells; and the Canine Unit, which would use dogs to help in screening and searches. In addition to these three core aspects of the work, an important part of the OSG's brief was also to break up the gangs that had been getting a foothold in the prisons. This would require gathering intelligence and splitting up prisoners who were key men in the gangs.

Introducing screening at the entrance to the state's prisons was a big leap forward. Difficult as it may be to believe today, but in 2008 Portlaoise was the only prison that had screening – and that was only because of the subversives. Because it already had a security apparatus (and despite the fact that it was an incident in Portlaoise that led to the setting up of our unit), Portlaoise Prison would stay outside the OSG operation until 2014.

New equipment, consisting of X-ray machines and walk-through metal detectors, were installed at the entrances to all prisons. This required a fair bit of building work and rearranging, and in the early days the screening area was like being on a small building site, with dust at our feet and the agreeable waft of cut timber filling the air. But there was huge urgency to get this up and running.

The new system represented a major upheaval – both for employees of the service and also for all visitors, including solicitors and barristers. Absolutely nobody was to enter the prison without going through the screening area. We even developed a saying about it. 'In God we trust, everybody else we search.'

The routine was exactly as you get in airports today. All metal objects – belts, keys, et cetera – to be put into a tray, bags through the X-ray machine, and then you walked through the metal detector. If the detector was set off, you were subjected to a full pat-down search. This stuff is routine for everybody today, even in court buildings, but back then it was seen as a radical departure.

Early doors, there was some hassle from prison officers who objected to the new regime. A few who had done their thirty years turned around, went home and handed in their notice. It wasn't that they had been bringing in contraband and were afraid of being rumbled; they just saw this new move as an assault on their dignity and not worth the hassle for them.

More just complained. Mornings were a particular flashpoint. You'd have the odd fella coming in grumpy; maybe he'd been out the night before or he'd had a row with his wife that morning. If he set off the metal detector, he'd be asked to raise his hands. There might be a moment when he'd have other ideas about what to do with his hands, like maybe close a fist. That was when I would have to step forward, calm things down.

These were the kinds of teething problems that were inevitable. However, the vast majority of officers knew that it was for their own protection. It would also mean fewer weapons like Stanley knives coming into the prison, which could end up being used against them.

There were no such problems from the governors or chief officers. They knew the times were a-changin' – and most of them were of a mind that it was a wholly positive change. They were therefore willing to put up with the inconvenience.

There were a few incidents, early on, which showed that the new regime was having an effect. One shocking case involved a woman who was coming in as a visitor. She was being patted down by one of our female officers, Fiona Holmes, who could feel a package underneath this woman's clothes. The woman was also holding a baby in her arms. She threw the baby up in the air as a distraction to allow her to grab the package of drugs and swallow it. Fiona literally caught the baby in mid-air – the child was only months old. We got to the woman in time to stop her swallowing the drugs, and immediately rang the guards. Fiona should have got a medal for what she did that day, possibly saving the child's life.

In the same vein, there was another incident in a visiting box when a father and son came in to visit another son in the prison. The visiting son had a baby with him. We could see that there was going to be a handover, so myself and another officer went into the box to stop it. Once we arrived and they copped what was going to happen, the visiting son picked up the child and threatened to throw the child on the ground if we didn't back off. 'I'll fuck him on the ground,' he roared at us.

We weren't going to take any chances. We escorted him, with the baby held aloft the whole time, to the main gate. Obviously, once he was outside, we rang the guards and the social services were also contacted. The incident was a lesson in how powerful a grip drugs have on some people. What was being threatened was insane.

The second element of our work was the cell searches. Prior to this, searches were of a cursory nature – you'd go in and search as you might in a room at home, looking for lost keys. Now, it was going professional.

John L and his chief officers devised a system, largely lifted from other prison services, whereby we set up a mock cell in Stack House and sent two officers in to do a proper search. One went left inside the door, the other right, to conduct what's called a circular search. I would have hidden in the cell maybe two SIM cards for mobile phones and a package of powder. The room would replicate a cell, with socks and jocks thrown around, books and the usual bits and pieces of a prisoner's personal property.

The pair would spend at least an hour or so doing the search and then swap places and do it over again. Every imaginable nook and cranny was searched. We had tools to take apart the frames of beds and light fittings. We had cameras that could be put down the toilet bowl to see if anything was hidden behind the cistern.

The mobile phones coming into prison are tiny fob phones, about the size of a modern car key. They can be bought in the shops that specialize in phones, and some are made without using any metal.

The tiny size means that there are all sorts of places where phones can be hidden. For instance, in a mop or brush there might be one little hair out of place. That left enough room to conceal a tiny phone which could be kept intact while the mop or brush was in use. Another trick was to leave a bit of excrement in the toilet with drugs hidden behind that, or the same trick with toilet paper.

A favourite was to take a pack of biscuits, bought in the tuck shop, open the pack at one end and empty out maybe half a dozen biscuits. Then you crumble one of them and put the phone in, before putting everything back on top, nice and neat. Only practised hands on the package would notice that something was amiss.

Every time we came across one of these methods, we put it on the OSG computer system to share with colleagues in all the prisons. When it was a one-off – like removing a small part from the back of a TV to leave a little cubbyhole for storing something – we photographed it and circulated it. All of this went towards building up a databank that would ensure little or nothing got past us.

In cell searches one golden rule we had was to replace everything exactly as we found it. Posters were put back up on the wall, care was taken with family photos and any personal items, and everything was left just as it was when we entered the cell. On occasion, if we thought it necessary, we took photographs before we began, just as proof of how we had found the place. That way, there could be no room for allegations that we were harassing a prisoner or upsetting him on purpose. The other consideration was the officers on the landing who, if cells were left in a state, would be the ones to bear the brunt of the retaliation or anger from prisoners.

The decision to search a cell was usually taken as a result of receiving intelligence or a tip-off. A good share of the working day for our members in the Operational Support Unit (OSU) was spent gathering intelligence. We had recordings of phone calls, to check what might be coming in or who was dealing inside or whatever. We also had access to the CCTV network in the prison, which was viewed to find out whether anything was being passed about. And then there was interaction with the officers on the landing, who, once they got over the new set-up, would pass on to us any little bit of information that mightn't amount to much in itself but would go towards building an intelligence file.

The OSU officers would then come back to me and say, for instance, that they had listened in on a call in which a prisoner asked his wife for fifty yellow T-shirts, which is quite obviously code to bring in a quantity of pills. Or we might find out that he is in bother over money and acting suspiciously. Every kind of detail would go to determining whether he was up to something. We put it all into the computer and quickly built up a database.

Once we decided that the timing was right to move in on somebody under suspicion, we acted. The searches always happened at mealtimes, when everybody was in their cells and there would be no chance of any aggro on the landing. We would walk in unannounced, not even telling the class officer on the landing. Then tell the prisoner he was going to be searched. More often than not, he might try something, such as saying he had to brush his teeth – anything to give him the opportunity to swallow or somehow get rid of contraband.

'No teeth brushing allowed. No nothing, just come with us.' Some would bitch and moan about their dinner going cold. 'Don't worry, we'll have a fresh dinner waiting for you when you get back.' And off we'd go with the prisoner, and leave some of our people to get on with the search.

The prisoner would be taken down to the screening area and stripped completely. Then he would be given a towel to protect his decency and told to sit in what we called the Boss Chair, 'Boss' being an acronym for Body Orifice Security Scanner. This was a throne-like contraption that could detect metals. If anything was secreted anywhere in the body of its subject, the Boss chair would detect it. (Some of the tiny fob phones sold in shops and online are marketed as 'Beat the Boss'.)

Once that was completed, the prisoner got his clothes back and was put in a holding cell until the search of his own cell was complete. It wasn't unheard of for our people to arrive on a landing and take as many as six prisoners away for this procedure.

Naturally, the new regime caused grief, and inevitably there were allegations that we wrecked cells. Within the first few weeks, we had the kind of incident that allowed us to nip these kinds of complaints in the bud and put down a marker. David 'Frog Eyes' Stanners was a Limerick gang leader serving a life sentence for the notorious murder of another Limerick criminal, Kieran Keane. He claimed that on our first in-depth search of his cell we had wrecked the place, including tearing up photographs of his wife and children and throwing them in the bin. What he forgot was that the bin was covered by CCTV cameras which showed he was the one who had done it. Within days of that search, he and his gang came out on to the landing with fists up, looking for a fight. A shemozzle of sorts ensued between the prisoners and officers, but it wasn't anything to write home about in the context of the kind of violence we were used to.

The claims Stanners made were considered by the class officer on the landing, who asked us whether there was any truth to them. If there had been, then the class officer could reasonably say that we were making trouble for him, wrecking cells and leaving him to deal with the fallout. We showed the class officer the CCTV and immediately he saw what was going on. His attitude then was, 'Fuck this, he's not going to rule the roost here!' For a while after that, every time we did the cells of Stanners and his gang we pulled the prison escort van, with its small uncomfortable cells, into the yard and threw them into it. That softened their cough.

The third element to the OSG work was the Canine Unit. Because of the nature of training dogs, it took a few months before we had this up and running.

We brought in three types of dogs. The passive drug dogs are those who are used to detect whether visitors have anything on them. Despite the job they have to do, these lads are big softies, mostly Labradors. They will just walk around the subject and, if they can get a waft of the drugs, they will nearly smile as they sit down to indicate. That's what we call it, 'an indication'. The only drawback is that tablets can't be detected by these fellas.

Then we have the active drugs dogs – usually collies – used mainly in cell searches. These lads are not, well, passive. If searching a cell, we would send one in thirty seconds ahead of us to get his bearings. These dogs do the business with drugs but are trained to detect mobile phones, and they do some great work. The third type of dog was our old friends from the first chapter in this book – the German shepherds trained as conflict resolution dogs. The best that can be said about these fellas is you won't mess with them. You don't want to ever be in a position where they are out for you.

Training dogs is a trial-and-error business. For every three that are initially selected maybe one might end up passing as an active drugs dog. One of the big factors in determining which dogs make it through is temperament. You can't have a dog that will bite somebody, or who doesn't have the basic patience required to do the job.

Some of the dogs were first class, while others wouldn't have smelt a rasher at a banquet in Bunratty Castle. We also had to regularly test them to ensure they were not falling down on the job. Every so often, we might take them off to Stack House and have maybe four officers standing in a room, one of them with drugs on him. If the dog went to any of those without drugs, he was out the door and taken away for retraining.

Each dog had their own dedicated handler. The dog would only work for that handler. All the handlers were trained in the North and it was a much sought-after number. The job was known as a 'dead man's job' because the only time one became available was when somebody already in service died or retired. For the dogs, the work was done on a reward basis – and the reward was nothing more than a plain old tennis ball.

The system we put in place was that we could randomly select visitors to be taken to a room adjoining the screening area, where the dog would be ready to do his or her thing. The visitor would be asked to stand on a line with hands down by their sides. The handler then brings the dog around the visitor, clicking fingers to get the dog to sniff high and low on the person. The dog doesn't touch the person but if he gets an indication he will stop. For instance, the obvious place the dog often stops is around the visitor's back passage, a favoured depository for drugs.

If the dog does give an indication, then we ask the visitor why this is so. If no reasonable explanation is provided, the visitor will then either be asked to come back some other time or possibly allowed in, but for a screen visit only. (That's a visit in which a full-height – countertop to ceiling – clear perspex screen separates the prisoner and their visitor. The area beneath the counter is solid so the screen is only needed from the countertop up.) If a dog indicates three times on a particular visitor, then that visitor is on permanent screen visits only.

Sometimes, solicitors or barristers would have to go through this process. None of them would be likely to have drugs but they could, for instance, earlier in the day have been in the criminal courts with defendants who smelt of drugs. The power of the dog's sense of smell was so strong that even contact at such a remove, hours old, would result in an indication.

Once things got up to speed, the dogs did good work. Before long, we were getting up to ten indications a day, sometimes as high as twenty-five on a Saturday. It would not be unusual to have up to 10 per cent of all visits on a screen-only basis within a short while.

Another incident, early on in the OSG, showed how quickly some of the criminals had copped on to the new regime. One day, a call came through from a service station just outside Portlaoise. The manager had some interesting CCTV footage he thought we might want to view. What he showed us occurred around the side of the service station, at a quiet spot. A young girl, about eighteen or so, met two older people there: one male, one female. The girl adopted a pose where she put her hands up in the air and the older woman opened the girl's jeans, pulled down her underwear and inserted a small package into her vagina. The whole process was obviously adopted to ensure that the girl, who would later be visiting the prison, had absolutely no contact with the drugs and should then be in a far better position to make it in past the dogs. As with a high percentage of those who brought in drugs, this girl was, in all likelihood, acting under duress.

15. Face to Face

Over the years in the OSG, we came across a truckload of innovative ways in which contraband was smuggled into prison. But the main route is, and always has been, through visitors. When everything is stripped back, the human-to-human contact that occurs during weekly visits is simply the best opportunity for the passing over of drugs and phones.

Here is a typical scene from the visitor box in the Midlands during my time. The visitor, usually female, arrives in and sits on her side of the table. The prisoner sits opposite. At some point after that, the visitor puts her hand inside her underwear, pulls out something, throws it across to the prisoner and he immediately takes it, puts it in his mouth and swallows. A shout goes up. Prison officers burst into the room. They take away the visitor and grab the prisoner in a headlock, trying, usually with no success, to get him to spit out the package of drugs.

Some of the children in the room – there are usually around six separate visits going on at the one time, many of them including children – look frightened. Some of the other visitors also are full of fear. The other prisoners are most likely just pissed off that their precious weekly visit has now been thrown completely out of kilter.

The offending visitor is brought to the screening area, where she will be held until the gardaí arrive, take her away and ultimately charge her with bringing drugs into the prison. She will be denied entry to the prison for a period, and when her visits resume they will be screen-only. If she is brought to court, she will in all likelihood receive a fine.

The prisoner will be taken to a strip cell, stripped naked and left in there in his poncho and jocks, in the bare cell, for two or three days. During that time, he will probably pass out the pills from his body in the form of solid waste. He will then root around in the excrement and find the pills or whatever he swallowed – sometimes it will be drugs in a condom. He will surrender a small quantity of what passes out in order to get back on to his landing, but he will retain most of the pills. The management in the prison can't do a thing about that – because, apart from anything else, who knows how many he swallowed and what number he has kept for himself? Back on the landing, he will be put 'behind the door', restricted to his cell for the down time in the evening, for a few weeks at least. That won't really bother him, because he will have his happy pills to keep him company. The visit, a brief chance for loved ones to maintain regular contact with each other for precious minutes, was sacrificed. And it won't take place again, for maybe months.

That scenario was played out, over and over again, during my time. It still goes on today. It shows that, despite the best security in the world, drugs and phones will get into prisons – unless you have some sort of inhumane regime, as they do in places like the supermax prisons in the USA. From my early days in the OSG, two things about smuggling contraband became obvious to me. The hold that drugs have over some people is so powerful that, if they could, they would readily sell their mother to get a fix. The second thing is that when needs must, in order to get something into a prison, people are capable of coming up with all kinds of creative ways to do so.

Before the OSG got off the ground in the Midlands, it

was relatively easy to bring gear in through visits. In the early 2000s, the Limerick gangs in the prison had a fairly free rein. This wasn't down to slack management. The nature of these gang members – the sheer numbers of them in the system, with their constantly shifting loyalties – meant that the main emphasis was on controlling them rather than strictly monitoring their visits. The priority was to ensure that the various factions were kept separate during visits, to prevent an outbreak of violence. Visits generally take place Monday to Saturday, but we had to open up on a Sunday to facilitate the separation. It was the sensible thing to do, because otherwise there would have been a constant threat of one or other of them getting stabbed during the coming and going from their landing to the visiting boxes.

The scene inside the visiting boxes when the Limerick gangs were receiving visitors was something else. It was pure mayhem, prisoners and visitors walking around and mixing, children wandering around the place, all of which meant it was easy as pie to pass on contraband. A few times, they even managed to swap jackets and the prisoner just returned to his landing weighed down with booty.

There were no pat-down searches, X-ray machines or dogs. Visitors were bringing in drugs but also vodka, brandy, gin and whiskey (and some more niche products: we discovered that David Stanners had a liking for Pernod – not an impressive feat of detection, because you could smell it on his breath). Because of its bulk, alcohol is one of the more difficult things to smuggle into a prison, but they managed it. At one point, the officer in the box spotted a hot-water bottle being passed over. On examination it turned out to be full of vodka.

One of the main issues around prison visits with the Limerick gangs was to ensure that all the visitors who entered the prison were accounted for on leaving, and none of the prisoners managed to swap places. This was a constant threat as far as we were concerned. All of that was to change after the OSG got up and running.

The early years were a useful learning experience. To a large extent, it was a game of cat and mouse, trying to stay one step ahead. There were all kinds of myths about how to outwit security that prompted visitors to try out different things. One was that the dogs couldn't smell drugs if the package was coated with Vicks VapoRub, the stuff you use to relieve cold symptoms. In reality, the dogs just refused to search, which for us was the same as an indication, so the visit was not allowed to go ahead. Another myth that did the rounds was that phones wrapped in carbon paper would get through the metal detector. Visitors tried that for a while, until they copped that it didn't work. At another point, it was all the rage to break up the phone, bring in the casing one day and the interior the next, and have a SIM card in the visitor's mouth. We copped on to that one, too, though some probably still got through.

The baby with the dirty nappy was used until we organized to have all nappies removed. Visitors would present at the screening area with the baby, and close examination would reveal the usual pong coming from the nappy. Who wants to delve into a nappy full of poo? After a while we realized we had to. So, a room was organized where there were changing facilities, as you might find in a restaurant. The visitor would bring the baby, and every nappy had to be taken off and put back on in the presence of a female officer. Unless, of course, it was full of poo, then the nappy was replaced. We had a supply of nappies on hand in the screening area, just for this purpose.

Initially, there was some trouble over this, with visitors

claiming breach of privacy and that it was affecting the children. But we were careful how it was handled. The female officer never touched the baby or interfered in any way. We also made sure that the area where the nappy was taken off was outside the range of the CCTV cameras for privacy. The reality was that babies were being used to bring in drugs, and our job was to stop it.

Another ruse was the hair tied up in a bun, which is a grand place to hide something. Once we copped that, we insisted that all women untie the bun and shake out their hair before entering. The visitor was entirely free to retie the bun once past the screening area. Hair became an issue in another way when hair extensions became a fashion statement. A woman wearing clip-in hair extensions would nearly always activate the metal detector, and we had to ask her to remove them. Sometimes, when other visitors arrived in the screening area, they would be shocked at the sight of a pile of hair sitting in trays – you could see it in their faces – but we usually said nothing and let their imagination run wild.

The lining of waistbands on tracksuit bottoms was another favoured location for hiding drugs in clothes left in for prisoners. Even when we discovered stuff in clothes, nobody could be held responsible, because whoever dropped them in was already gone and the prisoner hadn't done anything to receive the drugs.

Then we had the spray. There is a form of heroin that comes in a spray, and this made its way into prison through letters. The paper was then cut into tiny pieces and smoked. Again, it took us a while to cop on to that, but we did. They try something, it works for a while. We detect it and they try something else. That's how it went. And how it always will.

*

Each visitor box is a long room, effectively split down the middle by a series of tables. The centre of each of these tables will have a ledge, maybe six inches high. This is the divide between prisoner and visitor. Typically, there is enough room for four to six prisoners at any one time. On the prisoner's side there is a wooden chair nailed to the ground. On the opposite side there is a wooden bench which can seat at least three adults. Each prisoner is entitled to have three adults, plus a child or a number of children, on any visit.

At one end of the room, there is a high chair, where an officer sits overseeing the visits, a bit like the umpire at a tennis match. If anything arises, he or she can bring the visit to an abrupt end. Each visit lasts thirty minutes. When it's coming close to the end, the officer will hand the visitor a docket which records the time of the visit. The visitor needs this to be allowed out of the prison. Every visitor box has two CCTV cameras, one at each end; one is focused on the prisoners, the other on the visitors. The cameras are monitored live in the control room.

Officially, there is supposed to be no touching, but practically all officers will allow a hug at the start and end of the visit. The latter is the time when there might be an attempt to hand something over. You might say that cutting out any contact would reduce the chances of contraband being passed over, but this would be to deprive the majority of prisoners of a rare opportunity for human touch. We are not dealing with robots here and, arguably, it would be inhumane to deny brief contact to the majority because a small number are engaged in criminal activity.

Screen visits take place in a separate box designed especially for the purpose. These visits are generally used as a form of punishment for previous attempts to bring in contraband and often take place following a period in which visits have been banned. The full-height perspex screen separating prisoner and visitor prevents the passing of anything between them. To allow for conversation between prisoner and visitor, there is a hollowed-out section in the wooden counter which is sealed with metal grille covers. The door to the box is locked and there is no officer present, because it is simply impossible to pass anything across. At any one time, there could be up to a quarter of prisoners on screen visits only.

Then there is the lifers' box. This allows for a small bit of privacy for families of a man serving a life sentence. The room might have paintings on the wall, carpet and a few small couches and maybe some toys for children. There is also a kettle and tea or coffee. The visit is completely private, with no officer in attendance, but the room is monitored on CCTV. The special treatment is in recognition of the length of time that the prisoner is removed from his family. Some children will grow from toddler to adult, only knowing their father through visits.

Problems can, however, arise. Dessie Dundon, a gang leader from Limerick, was (and still is) serving life for murder. His girlfriend visited him regularly, and on one occasion she passed solid waste into a cup after having swallowed tablets outside. Three officers burst in on them, but Dessie had managed to swallow one or two of the tabs. She was taken away and Dessie was not allowed back into the lifers' box for about six months. His girlfriend was not allowed visits of any sort for a few months, and after that she had to endure another period of screen visits only. Not for the first time, I wondered about the price some prisoners and their loved ones were prepared to pay to get their hands on a small amount of drugs.

Once we had the operation up and running, we began to have some success. Everything is relative, though. Using dogs for detection meant that the prospects of visitors getting in drugs like heroin, hash or marijuana were greatly reduced. However, drugs will always find a way in, so the nature of the drugs being smuggled in changed. The next port of call for the dealers was tablets, many of them opiate-based, but crucially without an odour.

Some of the prisoners made light of the new regime. 'Ah, Mr Mac,' one of them said to me, one day. 'You're an awful man. It used to be hash for me, but now you have me on the mind-blowing tabs.'

Tablets could be easily carried. And with tablets there was nothing that would attract the attention of the dogs. Anything that involves the groin area is naturally sensitive, so detecting these drugs is always difficult. The only realistic chance of intercepting them is when there are attempts to hand over the stuff, usually in the visiting box.

This obviously puts more emphasis on the various ways of handing over the drugs. Typically, a row will start between a couple during a visit. Prisoner A gets to his feet and begins shouting at his partner. She responds. A shouting match ensues, raising the temperature in the room and attracting everyone's attention. Meanwhile, Prisoner B, sitting maybe at the far end of the visiting box, takes advantage of the distraction and gives his partner the nod. She retrieves a bag of tablets from her body and hands it over. Afterwards, Prisoner A may have to pay the price of being locked up for a few evenings, but he gets his reward of some pills from Prisoner B.

The Saturday Blu-tack job was another ruse that worked for a while. The visitor – usually a woman – arrives in the visiting box on a Saturday and during the course of the visit retrieves the drugs from her person. She has a piece of Blu-tack which she uses to stick the drugs to the underside of the table. The visit ends, she goes home, and the prisoner goes back to his cell.

The following day, Sunday, is reserved for cleaning out the visitor box, which is carried out by a trustee – one of the prisoners who are on special detail because they are well behaved and considered trustworthy. More often than not, this man is acting under threat. He would have been visited in his cell at some point over the previous days and told he was to retrieve the drugs when doing the cleaning. If he did as he was told, there might be the reward of a few pills. If he didn't, he would immediately come under threat of having his face cut up at some point. We copped this after a while, through accidentally catching a trustee on CCTV fiddling around at a table.

It is all a game, and you wouldn't want to take it too seriously; there will always be some new and inventive way of getting drugs in. If I was visiting a prison tomorrow and wanted to take in something, I'm sure I would have no problem concealing a bag of tablets and managing to get it in. Our job was to minimize the traffic, and I think we did that to the best of our ability and within the constraints that were always present.

What really struck me after a while was how creative some of these lads could be when it came to getting in contraband. Many among them were obviously intelligent, some very much so. You have to wonder how they would have fared in life if they were born into different families, in a different place, with a different postcode, and grew up with all the advantages of middle-class kids, where the emphasis was on education and getting a good job. I've no doubt some of them would be running big companies, or banks, or maybe even the country.

Another feature of the flow of contraband into prison is that it is often done under duress. Of course, you can have a partner or wife doing it against her better instincts, or as a result of emotional blackmail, but I'm talking here about real duress: the threat to the safety of a prisoner and his family. This is something that the criminal gangs excel at, and it plumbs real depths of inhumanity.

Take the case of a prisoner who has debts from drug dealing when he is convicted and begins his sentence. The debt remains, and now he has a problem when he enters prison in that there is no escaping it. He effectively becomes a slave to whichever gang leader inside the prison takes responsibility for the debt. He can't pay for it on the outside, so he must recruit his loved ones to do so, usually through bringing drugs into the prison.

Then you have the debt that is accumulated in prison. A man is convicted for the first time. He is taken from the court to prison, is disorientated, worried, if not scared shitless. In the prison a friendly neighbour wanders into his cell to welcome him to this new world. The nice man says he'll show him the ropes. The new prisoner must want to ring his loved ones just to let them know he's OK. This friendly face will offer the new prisoner a bang off his phone, in order to let the family know he's alright on his first night inside.

The following morning, this nice man re-enters the new prisoner's cell – except this time, he's not looking so nice and may be accompanied by a couple of mates. That will be €200 for the night's rent of the phone. A prisoner has access to a bank account, but only to buy stuff in the tuck shop or to transfer money, with the governor's permission, to a visitor. A new prisoner would be highly unlikely to get permission, because the suspicion would be that it's being done under duress. Thus, the new prisoner enters the world of prison debt. Repayment can be painful, not just for him but for his family on the outside. The prisoner has a choice. Ignore his oppressors and he will be cut up, his face slashed, and possibly worse. Or get his family onside to work off the debt.

The work, more often than not, will mean attempting to bring in contraband during visits. In extreme cases, it might require somebody to act as a mule, perhaps flying to Holland to pick up a suitcase of drugs. This is sometimes favoured by the gang if the loved one on the outside is an older woman, usually a mother, who might raise less suspicion on a flight to and from Amsterdam. There are also cases, albeit rare, where a prisoner's partner is forced into prostitution to pay off the debt.

During my time, when we discovered attempts to bring in gear, it was not uncommon for the visitor to break down and tell us the full story. She had been instructed by her partner that this had to be done, or he was going to be savagely attacked.

Of course, you might think this is an attempt to explain away her actions when she's caught, but after a while it's easy to spot the ones telling the truth, given what we might know about the circumstances of her partner, the prisoner.

In these instances, we would assure the woman – and it was nearly always a woman – that we understood the scenario. We would explain that we still had to go through the motions of calling the guards to arrest her, but we would sort her out as best we could.

Meanwhile, inside, word gets around that the visitor was arrested. This means she will be of little use for the foreseeable future, because she will be banned from visiting. That takes the pressure off the prisoner. He can't do anything, so maybe he is allowed to work off the debt some other way.

There were, I would guess, at least ten times during my years in the OSG in the Midlands when a prisoner came to me, or a colleague, confessing what he had been told his visitor must do in order to ensure his safety. This is the point where our duty of care kicks in. The obvious solution to protect him is to have him transferred to the protection block where he will be safe, unless they make a concerted attempt to go after him. That, however, does not kill the debt, and nor does it free his family from their obligations, as far as the gang is concerned.

So, in these incidents we often set up a ruse. We tell the prisoner to go along with what is planned. His loved one is contacted by associates of the gang and given the drugs to bring in. The drugs will have to be hidden internally in her body. She enters the prison and we nab her, either in the screening area or in the visitor box. She is detained until the gardaí arrive and arrest her. We fill the gardaí in on the background so, in all likelihood, the case never advances to a prosecution. Meanwhile, she is also banned from entry to the prison for a few months.

The prisoner would have to appear before the governor, to make a case to have her let back in, and the governor wouldn't even be in on what we had done. Once allowed back in, she and the prisoner are confined to screen visits only, for another few months.

The ruse once went pear-shaped on us. After the woman was arrested, and we filled in the gardaí, something went wrong. Contrary to every other time, the case advanced all the way to the district court. When we heard that, we were in a bit of a tizzy: *What if this woman walks into court and tells the judge that she was just playing along with us when she brought in the drugs?* There would be hell to pay. Thankfully, it never came to that. The judge was given a genuine sob story by the woman's solicitor; he imposed a minor fine, and we heard no more about it.

One other case was particularly depressing in how it unfolded. The prisoner in question was hitting sixty. I can't remember what he was in for, but he certainly wasn't a hardened criminal. He had a debt which, from recollection, was run up before he entered the prison. He was told what had to be done. He came to me in despair. I advised him to go through with bringing the drugs in and getting caught. There was no other way to deal with the matter, bar putting him on the protection block and installing 24/7 garda protection for his family, which just wasn't going to happen.

The gang knew his family background and had told him they wanted his daughter to do the deed. She was around nineteen years of age and had a learning disability. The disability was mild enough, but I don't think she was fully aware of what was going on.

Anyway, the prisoner rang her from my office. I was present for the whole conversation, and he got very emotional talking to her. She was told to expect a visit at home from some people who wanted her to bring a package to her dad in the Midlands. He didn't tell her what the package would contain. She was then to get on a specific train from Heuston Station to Portlaoise, and go straight to the Midlands.

As it was to turn out, nobody called to her home. Instead, she got on the train to Portlaoise and was met off it by two men who introduced themselves as friends of her father and drove her to a remote area. From her subsequent description, this appears to have been an area known as 'the Heath', about three miles outside the town. Out there, they concealed a package in her underwear and, from what we could gather, may have sexually assaulted her. Then they drove back to Portlaoise, dropped her outside the Midlands and drove off.

When she came into the prison, we went through the routine. She was brought into the room with the dogs, where there was an indication. She was held and the guards came. The poor woman was in bits as she was arrested and led away by the guards.

Ultimately, it worked. The prisoner was left alone, and no further work was required to deal with his debt. I'm sure the whole ordeal was traumatic for his daughter. But what was the alternative? If we had simply gone along with the official policy – called in the guards early, moved the prisoner – then his family would have been put in grave danger. The gardaí do not have the resources to protect every family in such a scenario, and you are dealing with people who have absolutely no morals.

16. Bad Apples

Early on in the Operational Support Group (OSG), one of our aims was to gather as much external expertise as we could. John L, the first governor, and John Kavanagh, who succeeded him, were very open to this. We organized to link in with the military police in The Curragh for some training, including for the new Canine Unit. As time went on, the connections we built up meant there was an open door any time we felt they could assist us, usually with advice.

In 2010, I suggested that we should make contact with the Customs and Excise people, with a view to gaining experience in searching vehicles. I got the nod for that, and a few of us were sent down to Rosslare to work with the customs officers in their routine searching of vehicles coming off the ferry from the UK. That was invaluable experience.

Our main relationship with an outside body was with the gardaí. I've always had a lot of admiration for some of the work the gardaí do in apprehending criminals. One case where I thought they did exceptional work was in solving the murder of Elaine O'Hara, which was a highly complex investigation. Only partial remains of Elaine's skeleton were discovered in woods at the foot of the Dublin Mountains, in August 2012, a year after her disappearance, so initially there was nothing to suggest how she had died. The coincidental finding of mobile phones, supermarket loyalty fobs and bondage gear in Roundwood Reservoir, and the presence of mind of a local young garda, James O'Donoghue, who followed up assiduously, and discovered the fobs were connected to the missing woman, put in motion a chain of events that allowed gardaí to piece together what had happened to her. They worked out that a Dublin architect, Graham Dwyer, had been grooming her over a period of time to participate in sadistic encounters that would culminate in allowing him to stab her to death, in fulfilment of his ultimate sexual fantasy. Dwyer was convicted of murder in 2015, and sent to the Midlands to serve his life sentence. I had lots of dealings with him, and in terms of his conduct, he was, and I presume still is, a model prisoner. He stood out for his obvious intelligence, and he always came across in a shy, respectful way. His mild-mannered demeanour was unsettling because, in addition to the disturbing picture of how he had manipulated Elaine O'Hara, his trial had included evidence of his extremely violent fantasies – centred on the torture, rape and killing of women. Still, I knew that a few of my colleagues approached him for advice on planning and related issues to do with extensions to their homes. As far as I was concerned, though, it was the job the gardaí did in apprehending him that stood out for me.

As I mentioned in Chapter 5 (Back Home in 'The Bog'), for a long time there had been tensions between prison officers and gardaí in Portlaoise Prison. By the time the Midlands was up and running, I felt these tensions were falling away. And then when the OSG was set up, it was time to look again at how we interacted. We made contact with the local gardaí, in particular, and built relationships. There was a realization that we were both on the same side and could help each other. From there, things improved and good relations with the gardaí yielded some great results, both for them and us.

One of the areas where the gardaí were a help to us was

in attempting to collar officers who were bringing in drugs. Prison officers are no different from men and women in other walks of life: there will be bad apples. The difference with our job is that the bad apples can do serious damage. Some of them see an opportunity to make money. Others just land in trouble, maybe through recreational drug use or by getting into debt with gambling.

From our point of view, a bent officer could do massive damage. One officer who is willing to bring in drugs is more valuable to a dealer on the outside, or gang leader on the inside, than a hundred visitors. Notwithstanding the operation of the screening, there are multiple opportunities for officers to bring stuff in. If I was still working in the service and was of a mind to bring in a big quantity of drugs, I would have no problem at all.

There will be some officers who attempt to bring drink in for their own use. Lads who had a drink problem might have a two-litre bottle of Coke in their bag and half of it would be vodka. There wasn't a lot we could do about that without creating a fuss, and you'd want to be 100 per cent sure of your facts to go down that road. Drinking on the job is a problem in prisons but, strictly speaking, it wasn't our problem in the OSG.

When somebody shows up and says he has cans of Coke in his bag, and it turns out to be cans of beer, you definitely confiscate it. Anything like that is a no-no, although we did relax things at Christmas time. A few cans, a bottle of wine or Baileys, being taken in by somebody going on night duty on Christmas week was something to which we turned a blind eye. In those situations, we might have a discreet word about not leaving any glass bottle around the place. That's the kind of thing that you definitely don't want prisoners to get their hands on.

All of that was relatively harmless. The main issue was to ensure that officers weren't bringing in drugs for prisoners – and in that respect, our relationship with the guards was certainly a big help.

Sometimes in the OSG, we dealt with the matter ourselves. There was a case in Cork Prison, in the early years, where an officer was bringing in alcohol for a prisoner. This officer had got himself into trouble with the prisoner, whom he had known on the outside. The officer was having marital problems and he leaned on the prisoner. The prisoner asked to borrow the officer's phone, one day. The officer handed it over, but when he came to retrieve it, he was told to get lost. His former friend then threatened to expose him for handing over his phone. So began a different relationship between them in which the officer was blackmailed to bring in alcohol and then pornographic videos.

Our lads in Cork eventually nabbed him. He was an eejit more than anything else, but he was told to hand over his ID, he was being pensioned off – and he wouldn't be getting his full pension, either. The alternative, as he well knew, was to bring the whole matter to the guards.

One early case in which we and the gardaí co-operated was that of Trevor Gleeson. We had gathered intelligence about Gleeson, an ordinary-rank prison officer in the Midlands, which suggested he was bringing in drugs. Some of it came from prisoners who knew he was a player. Once it gets to the stage that prisoners are aware of it, you know he's somebody to watch.

And watch him we did. Every day that he came through the screening area when I was there, I paid him particular attention. He was always carrying a cup of coffee, and while that is standard today, this was in the late 2000s when it wasn't as common. I had my suspicions about the coffee, so one day I bumped against him, as if by accident, causing him to spill it. Nothing of any significance popped out, but I had satisfied myself.

At that time, we were having regular meetings with gardaí in Portlaoise to share intelligence. I brought them my suspicions – by that stage, very strong suspicions – about Gleeson's activities. Following that, the gardaí put him under surveillance. They had their own intelligence on the outside, and eventually they reckoned they had enough to move against him.

The detective with whom I liaised kept me abreast of the situation. On 22 December 2009, this detective – we'll call him Pat – told me they had intelligence that Gleeson would be collecting a package that evening. As I explained at the start of the book, at Christmas the volume of drugs coming into prisons cranks right up.

Pat swore me to secrecy. As with any operation of this nature, surprise was a weapon. Any chance of Gleeson or his criminal associates being forewarned would put the kibosh on the whole thing. But I had a dilemma. Knowledge is power, and management in many walks of life is often obsessed with who knows what first, in order to demonstrate that they are all powerful. Or, to put it in plain terms, there is often a pissing contest between senior managers to make it clear who is the boss.

Two governors had asked – a mild way of putting it – to be kept informed of any operation against Gleeson. Quite obviously, both would want to be the first to inform Irish Prison Service headquarters in Longford of something like this. I asked Pat could I at least tell John L, my governor in the OSG. 'OK,' Pat said, finally. 'Him, and him only, absolutely nobody else.' The other person who wanted to be kept abreast was Ned Whelan, campus governor over the Midlands and Portlaoise. I knew I was going where I shouldn't, but I also filled in Ned. I admired him as a governor. But more than that, I wanted to stay on his good side for the sake of the OSG, as he had been a big supporter of ours within the system. In any event, I knew there would be no leak originating with either of those two gents.

That evening, the gardaí followed Gleeson. I was kept in the loop through my detective pal, who gave me hourly updates. Gleeson parked his car at Lourdesville, a residential part of Kildare town. A criminal figure, whom the gardaí knew, got into the passenger seat, and the two men drove a short distance. The criminal figure then got out and Gleeson's car began making its way out of town. The gardaí switched on the siren and gave chase. At some point, a plastic bag was thrown from the car. Gleeson pulled in soon after and was arrested. The plastic bag was retrieved and found to contain just short of €6,000 worth of benzylpiperazine, diamorphine and cannabis.

In the station, Gleeson told the gardaí that he had been acting under duress in attempting to get drugs to particular prisoners in the Midlands. He said that prisoners in the Midlands and their associates outside had threatened him that if he didn't do as they instructed, there would be repercussions. He said that, a few months earlier, he had picked up a package after being told to do so but had dumped the drugs rather than actually bring them into the prison. He had intended, he claimed, to do the same thing on this occasion.

Asked why, of all the staff in the prison, he was the one officer criminals selected to approach, he said he had no idea. He had not reported the threats made against him to the gardaí, or to the prison authorities, because 'they wouldn't even listen to you', he told detectives, referring to prison management.

In interview notes he was recorded as saying the following:

'I have been followed home, been intimidated by people from Limerick both inside the prison and outside. It's going on months, being pressured and pressured and being followed. I don't know why I agreed to meet this lad tonight and get it and throw it in a bin. That was basically it. And this man came in behind me [the detective]. I knew obviously what was in the bag, I knew it was drugs; I threw it out when this man came in behind me . . . He saw I was petrified when I got out. I don't know why I agreed to meet him tonight. I was afraid for my family, and now I will have no family . . . they are the most dangerous criminals from Limerick. Being followed is not a nice thing . . . I never touch drugs. I just did it to get my family out of it, out of their lives, when certainly criminals are telling you that there are people looking for you inside the prison . . . I am a nervous wreck. I can't sleep.'

Gleeson was charged with possession with intent to supply. The day after he was released from custody, he showed up at the prison and was brought before Ned Whelan. Ned was not a man to stand on ceremony. He told Gleeson in no uncertain terms to get the hell out of the prison. Officially, he suspended Gleeson. Initially, the suspension was without pay, but at some point after that he got his pay restored.

Three months after the incident, something else occurred which would feature at Gleeson's trial. CCTV footage at a local supermarket showed Gleeson talking to two men.

Gleeson would, in time, suggest that these men were part of the gang who were intimidating him. The prosecution would claim it demonstrated he was in cahoots with them. The court was told that the two men did have criminal convictions, but it was also pointed out that a prison officer could encounter or even know ex-prisoners from the time they spent behind bars.

The trial took place at Naas Circuit Court, in December 2012, three years after Gleeson had been caught and suspended. At the trial he made no issue about the details of having the drugs in his possession before throwing them from the car. His defence was one of duress, that he was acting out of fear and intimidation. The gang that was allegedly intimidating him was the McCarthy-Dundons from Limerick, a number of whom were serving long sentences in the Midlands.

The jury found him guilty of possession of the drugs, but crucially they disagreed on the charge of intent to supply. The following July, he was retried on the charge of intent to supply. At that trial, the video footage from the supermarket was introduced, but it became the subject of legal argument, particularly because of the late introduction. As a result, the trial judge dismissed the jury. Gleeson was never retried on that charge. In January 2014, he was sentenced on the possession conviction, for which he received an eighteen-month prison term, suspended for three years.

So, the ultimate outcome of this prison officer being found in possession of nearly €6,000 worth of drugs was a suspended sentence.

There was nothing to stop him returning to work, and he did just that, once he got the all-clear. He came back to Portlaoise Prison, where he was not greeted with open arms. In fact, most officers at every level gave him the cold shoulder. There is a fair bit of camaraderie in the service, we look after our own. But what he did was beyond the pale, as far as the vast majority were concerned. Bringing drugs into the prison, apart from anything else, makes our job more dangerous. While he was not convicted of actually bringing the drugs in, most of us had made up our minds that that was precisely what he was intending to do.

Soon after returning to the job, he was transferred to the Prison supply depot, which is basically a warehousing facility in Santry, north Dublin. It's my understanding that he left the job shortly after that. In 2018, the Court of Appeal overturned Gleeson's conviction.

The gardaí were also centrally involved in another case in which a member of staff was bringing in drugs, except this time it was a nurse. This nurse – we'll call her Florence – worked in the prison and she had a drug habit, as far as I could see. The usual signs – dilated pupils, slightly slurred speech at times – suggested to me that she had an ongoing problem. Despite that, there was nothing we could do about it without actual proof. We had our suspicions for some time that she was bringing stuff in, but nabbing her was going to be difficult.

First, there was little chance of doing so in the screening area. Staff were not searched in the same manner as visitors, because it simply wouldn't be practical. For instance, staff did not have to go to the room with the dogs. Just as lawyers or solicitors might have a waft of cannabis off them, so also might officers who were dealing with prisoners. When it came to searching staff, all we could do was to put them through the metal detector and give them a pat-down. We suspected Florence was carrying the drugs internally, and there was absolutely nothing we could do about that.

She worked nights a lot, which facilitated her distributing the drugs. She would regularly visit cells to administer drugs, such as insulin for those with diabetes. She would be accompanied to the landing by an officer but he or she would wait outside the cell door. Florence would go in and give the insulin injection while slipping the drugs to her contact. None of this was ultimately proven, but it was perfectly obvious to us that this was what was going on.

Our suspicions hardened when a prisoner came to one of my colleagues in the OSG and essentially ratted on her. He was pissed off because she had been getting greedy, ramping up the price. Through an informant in the prison, we got a handle on what she was about. After that, the informant kept us up to date on her movements.

I got on to my contacts in the local gardaí and told them that there was a good chance of us finding out when she would be carrying drugs to bring in, at which point they could nab her.

Some weeks later, we got word that she was meeting the dealer in Stradbally, a small town about ten kilometres from Portlaoise. I informed my garda contacts. She went to a garage in the town and from there to the Windy Gap, a forest a few kilometres away. Despite the tip-off from us, the gardaí did not intercept her. Afterwards, I learned that they had an issue with the informant in the prison, who was not operating on an official level with the force, and therefore there could be problems down the line in bringing a prosecution. His evidence would be severely challenged in court, as he was not a garda-approved informer.

We decided to give it one more crack. This time, we

bypassed the local guards and went to the drugs squad in Dublin Castle. I had a contact in there, and we had a private meeting with two of their officers. We told them what we were at. They were great. One said, 'We'll have it sorted within a fortnight.' We just had to give them a shout whenever we got word that there was to be a drop-off.

True to their word, they did just that. I passed the information on to them the next time it came through. They followed Florence on the bypass outside Portlaoise, after she had made the pick-up, turned on the siren and flagged her down. She was carrying alright, and she hadn't yet hidden the drugs internally. She told the guards that she was a nurse working in the hospital and that she was bringing the drugs in to work. She was arrested and charged.

In July 2016, Florence pleaded guilty in the Circuit Criminal Court to supplying a controlled drug into a prison. Later that year, she received a three-year sentence, with all but three months suspended on condition she enter a €500 bond and be on good behaviour for five years. She served her sentence in the Dóchas Centre.

In 2020, the High Court granted an application by the Nurse and Midwifery Board to cancel Florence's registration as a nurse. In a fitness to practise inquiry, the board found that she had, on one or more occasions around 8 January 2015, failed to maintain appropriate professional boundaries when she 'engaged with one or more prisoners regarding her personal circumstances'.

It also found that she had, around the same time, failed to report to prison authorities that she had been requested by one or more prisoners 'to convey illegal and/or controlled drugs into the prison in exchange for money'. And it found that around mid-December 2014, on two separate occasions, she had brought a quantity of drugs into the prison and had either given the drugs or arranged for them to be given to one or more prisoners for money.

All of that was nothing to do with us. We had done our job in stopping the flow. There were, however, a few repercussions. The local management in An Garda Síochána were livid that we had effectively gone above their heads and brought in the drugs squad. That required a bit of repairing, because it was important to us to maintain a good, working relationship with the local gardaí. In time, I think they forgave us – or at least learned to live with us, for our mutual benefit.

There were many other cases of what you might call bent officers that never saw the inside of a courtroom. In most instances, when we found something going on, it was just put to the officer in question that we had the goods on him or her and the best thing they could do would be to hand in their notice. Other times, if the case was not as clear-cut, the officer would be transferred to some posting where they couldn't do too much damage. Transferring somebody like that needed approval from IPS headquarters in Longford, but they would rarely ask any awkward questions about the matter.

One case of the latter occurred in relation to the seizing of a mobile phone. This was again something that originated with the gardaí. Word was sent through to me that gardaí in Dublin believed a prisoner in the Midlands was, at the very least, privy to gangland activity being carried out by members of his family on the outside. This included at least one high-profile murder, that of a criminal called Eamon Dunne.

By 2010, Eamon Dunne was one of the most notorious criminals in Dublin. He was believed to control a large share of the drugs market in the capital, but it was his propensity to kill, or order the killing of, others that set him apart. He had taken over a gang based in Finglas, following the high-profile murder of Martin 'Marlo' Hyland, in 2006. Hyland was a gang leader who had attracted the attention of the gardaí to the extent that many of his associates considered him a liability. According to one report, Dunne was suspected of being the driver of the car used to murder Hyland, who was shot dead in bed in a relative's house in Finglas, in north-west Dublin. A tragic element to that killing was that an innocent young plumber, Anthony Campbell, who was working in the house in question at the time, was also shot dead because he would have been in a position to identify the killers.

Four years later, in April 2010, it was Dunne's turn to die violently. He was attending his daughter's birthday party in a pub in Cabra, a few kilometres north of the city centre, when a man walked in, approached him and shot him dead. History was repeating itself as, according to garda intelligence, those plotting to kill him included associates of his own who believed that he was out of control. Some of those involved in that plot were believed by gardaí to be close relatives of our prisoner in the Midlands.

What the gardaí wanted from us was the prisoner's phone – everybody assumed he had access to a phone – which could yield some important intelligence. One night, well after lockdown, we surprised the prisoner with a search. He attempted to swallow the SIM card, but we managed to get our hands on his throat before he succeeded, and stopped him.

Afterwards, one of our guys in the OSG took possession of the phone and brought it home with him. I didn't know he had done this. That was an absolute no-no. Apart from anything else, the phone was potentially evidence that the gardaí could use in court, and at the very least it might be a source of intelligence for them.

Later, we formed serious suspicions of what was afoot. I don't believe the OSG officer was dirty – in that he was bringing in drugs or anything – but he was good friends with another group of officers, some of whom were based in Cloverhill in Dublin, who were known as the Colombians. They had this name because they were suspected of supplying cocaine to some staff for recreational use. None of that was known to management, but in the real world young people do a lot of socializing, including taking illicit drugs, despite the career risks for those working in places like prisons, schools or the gardaí.

When our man came in with the phone the next day, he got the head eaten off him. The most suspicious aspect to his 'error' was that when he returned the phone, there was no record of anybody having texted or called since it was seized the previous night. That was highly unusual. For instance, a while later, we seized another phone from the same prisoner (again, trying to help out the gardaí). That time, right through the night after we seized it and into the next morning, there were, I think, at least fifty contacts by phone or text, which was fairly typical.

Anyway, our suspicions were that the lad who took the phone home did so in order to protect his mates, the Colombians, as he feared their numbers might be on the phone. There was only one way of dealing with the officer in question. He was transferred out of the OSG. He was never confronted with the suspicion that he had wiped the numbers of his mates from the phone, but the mere fact of having taken it home was enough to merit a disciplinary response.

17. Getting a Handle on the Gangs

Gangs are a feature of modern prison life everywhere in the world, and Ireland is no different. As is well documented, organized crime in this country really took off in the 1990s through the activities of the likes of John Gilligan and the gang he built around himself. Before him, there was Martin 'the General' Cahill, but his influence never spread to prisons.

In this country, through the subversives, we had an early demonstration of the power an organized group can wield in a prison. The subversives acted as a unit and saw the advantages that could be gained when they were all in it together. Then the gang culture made its way into Irish prisons in the early 2000s, when the Limerick gangs, in particular, had a hold on sections of the Midlands.

At the turn of the century, crime in Limerick, and particularly the drugs trade, featured one of the most notorious families to come out of the city: the Dundons. They had been reared in extremely difficult circumstances, between Limerick and the UK, and the gardaí were of the opinion that they brought a whole new viciousness to the scene in the city. Before their rise, the Keane family from St Mary's Park had dominated crime in Limerick, but the leading member of that family, Christy Keane, was convicted on drugs charges in the late 1990s and received a long sentence. The family business was then taken over by Christy's younger brother Kieran, who was the prime suspect for murdering a former associate, Eddie Ryan.

In January 2003, Ryan's two sons – Eddie Jr and Kieran – went missing. A friend said he witnessed them being bundled into a car and driven away. The presumption was that Kieran Keane was behind their abduction and was likely to kill them. A few days later, Kieran Keane himself was lured into a trap by Dessie Dundon, who claimed that he was holding the Ryans. That night, Kieran Keane was shot dead on a quiet country road outside the city and his cousin stabbed seventeen times. Five men were convicted for the murder, including Dessie Dundon and David 'Frog Eyes' Stanners.

Both of these individuals were significant operators in the Midlands during my time there. They retained the power they had on the outside and gathered around them the same kind of foot soldiers they'd had in Limerick. Later, Dessie's brothers Wayne and John also began long prison sentences, and the Ryan bothers were also imprisoned at various times. The whole thing led to a toxic brew in the prison, one of the main issues being that loyalties kept changing. That, in turn, meant it was more difficult to separate elements who would be likely to attack each other.

Dessie Dundon was just twenty when he began his life sentence in 2003. In my experience, he was the most human of his family. Wayne was particularly vicious, and John was beyond relating to on any level, as far as I was concerned. Dessie knew how to use his fists. Once, before my OSG days, when I had him in on the punishment landing on C block, I was in a cell with him when he punched the wall twice. I remember thinking, *If that was my head, I'd be a dead man.*

On another occasion, I saw him and Warren Dumbrell in a fist fight. I can safely say he was the only man I ever saw get the better of Dumbrell in that kind of situation.

Early on in his sentence, Dessie was under some threat from rivals, and he formed an alliance with a Lithuanian gang led by a man whose name was Gintaras Zelvys. These Eastern Europeans were serious muscle. At one stage, every time Dessie left his cell he was accompanied by two of the Lithuanians. This association led, in turn, to an alliance between the two gangs on the outside. He would often ask for large sums of money to be transferred to his girlfriend who visited him regularly. Most of the time, we'd block that because we suspected the money was going to be used for criminal activity. (Prisoners don't have access to their accounts to withdraw cash, but they can request that money be transferred to a family member or visitor. We didn't have to agree with the request, and sometimes we didn't, particularly if it was a large sum and we suspected it was either being transferred under duress or with the intention of buying drugs.)

One day, Dessie's girlfriend arrived at the gates in this big car with two Lithuanians who could have passed for bodyguards. After that, we decided it was too much. We had him transferred out of D division, removing him from the Lithuanians.

I got on well with Dessie. At times. You could have the craic with him.

I might meet him on the landing and he'd say, 'Mr Mac, you're looking well, you must have lost weight.'

And I'd reply, 'Thanks, Dessie, I'll top up your phone with €20 credit for you.'

Before the OSG got off the ground, these Limerick gangs had a fairly free rein. As related earlier, the whole visiting regime had been adapted to accommodate them. All of that changed, once we had got into our stride in the OSG. Breaking up gangs meant there was going to be more peace and, crucially, less of a threat to other prisoners and to staff.

I knew all about the kinds of threats that could come from gangs, as a result of the death threat I received (described in the prologue to this book). It came in the days after we faced down the gangs whose drug-dealing we disrupted over Christmas 2012. Once informed of the threat by the gardaí, the prison service moved into action and installed major security apparatus in my home. I also got a briefing from the gardaí about security measures I should be taking, such as checking under my car for pipe bombs and that kind of stuff. I was told to take alternative routes to work and to keep changing my routine. We had panic buttons in the hall, in the bedrooms, flood-lighting around the house, changes of locks, alarms on all the windows, and we changed our door to one without a letter box. They wanted to put in a secure room, which we could rush into if the house was attacked and in which we'd be safe until the gardaí arrived. We passed on that one. It was just too much. I was also offered firearm training, which I declined.

I was sceptical about how genuine the threat was. In my mind, the gang in question was just trying to intimidate me. I didn't believe they would follow through on it. So, I decided to deal with it in the only way I knew how. One evening, without permission, I got a few of the gang leaders and brought them into the governor's office. I told them I wanted to know which of them was behind the threat, and I told them to leave my family out of it. They said it was nothing to do with my family, that I was the one giving them grief.

'Why don't you just fuck off out of here,' one of them said.

I said I wasn't going anywhere, and then he said they couldn't guarantee my safety.

That was it. Deep down, I really didn't believe they would do anything.

I was fortunate that Valerie took it in her stride. Of course, it bothered her, but she didn't lose it, or tell me that I had to pack it in, that we couldn't live like this. She trusted me when I told her that I was relatively confident we'd be OK. And as things turned out, we were.

Meanwhile, back in the Midlands, we had to be on our toes the whole time, sussing out which prisoners might be in various gangs. One of the first issues that arose when a prisoner from what you might call the criminal fraternity arrived down was to identify which gang they might be a part of. The first source of identification is address. It's like the number plate on a car. If he's from, say, the north inner city of Dublin, you could probably eliminate any gangs that might be based on the southside or the west of the city. Prior to the setting up of the OSG, all of this stuff was done on a cursory basis. There was no dedicated section documenting who was attached to which gang and, by extension, what trouble that could lead to. You obviously don't want rival gangs on the same landing or even division – or violence would be inevitable. And ideally, you want to break up gangs to ensure they can't use their power, usually through selling drugs and renting out phones.

We gathered intelligence and acted on it by enforcing strict segregation of gangs and transferring anybody who was getting too powerful. This wasn't possible in all instances. For example – and I'm getting ahead of myself slightly here – when I transferred back to Portlaoise in 2016, Brian Rattigan, a notorious criminal from Crumlin in south Dublin, was the leading gangland criminal in the prison. He ran his landing. Nothing moved without his say-so. Any time we shifted his henchmen to other landings, they just got replaced. There was nowhere to move Rattigan to within the system, so we just had to continue with a form of cat and mouse with him, taking out his key people and waiting to see who replaced them, before doing the same again.

The power to transfer a prisoner was a handy tool in breaking up the gangs, but of course it required the co-operation of management. Typically, I'd go to the chief officer in the prison and say we wanted a particular man moved. Nine times out of ten, there would be no problem, as the chief would be well aware it was in the best interests of the prison to do so. He would then have to get involved in some horse-trading with his equivalent in another prison, to see who he would have to take in exchange for the man to be transferred.

Apart from the domestic gangs, mainly from Dublin and Limerick, another problem we had to deal with in the early years of the OSG was the Eastern Europeans. By the time we were getting into our stride, the prison service had already experienced a surge in non-Irish-born prisoners. This merely reflected the changing population trends in society in general. At one point, up to 30 per cent of inmates in the Midlands were non-nationals. That seems like a high percentage, but it's just a reflection of the life chances of non-nationals at that time. Young, poor men are the biggest demographic who get drawn into crime and end up in prison. And a disproportionately high number of non-nationals were both young and poor. Inevitably, some of them also got drawn into crime and ended up in the system.

As is the case in any country with inward migration, eth-nic gangs were formed. As often as not, these preyed on their own people, who would be particularly vulnerable in a new country. But beyond that, these gangs just got involved in the general organized crime business. The gardaí, and subsequently the prison service, were to find out that there was an extra issue with some of these gangs. Many were more resourceful than their Irish counterparts, particularly as they would have experience of military training. In some Eastern European countries, certainly until recent years, military training was compulsory, with service required for two and sometimes even three years. As a result, those who got involved in crime had something extra to bring to the table. For instance, the average criminal in an Irish gang might have once fired a shotgun or have a basic knowledge of guns. These fellas, with their training behind them, knew all about weapons, how to use them, and, quite often, where to source them in their own country.

Once in prison, these gangs could then be at least as powerful as their domestic counterparts, and in many instances they formed alliances with the criminal gangs from Dublin and Limerick. One of the other problems we had with the Eastern Europeans was language – though things getting muddled in translation led to some lighter moments, too. We got great mileage out of an incident when a veteran officer we knew as Gazza, who was a native of Offaly, approached a visitor who looked to be in a hurry.

'Are you rushing?' Gazza asked.

She looked at him with a question on her face. 'Yes, yes, I am Russian. How did you know?'

On a more serious level, we monitored all the telephone calls to and from prisoners. But that wasn't much use if you didn't know what they were actually saying. After a while, we decided that we'd have to get a translator. The obvious port of call was the Courts Service, as translators were frequently used in court. We organized for a translator to come down to us in the Midlands occasionally. Naturally, we had to have security in place for the translator – because if word got out, she would be a target. I had a system set up whereby she would not have to sign in her full name, or go through the usual security checks – after all, she was already vetted by the court system – and would be known to staff on-site by her first name only.

Her work garnered acres of intelligence for us on the Eastern European gangs. And the beauty of it was that they were carrying on their conversations, thinking that we hadn't a clue what was passing between them.

The other issue with the Eastern Europeans was identifying who was in which gang. One form of identification was tattoos, which were very popular among those who had done military service. There was a good chance that the men with the same tattoos were in the one gang. We had access to their tattoos because every prisoner is photographed on entry, including any marks on their bodies. Before long, we set up a database of tattoos to identify who was with whom. You could have up to twenty or thirty prisoners in the same gang. From our database we could move to break up gangs, if things were getting in any way out of hand.

Then there was the traditional dress worn by some of the visitors to these foreign-born prisoners. When you are in security, every visitor is potentially bringing something in. When we saw, for instance, a woman in a burka we would ask her to fully identify herself before entering. She would be brought into an adjoining room and a female officer would ask her to remove the burka. If she refused, she was not allowed in. Nine times of out ten, they would comply. Similarly, women from some African cultures have colourful and large headgear. That would have to be taken off and searched by a female officer. And then there were Romanian women from the Roma community, who often had miles of flowing dresses and long skirts. Again, they would be taken into a separate room and a female officer would use a handheld metal detector to check if anything was being concealed. Unsurprisingly, inquiries and scrutiny relating to the clothing choices of people from cultures that were relatively new to Ireland were extremely sensitive matters. Sometimes, they felt it was racist. But all we were doing was our job. I don't care where you're from or what you look like – if what you are wearing could be used to bring contraband into the prison, then that has to be checked.

One of the most notorious gang leaders from Eastern Europe during those early years of the OSG was Dessie Dundon's pal, Gintaras Zelvys, a Lithuanian who was a violent criminal. He had been involved in crime in his own country before arriving here, and had convictions for robbery and sexual assault. He had a number of businesses, usually fronts for money-laundering, including a few in the cash for clothes business. That line was particularly useful to him, as it provided a front for moving stuff in and out of the country under the guise that it was clothes for Eastern European charities.

He started out in the north-east of the state but expanded into Dublin and beyond. He arrived in the Midlands Prison in 2007, after receiving a lengthy sentence for extortion and other crimes. Quite soon, it became obvious to us that Elvis, as we called him, was a major player. A physically powerful man, he was one of the few of his gang who spoke English. Any time we brought him down for a search, he was abusive and threatening, more often than not spitting out curses in Lithuanian – which, of course, went over our heads – but his body language was enough to tell us what he was trying to get across.

Elvis fitted the caricature for the gangster, right down to his partner: a woman who was straight out of the gangster's moll playbook. When she visited, she was always accompanied by a minder/chauffeur, and she was inevitably dressed as if she was on her way to a glamourous night out. She used to send Elvis some choice photographs in which she would be striking provocative poses in the nip, some including another woman.

One time she was visiting, we found a phone on her in the screening area. I genuinely believed it was an oversight – she simply forgot to leave her phone outside. She was detained until the gardaí arrived to arrest her, and the minder was immediately on his phone to a solicitor who came and had her out of Portlaoise garda station in jig time.

That was Elvis, a violent criminal with all the trappings I imagine teenagers who are drawn into crime believe to be the reward for their hard work. He and his gang were also responsible for one of the most ingenious ways I've ever come across of getting contraband into the prison.

Naturally, we kept a close eye on a gang leader of Elvis's profile and regularly searched his cell and those of his associates. On one such search we came across nylon fishing wire. Neatly wrapped up, there was about 300 metres of it. Now, it wouldn't be too difficult to get that into prison – the dogs, for one, are not trained to detect fishing wire! – but what exactly it was being used for we hadn't a clue.

Another search revealed a pair of high-powered magnets – and to this day we're not sure how they were brought in past the metal detectors. Now, we were scratching our heads. The third unusual bounty we came across was meat, and that really threw us. This was a kind of spiced beef soaked in vodka and kept inside plastic bottles. It was, we were to discover, a particular delicacy in Lithuania, which was usually reserved for special occasions, not unlike turkey at Christmas in this part of the world.

It was possible to see how they could get in the fishing wire and magnets, physically concealed, even if there was no explanation for doing so. But the meat? That didn't come through any visitor, unless it was in tiny amounts. And if they were smuggling in what was effectively a luxury, with probably no monetary value, what did that say about how easily they might be getting other stuff in?

The next piece of this jigsaw came through the gardaí. Word was sent to us that they had come across an Eastern European man in the town late at night, just on a routine patrol. He didn't seem to be obviously up to no good, but at the same time his presence raised suspicions, so they passed the information on to us.

At that stage, we looked at the possibility that somebody was entering the prison grounds with contraband in the dead of night, most likely over the wall. We got on to military intelligence in The Curragh, who would have had experience of rope ladders for scaling walls and all that kind of thing. We brought some officers down and examined the perimeter wall. Was it possible that an accomplice was coming down and getting over the wall with bagloads of loot and somehow getting it on to the Lithuanians' first-floor landing? Or could it be some kind of a dry run or a test for an escape attempt? The military boys looked at this every which way but came to the conclusion that maybe our imagination – or frustration – was getting the better of us. No rope ladder. Nothing that could point to an elaborate escape attempt.

I can't recall who stumbled on the next idea, or whether we treated it seriously at the outset, but somebody brought the whole thing back to the fishing line. What if there was somebody outside the wall with a fishing rod, casting a line over into the yard. OK, that's step one, and where to go from there? The magnets. Was it possible that our fisherman could cast a magnet into the yard? And then? Maybe Elvis's men had their magnet, ready to connect to the magnet being thrown in. Where would that lead but to a direct line? This would involve the fisherman reeling in his line, effectively setting up a pulley system, all the way from him to a window on Elvis's landing. It was ingenious. But was it possible?

We decided to take a look. I know absolutely nothing about fishing, but there was an officer on-site who was avid for the sport. I got on to him to lend us a hand, and he was up for it. We put him outside the wall at a spot near Stack House where there would be the possibility of getting a line over the wall, near a clump of bushes. He cast his line and in it went. One of our lads lowered a magnet from the landing in question and . . . *bingo!* They connected, and a line was set up. We knew, there and then, that we had cracked it. Later, we were to discover that the contraband was all put into a series of socks and the line pulled across and up into the cell block.

The next question was, how long had this been going on? It had been a few weeks since we first discovered the fishing line in one of the cells. So, it was at the very least that length of time, but more likely months. And that gave rise to another question. With such a line set up to bring in contraband, how much stuff had they manged to get in and how much was in their cells?

We decided to give a proper search. This was big-time

stuff, so we had to go in hard to retrieve whatever they had. The chief officer in the OSG, Ben Buckley, organized for us to get people from the other prisons for a special operation. And we went and took the cells apart. We had sledgehammers and wrenches and special screwdrivers that could take the bed frames apart.

The chief trades officer was present during the search, and he began to get nervous about what he saw as the damage that we might end up doing to some of the furniture, for which he was responsible. He asked us to stop when we began taking the bed frames apart, but I was adamant that we keep going. These prisoners were up to something, and we had to get to the bottom of it. Just as the trades officer was protesting, one of our lads swung an almighty belt at the bed frame and out fell a treasure trove of pills, syringes and phones. We all just looked at each other, and the trades officer said, 'I'll go and get a few angle grinders.' Once he had assured himself we were on to something big, he was totally on board.

The haul was something else: about sixty phones, 10,000 tablets and dozens of syringes. There was a big heap of socks in there, too! By the time we searched, they'd eaten all the meat. And God knows how many euros' worth of drugs and phones they had managed to flog.

Following the operation, we did something for the first and only time. We brought all the contraband to a common area and laid it all out on the floor for display, just as you might sometimes see the gardaí doing after a successful raid. It was just for our colleagues, though, to show them that this was the amount of stuff getting in and that we were doing our job in catching it. A little internal PR exercise, but it did no harm. And it did plenty for morale within the OSG. Later that day, our translator was on the job and she picked up one of Zelvys' men telling their associate on the outside to tell the fisherman to stay at home. The river had run dry.

Gintaras Zelvys was released in 2013, on completion of his sentence, and was immediately deported to Lithuania. He re-entered the country a short time later. On the morning of 8 May, he was walking with his wife into his cash for clothes business in Rathcoole, Co. Dublin, when two men approached him and shot him dead.

Another thoughtful ruse attempted by a gang, an Irish one this time, was the recycling truck. We first heard about it through the chief officer in the Midlands, Paddy Brennan. Paddy was not in the OSG but, like those in the regular service who saw our value, he was a big supporter. Paddy had one prisoner who was a source of some intelligence for him. This man, a Traveller, had his own little operation going, and some of his motivation for passing on intelligence was to stick it to a rival gang in the prison.

One day, in conversation with Paddy, the man told him what he had recently heard about the recycling truck. Every so often, a recycling company called and took away material: the usual stuff, cardboard and plastics, and such like. The system being operated was that the prison would contact the company when we had a load to be taken away. The load would never fill a lorry, so the company would say that it would call into the prison when it was on another run somewhere around the country. This would usually be within ten days or a fortnight of the initial call.

Paddy's snitch had it that the lorry was being used to bring in drugs and phones. The driver and his mate were in on it. They would arrive at the prison and park up at a docking area where wheelie bins full of stuff to be recycled would be brought down by prisoners to be loaded on board. Then, according to his intelligence, the wheelie bins would return to the different landings with the gear. It was simple yet highly effective.

Once we got word of it, we decided that the best way to strike was to let the lorry into the campus and then move in and search the lorry. This might sound like common sense, but it came with all sorts of problems. The Midlands and Portlaoise are separate prisons, but being on the same campus means that goods are brought into both prisons through the one entrance. The Goods Inward Gate, as it is called, is located in the Portlaoise compound and manned by Portlaoise officers. This is the entrance for foodstuffs and everything else required on a daily basis to run the two prisons. You may recall that Portlaoise was not under the remit of the OSG, on the basis that it had been operating to the very highest security standards since the 1970s. So, if we were to allow the lorry on to the campus, it would be passing through the Portlaoise security system. By definition, the officers manning the gate should be searching the truck and detecting anything that might be on it. A failure to do so would expose shortcomings in their security. While that wasn't the objective of our exercise, if things turned out as we expected, it could be an unintended consequence.

As usual, everything had to be kept tight. I informed the campus governor, Colm Bartley, who was in charge of both prisons. I asked him to ensure that, whatever happened, nobody would lose their job as a result of this exercise, and he agreed. Bartley was pro-OSG, and he was willing to go along with it.

After that, it was a matter of waiting. For the following week or so, I made sure that I was never further than ten or fifteen minutes away from the prison, available to go in on the shortest of notice once a call came through that the truck was on the way.

I was at home when I got the call and hopped into my car straight away. The truck arrived at the loading bay and the two men got out of the cab. They were both late middle aged, pushing for elderly. I told them to come with me and brought them into a room nearby. 'We know you've gear on that lorry,' I told them. They held their hands up, there and then, admitted the whole thing. The driver pulled four mobile phones out of his pockets, which were to be part of the consignment. I asked them where on board the stuff was, and they told me.

Some of it was in the cab and more in a trailer, and even more was strapped to the axle underneath the carriage, with masking tape. The gardaí were called and the men arrested. Despite their confessions and telling us where the stuff was, we didn't take their word for it and conducted a thorough search of the whole truck. That took nearly two hours and yielded nothing more than what the two men had already admitted. This had been just the third time they had come to the prison. The first had been a recce, and they'd brought in a certain amount on the second trip, but this was by far the largest haul.

The pair were charged but by the time the case came to court the driver had died. He had been an uncle of one of the leading gangland figures in Dublin. His mate was convicted, pleaded his circumstances and age, et cetera, and ended up with a suspended sentence.

The real fallout, however, was back in the prison. Apart from the lorry going undetected at the gate, the fact that the driver was so closely related to a well-known criminal was another black mark. Everybody who accesses the prison, from teachers to lorry drivers, has to be vetted. If there was any vetting procedure on that man, it was very flimsy.

The two officers who were on the gate that day, both of whom I knew very well, have never forgiven me, but I can't say I had much sympathy for them. Every officer who is willing to take the pay cheque has an obligation to do the job properly, and they obviously didn't. They got a bollocking from Bartley but there were no repercussions for their jobs, as had been agreed. What the whole case really showed up was how sloppy things had got in Portlaoise. This was a far cry from the days when it was regarded as the most fortified prison in Europe.

In some ways, time had overtaken the prison. Back in the day, the big security issue had been the possibility of escape and the potential for major political embarrassment.

Then the political situation changed with The Good Friday Agreement and the peace process. The main body of subversives, attached to the Provisional IRA, were no longer being incarcerated. Instead, it was the Republican dissidents, who were every bit as ruthless as their former comrades but lacked the organization or strength in numbers and resources. So things got a little slack. The political pressure eased, notwithstanding the ongoing threat that the dissidents were believed to pose.

You still had the heavies on E1, but their capacity to be a force in their own right was limited by the presence of the dissidents. While the worst of the worst, when it came to ordinary criminals, were still housed there, it didn't have the significance that it used to have. In such an environment, the old rules began to soften.

Meanwhile, the establishment of the OSG, in 2008, had led to a ramping up of security in all the other prisons. As they had advanced, it appeared that things in Portlaoise

Prison had continued to slacken. The case of the recycling lorry acted as a kind of catalyst to ensure that the remit of the OSG would spread into Portlaoise – and that is exactly what happened, in 2014. Now, we had the run of all the prisons in the state.

18. Ear to the Ground

As things went along in the OSG, we got a little more
sophisticated. Our first governor, John L, was the right man
to get the thing off the ground. His management style
was to give you space if you showed any initiative. If you
went to him with a good idea, once he satisfied himself of
its merit, he'd allow you your head and let you get on with
it. I got on well with him, but after eighteen months, John L
arrived at his pension age. After retirement, he moved
back to his native Kerry and sadly died after a short illness,
in 2020.

His successor was John Kavanagh, another man who'd
been around the block. Kavanagh had a different management style but was effective in his own right. Soon after he
took over, he brought three of us into his office for a chat.
He described how he wanted to work in circles, one inside
the other, drawing out these concentric circles on a piece of
paper. As the circles got smaller there were, he said, fewer
people in the middle, who had more to do. And then he
pointed at the smallest circle right at the centre and said to
us, 'This is where you are.' We were going to be at the heart
of the operation, knowing more about what was going on
than anybody else, and he wanted us to be aware that keeping that information safe would be a crucial part of our
jobs into the future.

One aid we would have was access to a private investigations firm. This was owned by a former garda who had worked
in intelligence, running informants. We were introduced to

this man and he brought us to meet some of his former colleagues in An Garda Síochána. This was to be a vital connection for us, particularly in providing some ad hoc training on how to run informants.

Apart from sex offenders, there is no more despised category of prisoner than 'a rat', as the informant is known. Just as the informant is a vital tool for the gardaí in dealing with criminals, so they also have huge value to a unit like the OSG in prisons. We need to know what is going on, who is moving stuff, whether there is any violence being planned, if there are any particular individuals – including prison officers – who are bringing stuff in. All of this was vital to the success of our operation.

A good class officer will usually have a rat on his or her landing. Their relationship will be informal and haphazard, but it will mean that the class officer has some handle on what's going on and whether something is going to blow. We in the OSG were operating on a different level, but we were plugged in to different class officers, who might pass on small nuggets of information here and there.

One example of that in action was when a class officer came to me and told me an informant of his said that a prisoner on his landing, who had a prosthetic leg, was up to something. This prisoner had used a courier business as a cover for moving drugs for gangs in Dublin. He was reputed to have been an excellent motorcyclist, but somehow he had come off his bike and had been lucky to survive, though he lost a leg. So, he already had the prosthetic one when he arrived in the Midlands.

The class officer had been tipped off that the prisoner was using regular trips from the prison to organize something. The trips were to the National Rehabilitation Centre in Dun Laoghaire, in Dublin, as part of his physical treatment.

On his return from one of those trips, I got some of our men to search him, including removing his prosthetic limb. He kicked up a stink about it, claiming that his rights were being abused and what have you, but that convinced us that he definitely had something to hide. And he did. Once we took off the leg, out popped nine top-of-the-range phones, worth about €3,000 each.

I went up to the Rehab Centre in Dun Laoghaire later that day. They showed me around and gave me a look at their CCTV footage. From that I was able to identify this fella who came into the centre wearing a high-vis jacket. His only call within the centre was to the unisex toilet, where he took away the contents of the sanitary bin. That, quite obviously, was where our man with the handy prosthetic leg had made his pick-up. I told the gardaí about it, in the hope that his contact might be back again, but word must have got out that the prisoner had been nabbed, because the man didn't show.

The new contacts we made in the guards through the private investigator were in the section known in policing circles, in Ireland and elsewhere, as Covert Human Intelligence Source (CHIS). This section runs informants. The garda CHIS team gave us an insight and knowledge, plus a degree of ad hoc training in the whole area. Why, you might ask, were the guards bothering to allow us this huge amount of access to their inner workings? Despite what many people might think, the security arms of the state don't operate as if they are all focused on the same goal. There are rivalries and divisions, even within the one organization. Frankly, we were given the kind of access that many within the force itself would never receive.

The simple answer is that there was something in it for them. Criminal organizations continue to be run on the outside when the leaders are inside. What we could garner and pass on could have all sorts of value in the fight against crime. Once these guards satisfied themselves that we were capable of being professional, they were willing to help us along.

Early on, I and another ACO were brought to a safe house that these lads operated. The house was on a side street, just off one of the main thoroughfares in Dublin's city centre. For all the world it was a simple mews house, just like the hundreds of similar homes in the area. Once inside, however, a different world opened up.

There were steel doors between some of the rooms. Every single nook and cranny was covered by CCTV cameras, although most of those were not visible to the naked eye. The windows looking out on the quiet residential street were bulletproof. And then there was the safe room. In the event of the house coming under attack, the person being guarded would be ushered immediately into this room, where everything would lock down. The only way to access the room if locked down would be to blow the door open. Inside the room, there was a single bed and a few bits and bobs, including a kettle, presumably in order to have a quiet cup of tea while people outside the room were intent on killing you.

Members of the CHIS team told us about their unique training. One exercise, for example, involved a couple of oblivious guards picking up a foreign national at Dublin airport to drive to a safe house. En route, when the car was stopped at traffic lights on O'Connell Street, this woman jumped out and began shouting that she was being raped. The woman, of course, had been primed to do this, to test how they would handle the situation. The guards, who don't carry official ID, had to calm her down and get her back into the car. That whole thing sounded pretty savage to me as a way to test if you could use your loaf.

They also have to take special precautions, like constantly changing the number plates on their cars. All of this is to ensure that any meetings they have with their informants don't give rise to suspicions. The seriousness of what's at issue can't be overstated. Informants are an interesting species in terms of their motivation, and even their psyche, but they are constantly in danger of being exposed and murdered. The people running them therefore have an enormous responsibility.

Selecting or identifying a suitable informant can be a job in itself. The person has to be reliable and capable of bringing you good-quality information, without giving rise to suspicion in his own environment. If they are doing it for ulterior motives – such as attempting to get some other criminal targeted or locked up – that has to be kept in mind. And from the guards' point of view, but not necessarily ours, the whole operation needs to be such that it can withstand robust testing in a courtroom, in case a prosecution relies on the informant. Our priorities weren't the same. We just wanted to stop the flow of contraband and break up gangs. Any evidence gathered that could go towards a conviction would be a bonus, but it was not our main focus.

The whole experience with the gardaí brought the running of informants on to a new plane for us. We had them graded: A, B, and C, with the As, obviously, the most valuable and producing the best information. At any given time when I was in the Midlands, I had between nine and twelve informants in place. Of those, one or maybe two were an A, and one in particular was what you might call A-plus.

*

The first informant that I worked, along with the guards, was a criminal who ran a business for cover and was plugged into several gangs. He had a reputation for moving stuff and accessing cars when required, and sometimes guns as well. He was already an informer for the gardaí before he was caught on a rap that was going to see him going to prison for at least a few years. I was brought to meet him – we'll call him Mr A – by the gardaí in the weeks before he was sentenced. We were sitting in a car in Balbriggan, in north Co. Dublin, and he sat in. Introductions were made, and then one of the gardaí said, 'You're going to work for this man or you can fuck off out of the car.' This garda knew his onions when it came to using psychology with informants. Mr A was by then relying to a certain extent on his garda handlers, who had made some representations for him in the legal system. Their intervention would see the chances of a long prison sentence being reduced. (As it was, he received three years.)

After the meeting, the garda told me that Mr A would need a short, sharp shock to realize that it would be in his best interests to work with me in prison. He was sentenced and began his time inside in the main committal prison, Mountjoy. Now, the governor of Mountjoy at the time was Ned 'Nike' Whelan, and Ned was a big supporter of the OSG. I went to see him and told him what exactly I needed in order to get Mr A onside.

Thus, Mr A was put in a four-man cell with three members of the Travelling community. As most people know, the Travellers have their own mores and traditions. In the confined space of a cell, petty rivalries and resentments can easily build up. And when you have three inmates from a tight-knit community, and a fourth inmate who is from outside that community and its culture, there is potential for an awful lot of grief.

After ten days in the cell, Mr A got the message. He sent word out through the governor that he was interested in talking to me. Ned then arranged for him to be transferred to the Midlands. Once he settled down, Mr A turned out to be a good asset to both the OSG and the gardaí during his sentence.

He was welcomed in the Midlands by prisoners who knew him on the outside, where he was popular. We set up a mobile phone system by which he could call me at any time. We supplied him with a phone, and I had a dedicated phone to receive his calls. Crucially, the calls were recorded not in the Midlands, as nearly all calls were, but in the prison service headquarters in Longford. The less that anybody on campus knew about this sort of thing, the better. Of course, there was a chance that one of the non-OSG officers might find the phone in his cell. But that was pretty unlikely, and we went with the risk.

Typically, I might get a call, I'd pick up the phone and just say, 'Go.' He'd relate a nugget of information, such as that a bag of drugs was coming in the following Tuesday through a particular visitor, or some prisoner had possession of a quantity of drugs or phones that were being flogged on a landing. That was all we needed to act. It was always a very brief conversation.

His contacts, and the circles in which he moved, meant he sometimes had info for the guards. Twice, that I'm aware of, he passed on his knowledge of where handguns were to be found, and other times he had information about car registration plates used in specific criminal activity. He would pass all of this on to me, and whatever was destined for the guards, I would pass it on to my contact. The guards never came back to me and said 'thanks', 'well done' or 'that turned out to be useful'. It simply didn't work like that.

Everything was businesslike and done on a need-to-know and maximum efficiency basis.

There were times when I, or the guards, needed to have longer conversations with Mr A, and special arrangements had to be made. Regularly, we would subject his cell to a search, which would necessitate taking him off to reception. Nearly every time we did this, we also searched a number of other cells on his landing, to ensure nothing would attract attention. Once he was taken down to reception, there was plenty of opportunity for me to meet up with him and discuss whatever was needed, including any messages the gardaí might want passed to him.

A few times, the gardaí wanted to talk to him so something more elaborate was required. On two occasions, we used what's known as a Section 22 for this. The section in the criminal justice law allows for gardaí to take a prisoner into custody for questioning about a crime being investigated. Mr A had had his fingers in a whole variety of pies when he was on the outside, so it would not be suspicious that he would be subjected to this.

The local gardaí came to the prison to take him off to Portlaoise station, then instead of going to the station they met up with our friends in the CHIS unit at some quiet point along the route. Mr A was transferred to the CHIS car, the cuffs were removed, and they drove off to a remote location outside the town where they had their chat with him.

When he was brought back to the prison, I had to walk him through his cover story. Since he was supposed to have been in Portlaoise garda station, I went into minute detail about the features in the station, including where the toilets were, what the holding cells were like, and so on – everything that would ensure that he could, if needed, give the impression that he had spent a few hours there. A number of the prisoners would have been hauled in for questioning under Section 22 and brought to Portlaoise, so if one casually asked him about the place, or whether he noticed something in particular there, he'd be able to engage as if he'd just returned. That kind of attention to detail was important. The nature of informants is that if one falls under any kind of suspicion, everything is blown up after that point in the minds of other prisoners. Even the smallest slip can have fatal consequences.

As things advanced with Mr A, we brought his wife into the picture. During visits, he told her stuff to pass on to us. I set up a phone connection with Mrs A but ensured that all the calls were recorded. That kind of precaution was necessary, because if things ever turned sour, she might have been in a position to make allegations of improper conduct against me.

We also got Mr A a new phone, passed on to him by his wife. We gave her the phone and allowed her to bring it for a visit. All she had to worry about then was passing it over, without being detected by the officer supervising visits, but for most handovers that can be managed easily enough.

Having served a good chunk of his time, Mr A received his reward for co-operating with us, which was a transfer to an open prison. This fell nicely for us, because there were problems in one open prison, Loughan House in Co. Cavan, where we could put a good informant to use. The place was being robbed blind by some members of staff at the time. Everything was walking out the door. Food, televisions, tools for the garden, you name it.

Mr A quickly got a suss on what was going on. He filled us in on who was involved and how it was being done. If the prison service had chosen to, they could have made a complaint about the offending staff members to the gardaí, once we had the evidence. It would have been a fairly straightforward prosecution. But like much else in the service, the prospect of any negative publicity was the greater concern, so the men involved were quietly let go.

Mr A certainly left his mark on the OSG as a first-class informant. He was ideal – well liked, well connected and careful. A postscript to his involvement occurred close to his release date. By that time, he was totally trusted by the management in Loughan House, to the extent that he was one of the trustee prisoners sent from the open prison to IPS headquarters in Longford, to do some work around the offices.

One day, I got a call from him. He was alone in the office of the then director of operations for the IPS, Brian Murphy. 'Mr Mac,' he whispered to me on the phone, 'I'm in the office of the head man. Is there anything you want here?'

I told him to fuck off and mind himself. And tried not to start laughing before I hung up.

One of the best informants I had during my time in the Midlands was a high-profile prisoner who was not part of the usual criminal fraternity. He actually came to me with information on the first day, and it turned out to be good. I was surprised at the approach, because I wasn't expecting it. Soon afterwards, I had a meeting with the CHIS gardaí and brought up the subject of this prisoner, his background and what I should make of him. They said he would be an A informer, no question about it. He wasn't looking for any specific reward – and from what I related about him, they came to the conclusion that he was intelligent.

The gardaí reckoned that he was driven by the idea that he was above the other prisoners and saw himself as being in cahoots with the prison service. They also said that he wouldn't be bothered with small-time stuff, would filter all that out himself, and only come to me with valuable information. Their forecasts turned out to be more or less on the button.

This man – we'll call him Mr Z (I would say Mr B, but that would be doing an A man like him a disservice!) – brought me some great stuff, including what some prison officers were up to on the landing. One of the nuggets he came to me with was that an officer appeared to be purposely running into Christy Griffin, a notorious gang leader from Dublin who was serving a long sentence for raping his partner's daughter. According to Mr Z, this particular officer appeared to be having words with Griffin regularly at opportune times, such as just before lockdown.

We checked it out on the CCTV cameras, and not only did we spot some of what Mr Z told us, but there were also times when we reckoned that the officer was interacting with Griffin outside the scope of the cameras, such as when coming in from the exercise yard. We had the officer moved and did nothing more about it. But it meant that if he was crooked and working for Griffin, we had killed his usefulness.

Another tip we got from Mr Z may well have saved a life. He told us that there was a plan to poison a prisoner through food from the kitchen. Somebody on the outside wanted this prisoner done and, from what we gathered afterwards, there was a contract of sorts put out on him. The job was to be carried out by a man who managed to get himself assigned to the kitchen. Now, one of the perks of working in the kitchen is that you can make up food to bring back to your buddies in their cells. The target in this case was a prisoner who was known to have a taste for curries, to the point that he would even swap up to ten cigarettes for one.

Mr Z told us that rat poison was to be added to a curry destined for this prisoner. We intercepted the food after it left the kitchen and took it away. It was sent to the lab for testing. The results showed that, in all probability, the strength of the poison involved would have made the prisoner very sick but would not have killed him. But there was no guarantee of that outcome. Who knows how the man's constitution would have reacted? In any event, it was far better that the attempt was stopped, and for that we were grateful to the quality of intelligence that came from Mr Z.

He was a valued asset for me but, like all good things, our relationship came to an end. At some point, senior management in the prison suspected that he was an informer and I was approached about it. I pleaded complete ignorance, of course, but they didn't believe me. I reckon their primary concern was Mr Z's high profile. If anything were to happen to him, it could have caused a huge stink. As a result, he was transferred.

19. Blocking Out and Listening In

The danger posed by mobile phones in prison was recognized even when the Midlands was being built, in the late 1990s. At the time, blockers were purchased, at huge cost, to ensure that phones inside the prison could not pick up a signal. The blockers were like large telegraph poles. They effectively operated as the polar opposite of satellite dishes – blocking, rather than picking up a signal.

Soon after the prison opened, the blockers were activated. They did an excellent job. Such an excellent job that they blocked calls for half of Portlaoise. These things work on a beam; the prison walls were not strong enough to stop the beam, so it spread out across the town and killed mobile phone signals all over the place. Those closest to the prison campus were worst hit. Not far from the entrance to the campus stands Portlaoise General Hospital, and within a stone's throw the town fire station. Cutting off mobile phone access to those establishments was a serious issue. So the blockers were deactivated – pronto! And that was the end of one attempt to cut out the use of mobiles in the prison.

While no longer used, the technology was kept on site. To the best of my knowledge, the blockers are still there in the Midlands, rotting away, a monument to another waste of public money. To be fair, the technology associated with mobile phones was not too advanced in the late 1990s. But still, the authorities should have had some idea of what was involved.

Over a decade after that failed experiment, I took a look at the whole issue of blocking phones again. The OSG was up and running by this stage, the job was exciting, and we were always looking at new ways to push the boat out even further.

I had heard about localized blockers being used in colleges – I think it was in the USA, in order to prevent students cheating in exams. I made a few calls, one thing led to another, and I ended up getting in touch with military intelligence in The Curragh. They used these local blockers in situations where they might be sent in to deactivate an incendiary device. These devices are often controlled by phone, so being able to cut the signal in the vicinity was a huge help to them. I was also in touch with An Garda Síochána headquarters in the Phoenix Park, where they used the same device.

It turned out that this kind of blocker was imported from an Italian company, which also supplied the Vatican with the blockers to be used when there was a papal conclave to select a new Pope. The conclave, as most people are aware, is conducted with a huge degree of secrecy. Despite managing for centuries to keep everything tight, the advent of mobile phones threatened the great old tradition. The same blockers were also used by the Italian government in Mafia trials, as a number of lawyers and judges had been the target of bombs set off by remote control.

It looked like these things might be the answer to all my prayers. After all, if the devices were good enough to keep a rein on cardinals from all over the world, they should do the job in clamping down on criminals running their gangs from inside an Irish prison.

I got in contact with the Italians, and they were interested in checking us out for their business. Every site was different, they explained – 'The Midlands ain't no Vatican,' I told them – so they had to come and physically inspect the prison. I organized for them to travel over, and they flew in and drove down to meet us. In the course of their visit we naturally showed them the old blockers, gathering dust and rust. The Italians pointed out that those blockers would be ideal for the kind of prisons they had in places like Saudi Arabia, built way out in the middle of nowhere. And because these lads were dealing internationally, they thought they could put the disused blockers in the Midlands to good use. They wanted to buy them, and we tried to organize that, but it came to nothing, probably over failing to agree a price.

Because any blocking would have to be localized, our main focus was on A block. This was a completely separate building in the Midlands, which actually stood on the campus between the Midlands and Portlaoise Prison. (This A block, not to confuse things, was entirely separate from the A block in the main Midlands building, which was one of the spokes in the wheel centred on the circle. Since then, the standalone block has been transferred to Portlaoise Prison.)

The block can house forty prisoners on five different landings. Each landing has its own exercise yard. There are no workshops or education facilities, and all visits to A block are screen visits only. Initially, the block was designed to be used for housing what you might describe as 'the worst of the worst' – those prisoners who were violent, unstable and determined to resist staff and the service at every turn. The idea was that they would be kept there until such time as they were willing to co-operate to a degree that meant they could return to the general population. Or to put it bluntly, A block was designed to put manners on them.

At various stages, some of the most notorious gang leaders were kept there. For a while, the three Dundon brothers plus their associate and cousin, Nathan Killeen, were all on A block. Leon Wright, another notorious criminal, and Warren Dumbrell – who has been in the system for most of the time, since before the siege in Mountjoy in 1997 – also spent periods in A block.

As an aside, there was also a time when Brian Meehan, who was serving life for Veronica Guerin's murder, actually asked to be moved to A block. He had got himself addicted to heroin in prison and decided that he needed to be removed from the general population to have a chance of cleaning himself up – which he eventually did.

Anyway, despite its relative isolation within the system, the big noises who were held on A block still managed to get their hands on phones. And these were the kind of individuals who could do serious damage through that connection. Information we recovered from phones seized often gave an indication of how some of these people were still micromanaging their criminal enterprises on the outside. For instance, you could have a text to an underling telling him to recover a drug debt from somebody, and if the money wasn't forthcoming to give the debtor a beating. You could have a gang leader ordering a murder from his cell. He could be issuing instructions about the next consignment of drugs being brought into the country. Using mobile phones, these gang leaders were still, to a large extent, able to operate from behind bars.

We brought our Italians friends to the block and they checked it out, seeing how much steel and concrete was present, and doing their sums. And then, as we were standing outside, one of them pointed to the bell tower of the nearby church of Saints Peter and Paul. There were about a dozen transmitters there for all the mobile phone providers, and just 240 metres away as the crow flies. It gave great coverage to A block.

We did a deal with the Italians for a number of these mini blockers, which would be used at different prisons around the state. These things were about the size of a suitcase that you'd be allowed carry on a Ryanair flight. Their strength was not just that they blocked a signal when required, but they could detect a signal without blocking it, and detect how many times there was a connection, either through text or a call, while the phone was off. The blocker would have to be placed within thirty metres or so of where a phone was located. To accommodate that in A block, we put the little suitcase up in the attic above any cell from which we suspected a phone was operating.

As a result, we could tell if a prisoner had a phone, and how many contacts were being made on that phone. Better still, the prisoner would have the phone turned off all day, to lessen the chances of detection, and then when he turned it on – say, late at night – all of the missed calls and texts would register on it. That, of itself, was a mini trove of information. The trick, as far as we were concerned, was to get our hands on the phone soon after it got turned on, when all that information was available, and before the prisoner had a chance to delete it. We conducted a number of operations on that basis.

We kept tabs on the phone activity in A block by some of the gang leaders there, such as Wayne Dundon. Sometimes, we would notice a signal showing up for incoming traffic. That would confirm that he had a phone, but the choice was to go in bull-headed or wait. So, we waited until he turned the phone on, long after lockdown.

Surprise was really important here. If he had any

indication that we were about to burst in, he would delete all the messages and, if luck was really on his side, deposit the phone up his back passage. If he managed to do that, there was little we could do to locate it. From his point of view, one way to ensure that the coast was clear to turn on the phone and respond to texts and calls was to keep an eye out through the flap on the door of his cell. The flap is about five inches wide and an inch deep; you can look up and down the landing for a few metres at the very least. The sight of somebody approaching would give him enough time to do what he had to do.

Of course, we were well aware of all this, so we approached accordingly. We got one man to crawl on his belly along the floor of the landing. He arrived at the door of the cell in question, got up and opened the door. At that point, four other OSG officers, togged out in riot gear, came barrelling down the landing and into the cell. Immediately, the target was poleaxed by the officers, knocked over, pinned down and generally incapacitated, in order to prevent him doing what he wanted to do.

After a while, some of the prisoners were expecting this. They would jam a broom handle up against the door from the inside, effectively barricading themselves in. Our response to that was to take the hinges off the door, which, of course, took a wee bit longer. One night, this scenario arose when we had targeted the Dundon brothers and Nathan Killeen. Everything went grand, but following our raid that night, Wayne Dundon made a complaint that I had hit him with an iron bar up to a dozen times on his back and neck. A complaint of that nature, under the circumstances, was deemed to be a Category A complaint and therefore had to be investigated by an external agent. The chosen investigator did a thorough job. Luckily, from my point of view, a control and restraint operation like that is all video-taped, so I had proof that there was zero substance to what Dundon was claiming. Apart from that, there were no marks or injuries to his body as would have been expected if he'd been battered with an iron bar. The investigation was a hassle, as far as I was concerned, but I knew it was all part of the cat and mouse game that went on between those of us in the OSG and some of the gang leaders.

We recovered a good deal of information this way, which we passed on to the gardaí. The blockers certainly served a purpose in our attempts to block communications between prisoners and their associates on the outside. But, as we discovered, any technology like that had a limited use in a prison located in the middle of town. However, listening in was a different matter, and one that brought our work on to a whole new level.

I touched in the previous chapter on the private investigations firm that the prison service had retained. Now, another area where this company came in useful was in setting up systems of surveillance. This was, in retrospect, a very serious business – which, I would have to admit, was legally dodgy. Back then, I didn't give it a second thought. Apart from anything else, I was following orders. I would honestly have to say that, if the same situation arose in the morning, I'd do it all again.

Around about 2011, we were convinced there were a few officers in different prisons in the state who were bringing in contraband, yet we couldn't nab them. We had discussions with the gardaí about our suspicions. They had their own suspicions as well, but resources were a huge problem. They explained to us that they simply couldn't put a prison officer under surveillance, as it would cost a fortune in man-hours. An Garda Síochána had, over the years, conducted this kind of surveillance on gangland figures. But they couldn't justify spending that level of resources in targeting a few prison officers.

But we had the use of a private investigations service. If the gardaí couldn't do it, then what was to stop us? We could do the surveillance and hand the results over to the gardaí. Of course, none of the surveillance material could be used in a prosecution, but we were going to provide a roadmap. For instance, if we could pinpoint through the surveillance when an officer might have drugs on them en route to the prison, a quick call could lead to a random stop, and there's your evidence. Aside from that, the details of a prosecution were not what interested us. We just wanted to do our job, which was to stop the flow of contraband.

We also realized we could use the surveillance for investigating others who weren't necessarily bringing in contraband but were up to no good. There were suspicions, for instance, about some of the work practices of some officers. Elsewhere, senior management in the prison had brought to our attention concerns that a few officers might be working for at least one of the major criminals who were locked up. Covert surveillance could be a useful tool for us.

We sat down with the private investigators and went through what was required. They could put listening devices and cameras into any location that we felt might yield results. They could also put tracker devices on vehicles, which would be crucial in finding out whether any officers were liaising with suspected dealers.

What they needed from me was physical details within the prison so they could determine where best to plant the devices. I was able to supply that, right down to providing photographs. We had cameras in the OSG, which we used to photograph cells before and after searches, to show that we had left the place as we found it. So, the sight of me with a camera wouldn't be that off. I went around at a quiet time, discreetly photographing fuse boards and panels where a device could be installed, right down to the kind of screws that were used, because these boys would have to be in and out quickly, no faffing around looking for an unusual screw-driver or other tool.

Nearly all the devices would be placed in areas where staff gathered or passed through. Therefore, the cameras and listening devices would be filming and picking up conversations from the vast majority of staff who were completely innocent of anything to do with criminality. There were privacy issues involved, but we didn't give that too much consideration.

Since all of this was covert, we would obviously have to provide the techies – as we called the boys from the investigations firm – with some sort of a cover when they came into the prison. We decided the best thing was to get our hands on a few badges for the security firm which fitted the CCTV cameras and other security features, and present the techies as regular security workers. Whenever they arrived to install or monitor kit, they were togged out in high-vis jackets. I met them at the gate and brought them to the screening area. I had my right-hand man on the X-ray machine and had briefed him to let them through, told him that it was kosher and that our chief officer knew about it. Once inside, I accompanied the techies wherever they wanted to go.

The tracker devices were a different kettle of fish. Some of these were on private vehicles, so the techies would do their job in the dead of night on a car or van parked outside an officer's home on, for instance, a housing estate. The tracker is a handy device that is only activated once the vehicle is up and running. The location of the vehicle can then be followed, and once it stops the device powers itself off after a short while. The main problem with the tracker is that it eats batteries, so it needs to be regularly changed.

We also put trackers on prison vans, which was a little easier and certainly less risky than placing them on private vehicles. For this, I would take out one of the vans and meet the techies on the roof of the car park in the Killeshin Hotel, on the outskirts of the town. They had identified that there was no CCTV on that part of the car park, so we could go to work there and apply the tracker to the underside of the vehicle.

Once the devices were in place, we were all set. The system was a success. From there on, we were privy to the movements and, in some instances, the conversations of officers who we felt were up to no good.

Apart from targeting those involved in contraband, there was another case that became the focus of our covert surveillance. This involved putting devices in the class office on one of the landings. There were suspicions that two officers on the landing were working for a criminal who was housed there. One of the officers had moved to the landing after the criminal was transferred there. As far as we were concerned, he was positioning himself nearby to be whatever help he could to the criminal.

The job here involved installing both a camera and a listening device in the office, in the hope that the two men, when alone in the room, might discuss their links to the criminal. The class office is a small room with a table and a few chairs, a sink, a kettle and a fridge. There is also a whole row of panels on the wall, all of which are connected in one way or another to the security systems: gates, CCTV cameras and all of that. The panels made it relatively easy for the techies to install their camera and listening device. The thing was set up perfectly, with relatively good quality, particularly on the sound.

Now, this was where the slog came in. It was my job to trawl through the endless hours of recorded tape. As you can imagine, most of what is recorded is boring and irrelevant. In any twenty-four-hour period you can have up to a dozen officers coming in and out of the office. Most of them do nothing of consequence whatsoever, but you have to keep viewing just in case. Then there are those whose behaviour when alone, particularly at night, shows they are sure that nobody is going to walk in on them or be in any way observing what they are at.

There was one guy who was obviously lazy about personal hygiene. More than once, in the dead of night, he got up from his chair in response to a call from nature. Except, instead of going to the toilet just down the corridor, he urinated into the sink in the office. A least once, I had the dubious pleasure of watching an officer masturbate.

When you view that kind of thing for the first time, it tends to be with eyes agog at the realization that this is going on in a workplace. After that, it's just a bit repellent. And then, of course, you'd cross paths with an officer you'd viewed getting up to something unsavoury. You're looking at this guy, him not having a clue that you have had an eye into his most private actions. Not really a position you'd ever want to be in with colleagues. It was difficult to get that image out of your head, but you had to.

Through all the mind-numbing boredom of acres of film, and the grimy insights into behaviour, we did get a result. One night, the two men who were the focus of the operation were alone in the office and they began talking about how they were working for the criminal. It emerged that one of them had a gambling problem.

From there, we got access to the man's accounts in the service's credit union. (We had somebody in there who was very helpful to us.) We then approached him and told him he could choose to either face a full garda investigation or take a short cut to retirement. Naturally, he took the latter option. The second fella was not as deeply involved, so he was given a transfer.

These operations were relatively harmless. You could argue that we were over the top in using covert surveillance to catch these men out. But once we had the equipment, it would have been difficult to resist the opportunity to use it. Soon, we would embark on operations that were more important. And, on reflection, more questionable in terms of people's rights.

20. Deep Sea Fishing

The surveillance was going so well we decided to up the ante. It was all about getting information, and where better to get it than in the visiting box. All prisoners had visitors, and the vast majority of what passed between them was of no interest to us or, for that matter, the gardaí. But there were some whose conversations we would love to have heard.

There are around 4,000 people in custody in Irish prisons and out of those maybe fifty are of major interest to the gardaí. Since building up contacts with various garda units, we would often get a request to monitor communications to and from a particular visitor. This might come from the drugs unit in Dublin, or one of the detective branches in Limerick. Now, there are three official routes of communication for prisoners: telephone, letter writing and visitors. Any criminal with half a brain would not communicate sensitive information over the phone or by mail, as he knows both are monitored. That leaves visits, which is exactly where our friends the techies came in.

The bugging of visiting boxes was a delicate operation. First off, it couldn't be done in the regular boxes, as the place would just be too noisy, so we had to confine it to the box for screen visits, and to the lifers' box. The first issue that arises is that the targeted prisoner must therefore be on a screen visit. But what if he, or any visitor, hasn't done anything to deserve being confined to screen visits only? Then we organized that a screen visit would be necessary.

When the visitor in question arrived at the prison, I would have signalled in advance that he or she should be brought into the room with the dog for screening. I would have told the handler to ensure that the dog sat down and gave an indication with this prisoner. The handler knew how to get the dog to do that, even when there weren't drugs present.

Once the dog did his business, I would tell the visitor that he or she had to go through a screen visit only, if they wanted to continue. There would be some hassle – understandably, because the visitor would feel aggrieved as they had no contraband on them – but that was the choice. Inevitably, the visitor agreed in the end to the screen visit. I would then take them to the visiting box and point to one of the benches to sit on. This, of course, would be the one in which we had installed the listening device. The device was voice-activated and planted close to the vent through which prisoner and visitor talked.

The installation and retrieval of the devices was another delicate operation. There are CCTV cameras in all visitor boxes, monitored centrally in the prison's control room. The cameras are switched off only when no visits are taking place, so it was during those brief periods that I or one of my colleagues brought the techies in to do their work. (The lifers' box was a lot more straightforward, as we just had to put the device somewhere in the room. There was also far less traffic or monitoring of the boxes, as the room wasn't used so often.)

We got a good share of information from these operations. Some of it was of use to us, in terms of plans to bring in contraband and goings-on within the prison. The bulk of it, though, we passed on to the gardaí. This could be as small as something to do with a prisoner's relationship with his wife or friend, or perhaps something about evidence from a crime scene that had to be dealt with, such as CCTV footage, or a piece of clothing that might be incriminating. There was bigger stuff also about the running of criminal gangs and, in particular, details about drug trafficking at a high level.

It didn't require huge man-hours to go over the recordings, as we would only have to monitor the times when visits occurred. Out of every ten of these visits that we monitored, we might get something in one, maybe a little Mickey Mouse stuff in two others, and absolutely nothing of any value in the remainder. That's not a bad return.

The operation also included listening in on conversations between prisoners and solicitors. This might yield some interesting nuggets of information, but it was also where things got hairy from a legal point of view. Solicitor–client conversations are privileged in law. Any messing with that, any monitoring of the conversation, is a total no-no and could lead, for instance, to the collapse of a trial, or even charges for interfering with the legal principle of privilege.

We weren't thinking about that when we monitored these conversations. As with the regular visitors, we duped some solicitors into diverting to a screen visit. They were put through the routine with the dog, and more than one solicitor was angry about the indication. They would then have a choice as to whether to abandon this consultation with the client and return home, most likely to Dublin, the journey having been a waste of time. Or they could go ahead with the screen visit, under protest, which is exactly what most of them did.

With hindsight, if you were to examine the scope of our surveillance operation, the monitoring of conversations with solicitors was the element that was most open to criticism. If it was ever proven, it could create quite a stink. But while all that information-gathering advanced our cause in general, there was one specific area of the surveillance in which we were desperate to get a result, and that was the targeting of Little Big Man.

This individual was a prison officer, and we're going to call him Little Big Man, or LBM. There were suspicions for a long time in the OSG that he was bringing truckloads of drugs into the prison. Various governors were also convinced that he was dirty. Our contacts in the gardaí independently had received intelligence to the same effect, but they had nothing solid on him. The first garda to tell me about LBM had previously been a prison officer himself, before retraining. I have to say, I wasn't that surprised. I knew the individual relatively well, and he would never have struck me as one possessing what you might call high morals.

He belonged to a younger generation of prison officers, who were operating in a different world. Over the years, conditions in the service had changed, particularly in relation to overtime. A new breed of jailer was now earning a lot less than my generation did, principally because the pay and conditions were nowhere near as good. Throw in the fact that this breed was growing up in a wealthy country – a vastly different country to the one I grew up in – and with much higher expectations.

In addition, the potential to veer off the straight and narrow can be much greater, in some walks of life. For instance, if a prison officer buys drugs from a dealer for recreational use, he or she is compromised in a way that your average accountant, teacher, nurse or carpenter isn't. If I'm a dealer and I know that you, the recreational user, is a jailer, I'm going to cultivate that contact, draw you in, because you can be really useful. I would make sure to arrange a few free samples of my product for you. I would also arrange that somebody take a photograph of us meeting, unbeknownst to you. Then I have you where it can really hurt. You do what I say or, at the very least, that photo could find its way on to social media, and you kiss your job goodbye, not to mind invite interest from the gardaí.

It should be emphasized that this kind of scenario arises with just a tiny percentage of prison officers, but the amount of damage that one or two can do is simply enormous.

So it was that we made a concerted effort to go after Little Big Man. I spoke with the techies, provided the information they required, and they went to work. The main method of surveillance used here was a tracking device. They fitted it to his private car, outside his home, in the dead of night. One aspect of this operation was that there was a certain risk attached to fitting and retrieving the devices. But these boys knew what they were at, and they were not rumbled.

From the surveillance we discovered that the officer would regularly leave his home and drive to Naas, which is fifty-five kilometres up the M7, heading towards Dublin. There, the tracker showed, he would go to a cul-de-sac where there was a disused silage pit. His vehicle would then stop, and he'd spend the next ninety seconds to two minutes in that spot. He would then return home, usually stopping off at an Applegreen service station for a cup of coffee.

There were other diversions. He sometimes travelled to Newbridge, in Co. Kildare, and stopped for a few minutes at a disused warehouse. And once or twice, he pulled in at a lay-by on a back road near Portlaoise on his way to work. It is certainly possible that there was an innocent explanation for these stops. But under the circumstances, from our point of view, it would be reasonable to conclude that he was picking up drugs to bring into the prison.

The techies tracked him for a few months and then we got to the point where we would have to act. One morning, he left home to go to work and stopped at a laneway outside the town, just past Telfords, the well-known builders' merchants. The time was now 8.08 a.m., so he was going to be late for work. In those circumstances, you would put money on the chances that his stop was to pick up gear. The techies phoned me to let me know. Now, we had a gold-plated opportunity. If the gardaí stopped him before he got to the prison, he was in trouble.

I made a phone call to consult with superiors on the matter. All it would take was a call to one of my contacts in Portlaoise gardaí. They would be only too willing to drop everything and haul in a big fish. But there was resistance. Now that the hour to act had arrived, there was reluctance to do so. While we dithered, LBM drove closer to the safety of the prison. Once he was inside, the chance would be gone.

I was told to hang back, leave it for now. Why? Some of our people had got cold feet. To collar LBM now would possibly, if not probably, expose that we were operating the surveillance. This would, of course, cause all sorts of headaches – if not a downright stink.

I didn't look at it like that. LBM was a big fish who was doing significant damage by bringing in huge quantities of drugs. Not moving against him when he was in an entirely compromised position was a dereliction of duty, as far as I was concerned. If I had my time again, I would have rung the gardaí myself that morning. The old saying that it's 'better to ask for forgiveness than permission' is well known in prison. I wish I had followed it that morning.

LBM showed up for work and went about his duties in his merry way. Later in the day, I had a conversation with one of my garda contacts, who was nearly as pissed off as me about the outcome. After LBM finished his shift that day, he went for his customary couple of pints in a local pub. Afterwards, he was stopped on the Portlaoise bypass by a patrol that had been tipped off about him, and he was breathalysed. His luck was really in that day, because he even beat the breathalyser.

LBM was never nabbed, even though I'd swear before St Peter at the gates of heaven that the fella was as dirty as they come. As time went on, he didn't feature on any intelligence radar, so I have to assume he pulled back at some stage. Maybe he actually copped on that he was on dangerous ground and stopped. As far as I know, he has no idea how close he came to having his whole life turned upside down, as would have been the case if we had nabbed him.

Not long after that, the surveillance operation was shut down. Changes of senior management in the prisons saw new people come in who didn't have the same level of interest in – some might say tolerance for – what we were at. So, the whole thing came to an end. I suppose, in retrospect, that mightn't have been a bad thing. Had we continued, it is perfectly possible that at some point either things would have got out of hand, or we would have been discovered – and that could have led to all sorts of problems.

The covert – and let's face it, illegal – surveillance operation would have remained a secret, most likely for evermore, were it not for events that prompted me to come clean about it, in 2018.

*

Let's fast-forward for a minute to 2018. The issue around the illegal surveillance got out into the public domain at a time when I and others were in dispute with the prison service. (The whole messy matter will be dealt with here in a later chapter.) As part of the dispute, I swore an affidavit detailing actions I'd been involved in over the years. One of these was the surveillance that had been undertaken, six and seven years earlier.

Once the affidavit was completed, I became frustrated that nothing was coming of it. I then contacted the co-author of this book, Mick Clifford, who had a track record of dealing with whistle-blowers. From there, the *Irish Examiner* published the details of the allegations I had made. When that was reported, there were questions in the Dáil about it and the Minister for Justice, Charlie Flanagan, ordered an inquiry to be conducted to find out whether there was any truth to the allegations. After all, this was suggesting that the prison service, a state body, was engaged in illegal activity against, among others, its own employees and solicitors.

The inquiry was conducted by the Inspector of Prisons, Patricia Gilheaney. I was interviewed along with others, including fellow OSG officers, governors and the management of the IPS. Ms Gilheaney also got sight of loads of documents from the time, held in the records of the prison service.

When her report was finally published, the following July – on the Friday before the August bank holiday weekend, a great day to bury news – it confirmed most of what I had alleged. In the words of the report, among the main findings were the following:

€29,000 was paid by the IPS to two private security firms in 2011 and 2012 for services including covert surveillance, tracking and CCTV and that these services were procured outside normal rules.

There is some evidence to corroborate the allegation that covert surveillance was carried out in a unit in the Midlands prison in 2011.

There is some evidence to support the allegation that covert surveillance was carried out in an office in the Midlands prison between October 2011 and December 2012.

There is no evidence to corroborate the allegation that solicitor/client consultations were deliberately monitored.

There is some evidence to corroborate the allegation that a tracking device was placed on the private car of a prison officer.

All of this was in line with what I had claimed. I claimed a lot more, but the evidence for some of it could not be found. For instance, the report found there was no evidence that conversations between solicitors and clients had been listened in on. Of course, there wasn't. How could there be? We didn't keep official records of recordings, and we certainly didn't keep records of the details that we passed on to the gardaí.

Then Ms Gilheaney's report came to the big question in situations like this. Who knew what – and when?

The evidence does suggest that in an effort to curtail the flow of contraband into IPS facilities, a small number of personnel within the OSG acted in a unilateral manner which was beyond the original remit of the OSG, that does not appear to have followed any standard procedural or operational guidelines and which fell outside of accept-able practice.

There is conflict of evidence as to whether these activ-ities were authorised by the then OSG governor. There is no substantive evidence to corroborate the allegation in the affidavit that these activities were carried out with the knowledge or authorisation of senior management within the IPS.

In plain English, the report suggested that myself and a few others took it upon ourselves to get involved in illegal surveillance in order to stop contraband coming into the prison. We did this off our own bat, and we kept the whole thing secret from senior management in the service. Not only that, but the report was saying there was a dispute over whether the governor of our own unit, John Kavanagh, even knew what we were doing. I don't accept any of that. Not for a minute.

I have no issue with Ms Gilheaney, a person of the high-est integrity, who did her best to complete a proper investigation. How close she managed to get to the truth is a different matter. Her investigation depended on access to records that existed and testimony from people who were there at the time. The nature of the operation was such that detailed accounts and records of what was going on were not kept. Wherever there was no written record to show that somebody had knowledge of what was going on, Ms Gilheaney was left with verbal testimony. Many of those interviewed had a vested interest in the whole issue. If, for instance, Ms Gilheaney ruled that they knew all about it and tacitly authorized it, such a finding could have a big impact on their careers. Under those circumstances, it would have been little less than jaw-dropping if anybody had implicated themselves. The only people who did that were me and a few of my colleagues – because, unlike everybody else interviewed, we had nothing to lose.

The outcome was that the department was able to say that the whole thing was down to a few lads who went off-side. The prison service did likewise, with the director general even issuing an email to all staff when the report was published, pointing this out.

That's all very neat and tidy, but a few awkward questions are outstanding. How did we manage to get the IPS to hand over €29,000 for something that apparently nobody in prison service headquarters knew anything about? Did a few of us just show up at Longford with an empty bag to be filled with all that loot? Then take it away and spend it as we saw fit? If I'd known it would be that easy to get your hands on money and spend it secretly, I might have taken off with my family on a world tour, courtesy of the IPS.

This, remember, was at a time when the state's arse was out of its trousers as far as the public finances were concerned. There wasn't a bob in the country. Yet the official position is that a big chunk of money was handed over to a unit in the prison service, to spend as they saw fit, with no real accountability for it, no questions asked as to what it was for.

At various times while that surveillance was ongoing, I was in discussions with governors and management personnel where it would have been obvious that we had access to information that was obtained covertly. I'm not saying that I, or anybody else, openly said to senior people, 'Well, we installed a camera in the class office the other day.' But it was obvious.

The other question is, where is the criminal investigation into this activity? Ms Gilheaney's report was referred to An

Garda Síochána. After all, this looked like a crime had been committed: it is illegal to put somebody under surveillance unless there is a court order allowing it. It is certainly illegal for anybody outside the gardaí to do so.

Any garda investigation into our operation wouldn't require a team of crack sleuths. Much of the evidence is in the inspector's report. Just use it as a roadmap. You might think the first port of call in such an investigation would be the man who made the allegation and who admitted his role in it. That's me.

At the time of writing, it has been two and a half years since the publication of Ms Gilheaney's report. No garda has knocked on my door looking to interview me. I haven't been arrested. I would happily co-operate with any garda who was investigating this matter. And not only that, but I could make their job easier by pointing them towards further clues that could yield more evidence and form part of a file. Yet despite the very public airing of this possible criminal act, despite the Minister for Justice, no less, saying what went on was wrong, there has been no investigation.

Why? Maybe because any investigation would have to face the reality that members of the force were aware of what was going on, and benefiting from it. Maybe an investigation couldn't look away from the fact that we had liaised with gardaí in trying to stop the flow of drugs and phones into prison.

If an investigation came to the point where all of that was uncovered, the choice for the investigating gardaí would be stark. Do they keep going and compile a file for the DPP? Such a file would include some highly embarrassing details that, in all likelihood, might ensure there couldn't be a successful prosecution. Do they charge colleagues with having knowledge of what might be a crime? What are the implications for the convictions of anybody whose conversations with their solicitor had been taped? They might try to claim that evidence in their case had been illegally obtained. Would a Pandora's box be opened? Far better not to go poking into those corners where trouble might find you.

In addition to Ms Gilheaney's report, the gardaí had more evidence handed over to them later, in 2019. I and others passed a file on to the Fianna Fáil TD Marc Mac-Sharry, who passed it on to An Garda Síochána headquarters. As far as I know, nobody has even been interviewed following the supply of that helpful information that shows a crime may have been committed. If all of this was down to a few allegedly dodgy officers like me, then why is it being ignored by the state's law enforcement agency?

The only time I was contacted by a garda was in late 2021. A few months earlier, I received an anonymous package in the post, which contained nine DVDs. On each one there were dozens of files containing acres of covert surveillance footage. I recognized this footage from one of the surveillance operations conducted in the Midlands. I had strong suspicions as to where the package came from.

After receiving it, I contacted the Inspector of Prisons' office, as it had been responsible for investigating the covert surveillance. I told them what I had received, and asked whether they wanted to see it. Next thing I know, a senior garda was ringing me from the headquarters in Dublin, demanding that I hand over the DVDs to him. For what? No investigation had been conducted, despite there being stacks of evidence on which to base a case. This material wasn't going to make any difference. So why did this senior garda want it? Surely not to watch it safely gather dust in some dark recess of a records office? I told him that I had given it to my solicitor and he could take the matter up there.

I have great time for the members of An Garda Síochána. During my career, I liaised with many and saw the best of some of those I met along the way. I have no issue with how the organization has decided to give this one a miss. But I circle back to the question: if, as the official line goes, the covert surveillance was all about a few dodgy officers going offside, why not come after us? I think we all know the answer to that.

The work I did in liaising with a private investigations company to install, monitor and harvest information from illegal surveillance was no different from anything else I did as an employee of the Irish Prison Service. I followed orders. That's not an excuse. If I was ordered to give a prisoner a clatter, or target some prisoner unfairly, or tell lies in order to further an agenda or whatever, I would refuse. In this instance, I was ordered to assist in stopping the flow of contraband and help out the gardaí. I genuinely didn't think twice about whether we were breaking the law. Was it possible we were infringing the rights of those we suspected of drug dealing or defrauding the state or working for dangerous criminals? Sure, but my job was not to compile a case that could be used in a criminal prosecution.

Did I worry that I might be breaking the law? How could I? I was working for the prison service, which is there to enforce the law as decided by the courts. The prison service is run under the arm of the Department of Justice, which is the main state organ in organizing the law. I was a small cog in the whole thing. If anybody really wants to find out who was responsible, they can start by looking a lot higher up.

21. Shining a Light in Dark Corners

Early on in my time in the Midlands as an assistant chief officer, I got first-hand knowledge of the spectre of suicides in prison. Later, when I was serving in the OSG, I got involved in a particular aspect of these tragic events which – I believe, and hope – has made some difference for the good.

Prison suicide is not a subject that gets huge publicity. I presume that is because of general attitudes towards those who are locked up. I am very aware that for practically every prisoner serving a sentence there has been a victim of the crime. That could be the bereaved family of a murder victim – not to mind the tragedy of a life cut short for the victim – or it could be a shop assistant on minimum wage, who has been viciously attacked by a junkie in search of a fix. It could be victims of child sexual abuse or adult sexual crimes like rape. The absence of any public feelings of sympathy towards prison suicides in general might be understandable.

Notwithstanding, there is something sad about a prisoner who takes his own life. To walk into a cell and see a man hanging from a window – to view a body, all life drained away – is a very strange experience. The expression on his face at the time of death can appear as if he is satisfied that he has passed across a threshold from a place where he could no longer live with some peace. It's a scene that is difficult to completely eradicate from your mind once you first come across it.

The strange thing is that, quite often, the prisoner who

takes his own life is not serving a long sentence. He may have a matter of months to go, in some cases, which would make you wonder why, once the shore of freedom was coming into view, he decided to do it then.

I have a theory about why some resort to it. There are prisoners who find themselves locked up for doing things that they deeply regret; things that, to the greatest extent, were attributable to being out of their heads on drugs. Addicts lead chaotic lives in which their primary concern is getting a fix; they will hurt whomever they have to in order to satisfy that need. Then, when the thick fog has lifted from their brain, and they finally have a chance of coming out the other side clean, it may be too much for some to face up to. The prospect of going back out into society is too much for them. If my theory stacks up, then it is particularly tragic.

Whatever your views about the circumstances that drive a man to take his own life, there is no doubt about one common factor in prison suicides: that is the huge number that can be attributed to untreated mental illness of one form or another. It is well documented that huge numbers of prisoners suffer with mental health problems. It is also undeniable that many of these people should not be in prison but in a setting that properly cares for their needs. The ultimate outcome is that there will inevitably be prisoners who end up suicidal. Of course, not all who fall into that category would be diverted from carrying it out if they had the proper treatment, but it's reasonable to assume that at least some would.

In Chapter 10 (Here Comes the Night) I touched on what those of us who worked in prisons can do to attempt to prevent suicides – which, in reality, is limited. What brought me back to the subject when I was in the OSG was considering what we should do after a suicide, in order to ensure that a man's death is dealt with both professionally and with compassion.

The case that sparked my interest in this whole area was a routine suicide – and to consider such a tragic end to a human life as 'routine' is, in itself, telling. The man was a Traveller and he hanged himself from the window. He left a long note, running to pages, about how he was unhappy but now he would be going to another world. It wasn't in any way religious – more attributable to a kind of fantasy. In that respect, the note was highly unusual. And after his body was discovered, word about it went around the place quickly.

Now, prison officers are nosy at the best of times. In this case, there was practically a queue of officers to get into the cell and see the aftermath of this man's death. They went in and rubbernecked, and before long the dead man was actually dragged out the door of the cell in which he had died. It was as if his body was getting in the way of the lads poring over the man's last letter.

The dead prisoner, who presumably departed this world in a state of despair, was left lying there on the landing. When the lads inside had satisfied their curiosity, they left and went back to their posts. Two of them grabbed the dead man and dragged him back into the cell. In the process of being dragged out, one of the prisoner's shoes had slipped from his foot. While two others were pulling the man back in, a third picked up the shoe. Initially, he held it in his hand, as if he wasn't sure what to do with it. Then he had a quick look around and just threw the shoe over his shoulder on to the netting strung across the landings to prevent stuff being thrown down to the next floor.

I watched everything on CCTV later. I thought the

behaviour of the officers displayed such a callous disrespect for a human being who, whatever he had done, had died in tragic circumstances. After that, I made up my mind I'd look into the way such matters were handled.

The contribution I could make in this area, as far as I was concerned, was in relation to preserving the scene. Out in society in general, any scene of death that might require investigation is preserved by the gardaí. That was not happening in prisons. Instead, it was open season for anyone who wanted to drop in for a rubberneck. The dead man's clothes would just be bundled into a bag and, say, the ligature discarded. Time and again, in coroners' courts all over the country there were instances where the relatively professional garda file on the investigation was in complete contrast to the reporting of a cursory and often slipshod inquiry from within the prison.

I went to the governor of the OSG, John Kavanagh, about this and made the case that the preservation of the scene in the aftermath of a death or a serious incident should be looked at. For instance, sometimes the cause of death might be questionable, particularly if the deceased was sharing a cell. And this wasn't just about deaths. Any time there was a violent incident in the prison, a garda investigation would have to take place. We in the prison service were always first responders in those cases; the first people on the scene. We had obligations to ensure that nothing was done to interfere with the garda investigation before it got off the ground. Up until this point, there had been little emphasis on preserving evidence in a prison setting. Bloodstained clothes, for example, would be thrown into a bag with boots and shoes, as if it was just a routine collection for the laundry. A weapon might be taken and kept in the class office, where any other officer could come in and pick it up to examine it or whatever. It was all wholly unprofessional.

Kavanagh gave me the nod to liaise with the gardaí, to find out about preservation of scenes. After that, myself and two other ACOs spent the best part of a year tic-tacking with the scene of crime gardaí for the Laois-Offaly division. They brought us through the basics and showed us the kind of training they received. This included proper attention being given to retention of evidence and the chain of evidence, along with preserving the scene.

We had to adapt to prison conditions. For instance, if a violent incident occurs when prisoners are going through the eatery, it is not possible to preserve such a scene. Unlike the gardaí, we couldn't seal off an area that was central to the functioning of the prison. So we got training in photographing the scene and were supplied with expensive, highly accurate cameras. We were also supplied with the white protective outfits that gardaí and patholo-gists use in the aftermath of a crime.

As with other aspects of our job, it was inevitable that we would put noses out of joint. If a senior governor arrived at the door of a cell, intent on inspecting it in the aftermath of a death or violent incident, we would not be in a position to deny him or her entry. But we would tell them that if they entered, then they would be obliged afterwards to hand over their clothes. They would also have to provide a DNA and fingerprint sample to the gardaí, in order to eliminate them from other samples that would be retrieved from the scene. That was not popular, as it was seen as infringing their authority. But we were satisfied it was the professional approach.

Out of all that, we devised a training programme, with help from the gardaí. I was tasked with delivering the programme to prisons around the country in order to train as many officers as possible. Our aim was to ensure that at least all class officers – who oversee landings – would be in a position to do everything absolutely correctly in the wake of an incident on their landing. The programme is now standard within the service and I'm proud of the role I played in bringing that about.

Through my work dealing with the preservation of scenes, and suicides in particular, I came into contact with the Inspector of Prisons at the time, Judge Michael Reilly. He was the second person to fill the role of inspector, which was created in 2002. The first holder of the office was retired High Court judge Dermot Kinlan; Reilly, a judge of the district court, took over in 2008. The idea of an inspector of prisons is solid, even if, as with much else, this country was late in getting it off the ground. The inspector is there basically to ensure that everything is being done properly. One comparison that could be made is that of the garda ombudsman's role in overseeing the gardaí.

The inspector's main brief is to ensure that prisoners are being treated correctly and according to the law. Prisoners can make a complaint directly to the inspector, who has rights of investigation, including the right to show up unannounced and ask to see a particular prisoner. In theory, the office has a lot of power. In reality, there are huge constraints to the job. From what I've observed, both prison governors and the management of the IPS ensure that the inspector doesn't hinder them too much in doing things however they want to do them.

Not long after he began, Reilly could see that deaths in custody were a problem. He went to the Minister for Justice and pointed this out. He said that the state could be in trouble with the European Convention on Human Rights, because these deaths were not being properly investigated. The minister asked him would he take on the role, and he did.

That was how I came into contact with Michael Reilly. He heard of my involvement in organizing the preservation of scenes and approached my chief, Ben Buckley, saying he wanted to talk to me.

I said no problem. He showed up one day at my house in his car, for which he had a garda driver. It was a hot summer's day and I invited both of them to come in.

Reilly turned to the driver and said, 'He's fine there.'

I replied, 'Judge, my house, my rules.'

The garda just smiled but stayed put. I brought the judge into the house but made a point of bringing a cold drink out to the garda.

It wasn't the best of starts between us, but after that we got on well. It became obvious to me that he took his job extremely seriously and wanted to fulfil the role of his office as best he could. Now, that might sound like nothing out of the ordinary, but you have to put it in the context of the environment in which he was working. If, for instance, the man wanted an easy time, nobody would have bothered him. Certainly, the less poking around he did, the more comfortable the IPS and prison governors would feel. The same goes for the Department of Justice, as far as I could see. The only people who would have been put out were the prisoners and their families

But that wasn't Reilly's way. He went into detail and wanted to know everything I did. I became a source for him. This wasn't a question of me ratting on anybody, but I think he recognized that I wanted these matters done properly and that I could show him what exactly went on at the frontline, so to speak. We met a number of times, both in my home and also in the Killeshin Hotel, in Portlaoise.

He would occasionally show up in the Midlands. On arrival, he would ask for me and I'd bring him wherever he wanted to go. This would often be associated with his investigations in the aftermath of a death, but other times he might be looking into something that I had given him a steer on. For instance, he was interested in the operation of the emergency buttons. Each cell has a button that, when pressed, lights up in the class office. A prisoner would use it at night for things like asking an officer to pass on some dust (tobacco) or a newspaper to another cell for his friend. It's also a means of calling for help if a prisoner isn't feeling well. Reilly wanted to ensure that all of these buttons were working properly. As far as he was concerned, it was the right of a prisoner but it could also be a lifeline.

He introduced a very humane concept for the bereaved families of prisoners. Sometime afterwards, the family would be invited into the prison to view the cell in which their loved one had died, and he would always arrange to meet families, to explain his investigation into a death and ensure that they were satisfied with it. From my dealings with him, he certainly did his job in a highly professional manner and rightly cared not a whit about whose toes he stepped on, in order to carry out his function. He died suddenly, in November 2016, while still in office.

One case that probably highlights an awful lot about what is wrong with prisons, and how they deal with mental health and suicide, is that of a man called Sean Hayes Barrett. I wasn't involved in the case, as it happened in Limerick Prison, but it did receive a lot of attention as a result of what emerged during the coroner's court.

Sean Hayes Barrett hadn't been in trouble with the law before his arrest, in April 2017. He was living in Limerick city with his girlfriend. He did have some mental health issues that had only become evident in recent months. In late March, he was admitted to the psychiatric unit in Limerick University Hospital. The mental health difficulties he was encountering included suicidal impulses. The extent of these difficulties required him to remain in the psychiatric unit for some weeks.

He left the hospital on 29 April. Venturing back out into the world, he was armed with medication to assist him with countering the suicidal thoughts, a prescription for a refill, and a letter of appointment with a psychiatrist for 4 May. Hours later, Sean was arrested after a minor altercation with a woman in a city-centre store. He told the gardaí that if he was free, he would commit crimes of a sexual nature. The gardaí who interviewed him were concerned about his mental health.

That afternoon, he was brought before Kilmallock District Court. Judge Marian O'Leary was told that gardaí were objecting to bail on the basis of the threat to commit crime that Sean had made. The main thrust of the hearing was concern over Sean's mental health and whether he was a danger to himself or others. The judge remanded him to Limerick Prison. Both the prosecuting garda and the defence solicitor appointed on the day told the court they would each contact Limerick Prison to alert staff to Sean's condition.

Sean Hayes Barrett was admitted to Limerick prison at 5.25 p.m. on Saturday 29 April. On entry, his medication, prescription and record of appointment with a psychiatrist were taken from him. These items were not recorded with his other possessions. The subsequent investigation by the

Inspector of Prisons found no evidence that the nursing staff were informed by officers at the main prison gate that Sean had medicine and medical records in his possession.

Both the solicitor and the prosecuting garda contacted the prison, as they had told the court they would do. These contacts were not made known to the Inspector of Prisons in the subsequent investigation.

On the day he was admitted, Sean was interviewed by a nurse who recorded that she 'advised (Sean) his medication did not arrive with him . . . he will have to go see a GP'. This was effectively referring him to a doctor to determine whether he required any medicine, despite the medicine already prescribed having been taken from him in the prison.

Following the interview, he was placed under 'special observation', the category for vulnerable prisoners. He was housed in a two-person cell on his own. Whatever the reasons for this, it increased his sense of isolation. There are two dedicated psychiatric cells in Limerick Prison, but it is unclear why he was not referred there. Most likely, this was due to capacity issues.

Sean went two days without receiving his medication. He phoned his girlfriend on the day after his admission, and every day after that. She attempted to get an appointment to visit him. Every prisoner on remand is entitled to a daily visit of not less than fifteen minutes, yet Sean's girlfriend 'found it extremely difficult to make an appointment', according to the inspector's report.

Eventually, she was given an appointment for 8 May – which would have been nine days into Sean's imprisonment, had he lived. The failure to allow his close friend to visit, combined with being alone in his cell, could only have heightened his sense of isolation.

During their phone conversation on 1 May, he told his girlfriend he had not yet received his medication. She contacted the hospital and was told that prison staff had been provided with details of his medication. The Inspector of Prisons found that he was provided with the medicine on the evening on 1 May, and every day thereafter.

On 2 May, during a conversation with his girlfriend, Sean said that he had received his medication the previous night, but he didn't think it was his normal dose. During this call he told her that 'the isolation is too hard on me'. As a remand prisoner he would have been spending twenty-three hours daily alone in his cell.

Sean was back in court on 5 May, and further remanded to the prison. That evening, at 8.09 p.m. Sean was given his medication by a nurse and locked up for the night in his cell. As a special observation prisoner, he should have been checked in on every fifteen minutes during lockdown. This is designed to minimize the possibility of self-harm, in particular. During the night, Sean should have been subjected to thirty-nine checks under this rule. In fact, he was only checked nine times, with the intervals between checks varying from twenty-eight minutes to, in the worst case, two hours and fifty-four minutes.

The failure to properly check special observation prisoners has been a feature of investigations following a number of deaths in custody in Irish prisons. In this case, the governor of Limerick Prison, Mark Kennedy, told the Inspector of Prisons that an incident occurred on the night in question in another part of the prison, which required the deployment of extra prison officers. This incident persisted for two hours and meant there were fewer officers available to check on special observation prisoners.

The Irish Prison Service has a policy that allows for extra

officers to be called into the prison in the event of an incident arising. No call was made to any off-duty officers on that night.

Sean Hayes Barrett was checked at intervals that averaged around an hour, throughout the night. A prison officer looked in on him at 2.54 a.m. The next check was at 4.08 a.m. Fifty-four minutes later, an officer looked in and saw Sean with a ligature around his neck. Efforts to resuscitate him were unsuccessful. He was pronounced dead at 7 a.m. on 6 May 2017.

The CCTV footage for the night/morning of May 5/6 went missing within the prison system. This failure to retain footage from a period prior to a death in custody had happened on a number of occasions and has been the subject of criticism from successive inspectors. In this case, a chief officer was 'commended for his diligence in making the written record of the CCTV footage'.

At the inquest into Sean's death, in November 2019, his father's solicitor, Jerry Twomey of Frances Twomey Solicitors, questioned Governor Kennedy on a number of issues that arose. The governor agreed that prison officers were not aware that Sean was a special observation prisoner.

'We weren't a hundred per cent that the officers on the night got the up-to-date special obs list,' Mr Kennedy said.

The governor also agreed that, despite the incident that occurred in the prison on the night, nobody made the call to draft in extra staff in order to cover the special observation prisoners.

'We didn't abide by our own protocols,' Mr Kennedy said. 'Our own protocols were that he needed to be checked every fifteen minutes, and that didn't happen. It is fair to say that this case was a landmark case and, as a result of Sean's death, the whole system has changed throughout the prison service.'

Significantly, coroner John McNamara recorded an open verdict in the case. He said that under the European Convention on Human Rights the state had a positive duty to prevent deaths where possible and 'it appears to me there were systems failures in respect of Sean Hayes's incarceration'.

He said the nature of Sean's death 'on the face of it would imply that it was a suicide', but taking the systems failures into account, he was not happy to record a verdict of suicide.

The case of Sean Hayes Barrett has been well documented through the coroner's court and the Inspector of Prisons' report into his death. Many others go below the radar. The problems that arise, both leading up to and in the aftermath of a suicide, are still there, despite the best efforts of some of us to ensure that things are done better.

22. The Murky Depths of The Bog

None of us can outrun time. By 2016, I was fifty-three, still in good shape, but maybe needing a little change of direction. The job in the Midlands was full-on from a physical point of view. The prisoners tended to be young, full of beans, and sometimes ready for aggro at the drop of a hat. The threat of violence is there for all who work in the service, but in the Operational Support Group we had to constantly deal with low-level physical stuff. For instance, you're doing a search and you go in and wake a prisoner. He has a phone and tries to 'cheek it' – shove it up his back passage – and you're into pulling and dragging and trying to restrain him. That kind of thing is a constant. And it's no big deal when you're young and in top shape yourself.

Early on in the year, my chief, Ben Buckley, asked me would I consider transferring across to the OSG team in Portlaoise. He wanted somebody in there to shake things up a bit. There was also a concern about the upcoming 100th anniversary of the 1916 Rising. Portlaoise still held the subversives, by now reduced largely to dissident Republicans. But the prison authorities feared they might attempt to mark the centenary by staging something spectacular to embarrass the government.

At first, I wasn't sure about the move. It would certainly be easier from a physical point of view. Portlaoise had by then taken over A block (where we had used the phone blockers). The block housed some of the most notorious prisoners in the state, but apart from that, Portlaoise had about a quarter of the number of prisoners that were in the Midlands. And they wouldn't be as messy or as young.

There was another attraction. Officers in Portlaoise are entitled to an 'environmental allowance' because of the presence of the military in the prison. That wouldn't sway me, normally. But if you get it for more than three years, it goes towards your pension entitlements. Given the stage I was at, this kind of thing would have to be a serious consideration.

Then a small incident that was nothing out of the ordinary made up my mind for me. It was a routine visit by a young lad of nineteen, but we could see that he was all set to pass over contraband, so we barrelled into the visiting box to take him away. He resisted fiercely and we had a job, with all the usual pulling and dragging and lashing out, to get him to the reception area. Then when he calmed down, I had a chat with him and he told me he was the father of three children. I was sitting there listening to him, and wondering whether dealing with young fellas like this was what I really wanted to do at this stage of the game. Apart from anything else, the number of visits in Portlaoise was only a fraction of that in the Midlands.

So, I picked up the phone and rang Ben Buckley. 'Alright,' I said. 'I'll go.'

From where I am now, I can safely say that it was not one of the smartest decisions I ever made. Despite my long years in the job, I had no idea what I was letting myself in for.

Portlaoise had changed hugely in the sixteen years since I had worked there, before departing to the Midlands. The subversives didn't have anything like the same clout as they had enjoyed during the height of the Troubles. Their numbers were greatly reduced – and in some respects they didn't have the same discipline, either. The heavies' landing on E1 was now for general use; a new C block had been built, where some of the serious crims were housed. The likes of John Gilligan and Christy Kinahan were long gone, although Brian Meehan was still there. The garda killers and the high-profile Provos had all been released. By 2016, there was one prisoner who stood apart from all others in Portlaoise, and that was Brian Rattigan.

Rattigan had spent most of his adult life in prison. He was just twenty-one when he was involved in a stabbing incident, in August 2001, in which Declan Gavin, also twenty-one, was killed outside an Abrakebabra fast-food outlet in Crumlin. That was to be the first of sixteen violent deaths, all of which were attributed to a feud between rival crime gangs in the Crumlin-Drimnagh area. By 2003, Rattigan was arrested and committed to prison. He was convicted of the murder of Declan Gavin. Over the following fifteen years, a series of legal cases ultimately saw the Supreme Court set aside the conviction because of comments from the trial judge, and Rattigan then pleaded guilty to manslaughter in the case.

Meanwhile, in Portlaoise, Rattigan continued where he had left off in building a crime business. Despite being locked up, he managed to retain his status as a leading gangland criminal. That hit a hurdle in 2008, when a unit from the Drugs and Organised Crime Bureau raided a house in Walkinstown, not far from Rattigan's stomping ground in Crumlin. They discovered 5kg of heroin and a Nokia phone in a shed at the back of the property. The heroin had a street value in excess of €1m. From subsequent mobile phone traffic, the gardaí were able to determine that Rattigan had sent messages to his then partner as the net was closing. 'Get rid of your phones quick,' he told her.

The gardaí also discovered paperwork at the house, which included a list of those who were working for Rattigan and the weight of heroin assigned to each dealer. These low-level operators had been given code names such as 'Dicko', 'Paret Man' and 'Lips'.

Meanwhile, more gardaí raided Rattigan's cell in Portlaoise. They surprised him when he was on the phone. Once they burst in, he threw the phone out of the cell. On it they found more evidence linking him to the drugs. The gardaí also recovered notes in his cell to bolster their case.

In 2013, the Special Criminal Court convicted Rattigan of dealing drugs from prison, the first such conviction of its kind. He was sentenced to seventeen years, much of it backdated to 2008. (In the end, Rattigan served eighteen years and was released in August 2021.)

When I arrived in Portlaoise, Rattigan was the undisputed gang leader in the prison. He was housed in C block and more or less ran the whole block, not to mind his own landing. As I described in Chapter 17 (Getting a Handle on the Gangs), there was only so much we could do to limit his power, apart from transferring prisoners whom we believed were key men for him. But they were simply replaced.

Rattigan didn't smoke and demanded that nobody in his immediate environment did so. If he arrived in the recreation room and a couple of prisoners were playing pool and having a cigarette, they left immediately. There was no question of anybody challenging his power in any manner at all.

In the visitor box, he constantly changed places with other prisoners, presumably on the basis that he thought some of the boxes might be bugged. (Obviously, this wasn't just paranoia on his part.) He might be in seat number one, and after ten minutes he'd get up and indicate to his visitor to do likewise. He'd go to seat four and tell the prisoner there to move. Nobody was going to argue with him, or ask to be left alone. The prisoner just got up and moved.

His cell was always kept clean, and he was no real bother. We were constantly searching him and his cell, but rarely came up with anything. When he was convicted of dealing from prison, he also faced two charges of possession of mobile phones, but he was found not guilty on those. His status was such that he would have underlings holding for him whatever he wanted.

Only once did the possibility of hassle arise between me and him. I arrived at his cell, one dinner time, to take him down to reception while two of our lads searched his cell. He got agitated, which wasn't like him, and made like he was going to resist.

'Brian,' I said, 'you can come with me or I'll have four lads up here from Control and Restraint, and they will take you down one way or the other.'

He hesitated for a minute, laughed and came along.

That was Rattigan. As cool as a cucumber but undoubtedly highly dangerous, as shown by his past crimes and his ability to build and run a drug-dealing business behind bars, where he had been for most of his life.

Controlling and monitoring the activities of the likes of Rattigan would be a job in itself, in normal circumstances. But there was little that was normal about the environment in Portlaoise. It was as if its special status, going back to the 1970s, and the role it was perceived to have played during the Troubles, somehow stopped the place advancing into the twenty-first century. Anything that smacked of progress was regarded with suspicion, as far as I could see.

There were good officers in there, but there was also a large cohort who just didn't want any hassle, and that was their priority, rather than ensuring that a proper job got done.

Two incidents that occurred during my time there said plenty about the culture of the prison, how it was run, and where the priorities lay. Neither involved me or the OSG, and both concerned A block, which held some of the most notorious prisoners in the system.

On the morning of 4 May 2018, fifteen officers left their posts in A block. This was done as a form of protest because an officer had been assaulted the previous day.

Prison officers get assaulted. That, unfortunately, is part of the job. All efforts must be made to ensure the safety of officers, and prisoners must know that if they ever go down that route, there will be a price to pay. There are processes for dealing with any incident of assault.

In this case, however, the officers decided that they were not happy with how the matter was being dealt with, so they just walked off the job. Cast your mind back a minute to the chapter on the defaulters (see Chapter 6) and how, in 1997, the men who had held the officers hostage in Mountjoy were separated from the general population when they were brought to Portlaoise. That followed a threat from the officers to go on strike if something wasn't done. As far as I'm concerned, that was perfectly understandable, considering what these dangerous criminals had done to our colleagues during the siege in Mountjoy. But it was a threat to walk out. We didn't actually do it.

Now, in 2018, we had a scenario on A block where an officer had been assaulted, and while that was traumatic for the officer, it wasn't in the same category as what had occurred in Mountjoy. Yet despite that, the officers just walked off the job in protest. This was completely unprecedented. Prison officers, like the gardaí, can't just down tools and walk off the job, as if they were employed in a factory or office, and work just comes to a halt. Leaving your post means that a serious security problem could blow up. Despite that, the lads just walked.

The campus governor, Ethel Gavin, reacted quickly. She managed to persuade other officers to agree to be deployed temporarily to A block, to ensure that nothing dangerous could develop. Ordinarily, officers – like workers anywhere – would be reluctant to cover for what were effectively striking colleagues. It is a tribute to Ethel Gavin's skills and her status among staff that she was able to defuse what could have been a major incident.

Later in the day, some of those who walked off the job returned, and others went sick. There was an urgent inquiry into what most within the service would have considered their reckless action. The outcome was that the officers would be transferred to a Dublin prison. I think it's fair to say that the punishment reflected the seriousness of what had occurred.

Then something strange happened. The transfers were halted and suspended for twelve months, conditional on good behaviour. The officers had to sign a declaration that what they did was 'without reasonable excuse' and that their actions had 'placed the welfare of colleagues and the security of the prison at significant risk'. None of that was in keeping with the code of discipline within the service. Personally, I couldn't see any situation where officers in any other prison would have got such favourable treatment. In some ways, it was a bit like being told to write out lines as a punishment when we were back in primary school.

Worse was to come. Ethel Gavin, who had risen to the challenge, was effectively demoted. She had been acting governor of the campus – overseeing both Portlaoise and the Midlands – and she was told she would now revert to being governor of just the Midlands. A chief officer and ACO were also transferred, although that was reversed after various appeals. The whole thing was a bad joke. The men who had abandoned their posts got a slap on the wrist, and the manager who had handled the situation with a high degree of professionalism took the rap.

Up until that point, Ethel Gavin had been viewed as a star within the service, put forward by Longford in the media, including taking part in a series that had been done on TV about the Midlands. She was a highly regarded and effective manager. Yet it would appear that she was sacrificed in a move to appease the officers' union, the Prison Officers' Association. The whole affair demonstrated that the POA had a tight grip on Portlaoise, and it would certainly appear that Longford was willing to go along with that for a quiet life. Ethel Gavin ultimately retired early. I am not alone in believing that she was a fine public servant who got messed up by the system and ultimately left, in disillusionment.

The other incident that gave an insight into the culture in Portlaoise also occurred in A block. In May 2019, a prisoner on the block, Freddie Thompson, made a complaint to the governor. Thompson, who had been known as 'Fat Freddie', was serving a sentence for murder. Prior to his detention in 2016, he was reputed to be a major figure in the Kinahan crime cartel. He was convicted in 2018 of a murder that was reported to be part of a feud in which the Kinahan gang was involved.

The complaint he made to the governor of Portlaoise was highly unusual. He said that three basic-rank officers on the block were constantly undermining three more senior officers at management level, and their work. At the time, these managers were trying to make some changes on the block – for instance, access to a library and a few other initiatives – designed to lower tensions and hopefully lead to a better environment for staff and prisoners alike. Apparently, these efforts were being resisted by the junior officers, who preferred the status quo.

Thompson's complaint included allegations that the junior officers were telling him and other prisoners that the senior men were people 'who will tell you they will do something and then not do it, persons not to be believed'. One of the senior men was also referred to as 'a fucking idiot'.

Earlier in this book, I've pointed out the importance of trust with a prisoner. If you tell him you will do something, then you must do it, or you'll sour relations completely. Thompson's allegation should be seen in that context. Thompson also claimed that what was being done to one of the senior officers, in particular, 'may put his life in danger if prisoners were to believe that he was lying and could not be believed'.

This stuff was dynamite, if there was any truth to it. The governor correctly deemed it to be a Category A complaint, which typically might be an assault or serious threat. That, in turn, meant it had to be investigated by an outside agency, and so the IPS retained an external investigator, John Naughton, to do the job.

John Naughton interviewed a whole range of prisoners and staff, including the governor, John Farrell, as part of his investigation. He also had access to an array of documents. Much of his final report was later leaked to the *Irish Examiner*.

In the report, Thompson related his experience. He told

the investigator he had nothing to gain from making the complaint, and even though it could cause him problems, he wanted it investigated. He said the three senior officers had supported him and other prisoners with matters on the block, such as setting up the library and trying to arrange open visits with family.

Other prisoners on the block echoed these sentiments, but there were a few who claimed to know nothing about any of it. Neither did two prison officers who were interviewed. Another, a senior female officer, had been told by a prisoner that some staff were 'winding him up and telling him lies'. She also told the investigator that 'she did believe that undermining comments were made, even though never made in her presence'.

John Farrell told the investigator that he had been aware that some of the new initiatives he had introduced were 'subversively resisted by some officers'. He had been told about disparaging comments being made about some of the senior officers, he informed the investigator. That prompted him to issue a general instruction to staff, in April 2019, titled 'Appropriate communication'. In it he emphasized that staff should be respectful of each other and not make any negative comments about other officers to prisoners.

The three senior officers about whom the disparaging remarks were allegedly made all gave evidence. One mentioned that when he started on the block, in June 2018, one of the basic-grade officers told him soon after his arrival, 'We do not like you, we did not send for you, we do not want you, you won't be staying. We will run you out of A block.' The basic-grade officer denied that he said this.

The three officers who were accused of making the comments also gave evidence to Naughton. All three denied resisting change or making disparaging comments about their colleagues.

John Naughton completed his task in late November 2019. He found that 'there was a lot of resistance to the regime change that was being implemented by Governor Farrell and his team in June 2018'.

He noted that he found one of the three basic-grade officers 'guarded and not forthcoming at interview'. He stated that another of the three had said that Freddie Thompson's complaint was fabricated and without foundation. The investigator stated, 'I do not accept that this is the case.'

Naughton found that it was 'undeniable' that some officers were making comments to deliberately try to undermine the work of one of the senior officers.

In conclusion, the investigator stated:

Based on my review of all the evidence gathered, and taking into account the statements of the complainant, witnesses and prison personnel, documentary evidence of the issues involved, I am of the opinion that there are grounds for the complaint.

The result was unprecedented in a prison setting in this country. An independent investigation had concluded that three officers had undermined their senior colleagues, possibly putting their safety in danger, by making disparaging and untrue comments about them to some of the most dangerous criminals in the state.

What followed, in the handling of that result, was just as worrying. In situations like this, it is up to the relevant governor to issue disciplinary proceedings or nominate a colleague to do so. For some reason, Naughton's report was not passed on from IPS management in Longford to the governor for seven months. Why it took that long is any-body's guess.

Once received by the governor of Portlaoise, he passed the issue on to a colleague. This governor agreed with the findings and recommended that there be extra training for the basic-rank officers who were found to have trans-gressed, and that the governor of Portlaoise remind all staff of the importance of not undermining the work of others. That was, more or less, letting them off completely.

There was no disciplinary process. It was reported at the time that the reason for this was 'the passage of time' since the complaint. Well, one reason why so much time had passed was because the report had lain dormant in Long-ford for seven months.

So, that was the end of that. Once the lack of action became known to many of us in the prison, and in other prisons beyond, there was a sense of shock. The three men had been found guilty of the most egregious breach of dis-cipline, putting their colleagues in danger. Yet they walked away with a slap on the wrist.

As for the senior officers who had been targeted, only one of them remains in the job today. The other two were granted stress-related sick leave initially, and were out of the job long-term. Both are progressive officers who wanted to get things done in the prison for the benefit of all. Their contribution to the prison service will be sorely missed.

Those two incidents give a flavour of the kind of atmos-phere I was working in, soon after arriving back in Portlaoise. Most of the officers in the OSG had been recruited directly from the prison, and so they were embedded in the culture. To be fair, around a third of those in the OSG in Portlaoise were good workers. But the rest were mainly concerned with their own sense of entitlement, and getting up every morning to find something to moan about. Small things like taking DNA samples were a big deal.

'I'm not putting my hand in any lag's mouth,' an officer told me, one day. He was talking about the swabs.

'You don't put your hand in anybody's mouth,' I told him.

Another day, I told a fella to compile an intelligence profile of one of the prisoners. He told me he hadn't been around when the computer course was given, and he didn't know how to operate it. Another profile that I requested was returned with four lines of information, when the standard was at least ten pages. All of this was completely basic stuff for which officers in any other prison would probably just get a bollocking – and they would know that they had it coming, and had to do better. No big deal, that's standard in any workplace. In Portlaoise, everything was considered an assault on the dignity of lads who'd had it too good for too long.

Even commandeering an office of sorts for the OSG was a big deal. In the end, we were shoved into what was effectively a tea room for staff. One day, I walked in and a few lads on their break were watching horse racing on TV while my staff were trying to work. I went ballistic, as you would.

The shoddy work infected all aspects of our job. The cell searches were a joke sometimes. On one occasion, I watched on CCTV as two officers conducted a search. They walked into the cell and walked back out thirty seconds later. A proper search would take at least forty-five minutes. When I confronted the pair about it, their response was that I had no right to be viewing their work on CCTV.

Many of the problems then fed back into relations with the POA. In sixteen years working at assistant chief officer level in the Midlands, I had never encountered problems with the POA. If an issue arose about a staff member, we sat down and ironed things out and moved on. Portlaoise was a completely different ball game. The smallest thing was blown up and used as some kind of a bargaining tool rather than a problem to be sorted out for everybody.

A lot of what I came up against could be distilled down into relations with one officer, in particular. This man was as useless as an ashtray on a motorbike, but he could moan for Ireland. Repeatedly, I had to pull him up over his failure to do the most basic aspects of the job. He made a whole raft of complaints about me, the most laughable being that my failure to allow him a break at the usual time – because we were under pressure on that particular day – meant that he had been denied a hot meal, because the kitchen was closed by the time he was free. Portlaoise Prison is in the middle of a town with about two dozen outlets where you can get a hot meal, yet this man appeared to believe that he was so oppressed on the job he was denied proper nutrition.

The issues with this officer, and the support he got from the POA, eventually led to an investigation into his complaints by an external investigator. The complaints he had against me were under twenty-four different headings. The report was compiled at huge expense, running into tens of thousands of euros. When it was completed, the investigator concluded that there was no basis for any of it, bar the detail that on one occasion I had a 'meeting' with the officer about his performance in an area of the prison that wasn't private enough. The investigator also noted that the claims that had been made did not merit an investigation of the nature that he was tasked to undertake. The officer appealed the decision but got nowhere.

That goes some way to summing up the kind of culture that I faced when I returned to Portlaoise. I got plenty of support from Ben Buckley and from the chief overseeing Portlaoise, Ger Dowling. But the resistance to change was staggering. I had been sent in to shake up the OSG in the prison, but in some ways, it was shaking me up. Anyway, I just got on with it, did what I could with those who were willing to do a proper job, and tried to avoid the noise. Unfortunately, the noise was just about to get a lot louder.

23. Away With You

The weather was warm, a lazy late summer sun beating down, and I was mowing the grass at home. It was 24 August 2018. I felt a buzzing from the phone in my pocket, pulled it out and turned off the mower. On the line was the governor of the Operational Support Group, Pat Kavanagh, who had taken over from his namesake, John Kavanagh.

'I have some bad news,' he said.

After nearly two and a half years back in Portlaoise, I was to be transferred out of the OSG with immediate effect and back on to the floor at the Midlands Prison.

The reason?

'Staff safety.' The call was short and sour.

I was left in shock. It felt like being told that somebody close to me had died completely unexpectedly.

Transferred? I had, over the years, come across loads of cases in which an officer was transferred. There were even times when I was involved in uncovering wrong-doing that led to a transfer. Every time, the transfer was a form of punishment, and not for a minor issue. Fellas who had been caught engaged in low-level fraud or even, in a few instances, bang to rights over bringing in contraband, or involved in an inappropriate sexual relationship. Those were the kinds of issues that led to a transfer, which brought with it a stain. If you were transferred, the first question anybody asked was, what did you do? In the days after I was told, I must have had between thirty and forty calls from colleagues asking me what I had done.

When I went to a solicitor, he understandably told me to drag out any skeletons that were in my closet. There were none.

I hadn't done anything. The excuse of staff safety was laughable. This was in relation to the officer who had claimed I was bullying him. As related in the previous chapter, the outcome of an investigation was not just that I was innocent of practically all the charges, but there never should have been an investigation at all. The whole thing was baffling.

I rang my chief, Ben Buckley, and guess what? Ben also had just got word that he was being transferred out of the OSG. He was to be assigned to what was effectively a made-up job in Cork. From that, it was obvious to me that this had nothing to do with staff safety. This was a move to get rid of us from the OSG, as some form of power play. Ben, who had given tireless service to the unit since it was set up, was not a favourite of management by 2018. Maybe they thought that he had acquired too much power and influence, and they wanted to get rid of him, irrespective of what damage that might do to the unit. If that was the case – and it's difficult to see anything else – then it must have been decided that I would have to go too, simply because I was seen as Ben's right-hand man. A third senior officer in the OSG, Ger Dowling, was also to feel the cold wallop of management targeting those who were now out of favour.

Had Ben Buckley – and, by extension, myself and Ger Dowling – become too powerful? I haven't a clue. We did our jobs, no more. None of us were involved in office politics or the kind of manoeuvring where people are jockeying for position. We had got a reputation for being efficient, certainly with outside agencies. Whenever the gardaí wanted to liaise with somebody in the prison, it was to us they came, because they knew who they were dealing with.

Just for clarity, none of this upheaval had anything to do with the kind of operations that I have written about in this book. The surveillance, for instance, had been stopped years previously. That would have been buried and forgotten about for ever, except that I, in the course of the dispute I had just been launched into with the prison service, would bring it out in public.

I had a record that was clean as a whistle. I had never over the course of my career been 'half-sheeted', the terminology for disciplinary action. Not once. I had been asked to apply for promotion to chief officer, and had twice been put on panels from which chiefs were drawn. Campus governors had recommended me for promotion. I had never once even so much as been brought into a governor's office for a bollocking.

Big revelation: one Christmas week, I called in sick after dinner one day and went on the beer. Once in thirty-one years. I invite you to measure that against your own record, whether you are in management or on the staff of any organization. When I was forced to look back over my career for anything that could be used against me, I was surprised myself at how clean my record was. Yet here I was, being transferred on the trumped-up basis that I was a threat to staff safety. I wasn't going to take that.

The day I was to report to my new job, I went in and met the governor of the Midlands. He had no problem with me. He said that he had been told another officer in the OSG was going to supervise me as I emptied my locker in Portlaoise. My exit from Portlaoise was to be supervised, as if I was a person who could not be trusted and was being transferred for having done something. I told the governor I was going on sick leave, with immediate effect. I would be out for three months while the whole thing was dealt with in the courts.

Over those months, my solicitor brought a legal action to stop the transfer. It came before the High Court and the court quickly came down on our side. I was staying put. Then the IPS decided they wanted another bite of the cherry and they transferred me again, presumably assuming they had done something procedurally wrong the first time and were going to get it right now. Everybody went back into court and, once again, the judge ruled in my favour. I was not to be transferred.

The whole farrago prompted Ben Buckley to retire. He had reached his thirty years' service and, totally understandably, wasn't in the mood to put up with this faffing about, but it was no way for a career like his to be brought to a close.

I had a different approach. I was coming up to my full service, and before all this kicked off, I was veering very much to retiring once I hit the thirty years, but not now. If they thought they were going to slap me around to push me out the door, they weren't thinking straight. I decided I'd go at a time of my own choosing.

Returning to Portlaoise, in December 2018, was no joke. I could see I was going to be frozen out. For instance, my access to the camera security and IT systems was completely curtailed. Before this blew up, I would have been given total access across the prison, as was proper for somebody doing my job. After I came back, I could access maybe a dozen cameras. There were other little moves, such as cutting down on the number of officers at my disposal during a shift. Previously, I had responsibility for setting out the work detail for the OSG in both prisons, but that responsibility was taken from me. The general thrust of things was to make my life difficult, wear me down, inch me closer to the door.

I know now that these tactics are not unusual in a situation where a person has fallen out of favour. What is amazing is the amount of energy that is put into this kind of thing. Getting the job done becomes secondary to making life as difficult as possible for the targeted employee. You have to wonder about what interests are best served when this is the focus of so much energy.

I am not a shrinking violet. The work I was involved in all my life required a certain toughness, and I don't think I was ever wanting in that department. Over the course of my time in the OSG, I had been involved in getting rid of staff who had not been doing their job properly, to the point that they were a danger to security. On those occasions, the evidence of wrongdoing was presented to the staff member and he or she was told to deal with it. This was completely different: there was no evidence of wrongdoing on my part, because there *was* no wrongdoing. There was just a decision that my face no longer fitted in the regime. Instead of using my experience in the best interests of the OSG, the goal was to push me out the door as fast as possible.

What really got to me during those last years in the service was that, for the first time in all my career, I didn't enjoy going into work. I have known enough jailers over the years who could whinge for Ireland about the job. There was always something wrong with these lads. It was as if they got up in the morning wondering how many things they could complain about on that particular day.

I like to think I was the opposite. As with any job, there

were days – and even long stretches – where there was stress. There were people I had to deal with who were a pain in the neck. And there were sometimes policies or procedures handed down from on high that I thought were stupid or counterproductive. But none of that is unusual in even the best of set-ups: whether you are a professional sportsperson, working at the checkout in a shop, running your own business, or even running the country.

The point is, I enjoyed the job. I actually looked forward to the day as I drove into the prison. I got a kick out of the challenges, solving problems that arose. I think I managed personal relations positively, whether it was with management, staff or prisoners. I felt I was making a contribution, I put in long hours, and I was grateful that I was being well paid to do it. And while I'm no management guru, I would imagine that when people are coming into work contented and in some way fulfilled, they are far more likely to be working well, in the best interests of all concerned. After the hassle blew up, much of the good was drained from the job for me. I soon found that my focus had switched from the best way to do the job to looking over my shoulder for the next attempt to stick it to me.

While I was frozen out by management within the OSG, I was not left completely out in the cold. Beyond my unit, there was support from plenty of colleagues and from the wider management within the prison system. Everybody, from Ethel Gavin – who was, by then, governor of the Midlands – down to staff on the floor in the Midlands and Portlaoise, still had plenty of time for me and understood the position I found myself in. I'm damn sure that many among them were also saying, there but for the grace of God go I.

*

In any event, I wasn't going to take it lying down. I decided to launch a legal action against the IPS, for the manner in which I had been treated. As part of the process, I swore an affidavit about the operations I had been involved in during my time in the OSG. If the prison service was trying to paint me in a negative light, then I was prepared to come clean on how exactly the service operated. I included in my affidavit many of the incidents that are laid out in this book, including the surveillance, the use of informants, and the shortcomings that I found in dealing with the aftermath of deaths in custody.

As I wrote earlier, I had leaked the affidavit to the co-author of this book and it was published in the *Irish Examiner*. On the day it was published, there were questions in the Dáil and the Inspector of Prisons was ordered to conduct an inquiry into the matter. A copy of my affidavit had previously been sent to the Department of Justice, before it ended up in the newspaper. Yet it was only when the matter became public, via the *Irish Examiner*, that there was any urgency about investigating it.

I have described in Chapter 20 (Deep Sea Fishing) how the inspector, Patricia Gilheaney, reported on the issue of surveillance. She also looked at the other matters and concluded that there was some evidence that they had occurred; she also accepted my allegations about the deaths in custody matter and that I had interacted with her predecessor, Judge O'Reilly. In my opinion, the investigation didn't go far enough. But there has been a long-standing issue over the weakness of the powers that the inspector has to oversee the prison service. Everything I put in that document was based on fact. Apart from anything else, why would I compromise myself, or any action I was taking, by telling lies?

Once that affidavit became public, there was no going back as far as my status was concerned – that bell could not be unrung. Prison headquarters in Longford simply couldn't have any officer revealing the state secrets, and trust him in any way thereafter.

The incidents in Portlaoise mounted up. One made me particularly angry because a female officer was dragged into it in order, in my opinion, to get at me. This officer was under my charge and she lived with her mother, who was going through some severe health difficulties. As a result, the officer was late for work a couple of times, one week in September 2019. After discussing her home situation with her one day, I allowed her to leave work half an hour early, to attend to an aspect of her mother's care.

There is nothing unusual in that. If somebody has something on, even such as attending a big football match, accommodations are made. This was far more serious than a football match – and I doubt any manager with compassion would have done anything different.

Yet both she and I were told we had to answer for five disciplinary code breaches. If found guilty, these could have resulted in a fine or suspension, or if the breaches were found to be really bad, dismissal. I had never experienced anything like this in my whole career. I had no problem in dealing with it, either. But it really got to me that they had to drag this female officer, who was already under stress, into the whole thing.

Once more, I went down the route that appeared to be the only one that got Longford to pay attention, and that was going to the media. I contacted Mick Clifford at the *Examiner* again and gave him the details, which he checked out from his end. I don't know what time the newspaper hit the shops that morning, in either Portlaoise or Longford, but by 11 a.m. I had been informed that the disciplinary actions against me would not be proceeding. Oddly then, when everything was hidden behind the walls of the prison, the way to proceed was to discipline me, yet once news was out that this was happening, suddenly that plan was abandoned. It seems a very poor way to run an organization, not to mind deal with staff over matters affecting their careers. Eventually, the female officer was also cleared. But for me, over a period when I experienced some very shabby treatment, this episode represented a real low point.

Things were changing in other ways, as far as I could see. The whole operation was looser than ever would have been allowed when Ben Buckley was the chief officer. I began noticing this in different ways. One day, we were all sent to Mountjoy for a big search operation. As usual, it was arranged to start early in the morning when the prisoners would be caught off guard, and to ensure that the governor could have his prison back before the afternoon.

We went up and did the usual, finishing the job not long before one o'clock. Once completed, those of us who had come from Portlaoise were told to take the rest of the day off. I couldn't believe it. The search had meant that there was a skeleton staff on duty back in Portlaoise, and while this is manageable over a short period, you certainly wouldn't want to see it persisting for a full day. On a basic level there was a security matter to address.

I brought this up but was overruled.

The looser approach then began to show itself in other ways. I suspected that some officers were clocking in for hours that weren't being worked. This is not to suggest that management were knowingly allowing this to happen, but there was certainly an environment where some thought they could get away with it. For instance, I came across one officer who managed to clock in for thirty-three extra hours one week. Those hours were down as overtime, so he was getting paid 1.8 times the normal rate, which works out at being paid for practically sixty hours' work *for the overtime*. That's a substantial amount of money to be walking out the door through the fraud of one just one officer.

I wrote to the management in Longford about it, pointing out that this was fraud and was impacting on the service. Very little came of that. Maybe it was just that they had me categorized as a troublemaker because I didn't go quietly, but one way or the other, nobody looked into it. So, I made a protected disclosure, forcing them to act.

The outcome of that was an investigation by the professional consultancy firm Mazars. That is still going on at the time of writing, which is a story in itself. I'm sure the consultants are doing all they can to advance it and bring it to a conclusion, which makes you wonder what's holding it up.

There comes a time to call time, even if the manner of your going is not what you ever would have wanted. At some point in 2019, I decided that, just for the hell of it, I would hang on until the governor of the OSG, Pat Kavanagh, retired. And then I'd go. It was a little marker for me – and yes, it does indicate a stubborn streak.

Pat Kavanagh was retiring in early 2020. On the day he was about to go, I was in his office and addressed him as 'Pat'.

He told me, as was his right, that I had to address him as governor.

'Only for the next two hours, Pat,' I replied. Relations between us had never been great, but they were in the bin at that stage.

A few weeks later, I handed in my notice. My last day in

work was nothing really out of the ordinary. I did go around both prisons to say goodbye to people I'd known down the years, including a number of prisoners. In the evening, I went out and bought fish and chips for a group of those on the OSG with whom I was still close. Some of them I had worked with through what were the most rewarding times of my thirty-one years in the service.

The assistant chief officer usually doesn't finish up until about half-eight, which would be forty minutes or so after most of the staff on the unit I was overseeing had left. I was alone for that period, with plenty of room to reflect and look back on my time in the service. I didn't receive a phone call from Longford just to say goodbye, as might be the case with many public or private organizations. I didn't even get the standard goodbye letter that is presented to all who retire from the service. Relations with headquarters had gone beyond all that. They were delighted to see the back of me.

I'm not one for great introspection, but it was a major event in my life. The prison service had been more than a job. Long hours, and the sense of camaraderie that is needed in a job like that, meant that this wasn't a nine-to-five number outside of which you rarely encounter work-mates. It had been a way of life. And then my time in the OSG – engaged in work that lived with you even when you were off duty – ensured that the job dominated my whole existence.

We all have regrets. Like everybody, I had some, but none out of the ordinary. I had enjoyed a good career, and it had given me and my family a good life. I also managed to have something that I think makes a massive difference in any-body's life – luck. Sure, it would have been much, much better if things had not ended as they did. My last two years in the service were dark, frustrating and often painful, but I had no regrets over how I handled them. The main thing was, that experience did not overshadow all that went before it, stretching back over the years since I first walked into Mountjoy as the greenest of recruits.

I finished up that evening, and walked out the gates of the prison with my head held high, looking forward to getting home and the prospect of myself and Valerie popping out for a quiet celebratory drink. We had organized to fly out for a sun break in two days' time, to mark the start of this new phase of life. As I heard the gate close behind me for the last time, something strange happened. Up ahead, in the car park, I saw Brid Curran standing there. Brid was a long-time friend from the OSG, and an outstanding officer.

'What's going on?' I said.

'Valerie's taken your car home,' she said. 'You didn't think we'd let this pass without marking it.'

Then around us, like something out of a movie, all the other faces began appearing: friends and colleagues with whom I had soldiered and who had stood by me in the darkest hours of the grief with Longford. It was a complete and utter surprise. They had organized a night out for all of us in the Bridge House, in Tullamore. And with that, I hopped in one of the cars and pulled away from prison life.

24. Looking In Through the Out Door

You don't spend over thirty years of your life in an institution without gathering some thoughts about how it's run, what's wrong and what could be done better. What follows are a few observations I picked up over the course of my career.

Regularly, if I'm in town in Portlaoise these days and I'm passing the campus, I see some fellas who have just been released from either Portlaoise prison or the Midlands. More often than not, they will be walking out the gates with a black bag full of their worldly possessions. Some will have homes to go back to, others will be bound for hostels in which to stay while they attempt to get their feet on the ground. And within the latter group there will be some for whom hostels and other forms of temporary accommodation will be their lot into the future.

In theory, these released prisoners will have been rehabilitated. During their term inside, efforts will have been made to show them the error of their ways. The system will also have equipped them to come out a better person, intent on contributing to society rather than attacking it. After all, a key aspect of imprisonment is supposed to be rehabilitation. In my experience, all sorts of noises are made about rehabilitation at official level but, in reality, the whole thing is balderdash. At least some of this is down to the fact that society in general isn't interested in whether prisoners emerge from their detention better able to fit in to society.

Take somebody at the lower end of the criminal scale,

say, serving two or three years for a series of shoplifting offences. He comes out and applies for a job. The employer will want to know what he was at for the last few years. And once he fesses up, the whole atmosphere changes and he is unlikely to be employed.

One reason for those kinds of negative attitudes from employers is that most people in society don't really believe that prisoners have been rehabilitated, and with good reason. The released prisoner may well have spent his time inside twiddling his thumbs, rather than learning how to be of use to society or picking up some skills.

In the Midlands, for instance, only around a third of the prisoners are engaged in something useful on a daily basis. When the other modern prisons like the Midlands, Cloverhill and Wheatfield were built, at the turn of the century, the idea was that they would provide every prisoner with a job or a course to attend. That certainly hasn't worked out. The majority spend most of their time maybe doing laps out on the exercise yard, or playing pool in the recreation rooms when available. Not all of them would necessarily want to be doing something, but if given a purpose they might embrace it, try to focus, and work to better themselves. From what I've seen, there is no willingness from on high to put in the effort to create that kind of atmosphere.

To be fair, the facilities provided for the minority are not too bad at all. When I started out, prisoners just did their 'bird' without anything to occupy them during their sentence. They certainly didn't learn anything. The only exception to this was the Provos, who engaged in everything from making bodhráns to applying for Open University courses, even in the days before computers were introduced to prison. For the ordinary prisoner, though, very little of that was available unless they were of a mind to go chasing it, which precious few were.

That has changed, over the years. People like Sean Wynne, whose work in Portlaoise I described in Chapter 7 (Getting to Know the Heavies), did Trojan work in introducing and developing education and courses. He brought the Leaving Cert into prisons, and after a while this was adapted to ensure that the subjects and courses chosen would provide some skills, such as metalwork and woodwork. That aspect of things has improved hugely. Prisoners learn genuine skills, and courses now lead to recognized qualifications. Literacy levels have also improved hugely.

That, though, is still for the minority. Most prisoners learn very little, do very little of use, and emerge at the end of their sentence arguably having regressed rather than been rehabilitated.

Rehabilitation isn't just desirable but vital, in my opinion, for one category of prisoner: the sex offender. In the Midlands, well over a quarter of the 840 or so prisoners are sex offenders of one kind or another. Yet treatment facilities in the prison have only been introduced in the last few years. The number of treatment places is still nowhere near what is required, but I suppose it is a start. I'm not suggesting that every offender would jump at the chance of treatment, but some definitely would, and only positive results could come from making sufficient provision to treat as many as possible.

Then there are those who are beyond any kind of rehabilitation in prison, simply because they should not be in prison in the first place. There have been studies that show up to a third of prisoners in the system have mental health issues. Many, if not most, of those would more suitably be detained in a secure psychiatric facility. When I was the

ACO in C block in the Midlands, I was often blue in the face trying to get the Central Mental Hospital to take prisoners, but there was little capacity available. They have about forty beds. Any time I did manage to get a prisoner transferred, it was something of a miracle. But that is how society is organized. People who should be in hospital are instead shoved into prison. Much of this is simply down to money. It would cost more to increase the beds in somewhere like the Central Mental Hospital, so offenders are put into prison instead, and everybody pretends that this is all normal and appropriate in a so-called civilized society.

Again, let me say that, of course, I appreciate that for every prisoner in the system there is a victim out there, who has, more often than not, been physically attacked and traumatized. Prison is necessary and, even with the best will in the world, there simply wouldn't or shouldn't be an alternative for many who are locked up. But there is a much better way of doing things, if only the will was there. Some of it would require little by way of extra resourcing.

A recent innovation in the Midlands and Portlaoise has been the introduction of resettlement officers. They are detailed to prepare prisoners for all the challenges they will face on release, such as reintegrating with family, or how to apply for social welfare payments to which they are entitled. That is positive, but it has come late and needs to be properly implemented and expanded.

To some extent, the basic yet vital aspects of preparing for release are still largely taken on by chaplains in the prisons, on a purely ad hoc basis. These people do great work, but they don't have the time – or, in some instances, the specialist knowledge – to do it properly. There really has to be a way to better prepare for release people who have been locked up for sixteen hours a day, seven days a week, often for years.

Better use could also be made of the open prisons like Loughan House, in Cavan, and Shelton Abbey, in Wicklow. Any prisoner who is serving a sentence of more than a few years should be automatically sent to one of these places before release, just to ease them back towards normal life. And in that regard, there is no open prison for female prisoners, which is definitely something that is badly needed.

I did see some positive change over the course of my career. In-cell sanitation has been a huge advance. The days when prisoners had to use a pot, and hurled parcel bombs out the window at night, are largely gone, and rightly so. The introduction of a TV for every cell has also been a big development. Apart from anything else, it has done wonders for the mental health of many prisoners.

The building of new prisons – including Cork's new prison – has been positive. The modern infrastructure makes the job easier and provides a more humane environment. One of the biggest changes has been the introduction of nurses into the system, which started around twenty years ago. This was long overdue, and at the very least it means that basic medical assistance is available at all times in the prisons.

Those were a few of the positive changes. In the area of management, there has been a lot of change also, but I can't say it has been for the better.

And now, one final insight into how things have changed for the worse – an incident known among officers, particularly those who are familiar with the prisons in Portlaoise, as Bloody Sunday.

On Sundays, a skeleton staff looks after the prison, as it

might be in many other walks of life. There is a Sunday allowance that amounts to around €300, so working the shift is popular. On this particular Sunday, a good share of those on duty – reportedly up to forty officers – took off for Ramsbottom's pub in the town for a few lunchtime pints. One thing led to another, and before long the whole crew got it into their heads that they were entitled to an afternoon off to go on the beer. And go on the beer they did – with a bang.

The accounts of what occurred may have been embellished over the years, but here are a few details where all versions overlap. The pints flowed freely, and everybody was getting nicely toasted as the afternoon turned into evening. At one stage, the gardaí were called about an incident. As the evening wore on, about six of the male officers found themselves in the car park of the pub, engaged in what was literally a pissing contest. The winner would be whoever could loop his urine farthest across the tarmac. A motorist approached them to complain. When one of the officers turned to address this man he was mid-flow, and some urine ended up on the poor motorist's trousers and shoes. A complaint was made to the gardaí about what was going on.

Later, outside a nightclub, the bouncers wouldn't let one of the officers in, because he was too inebriated. This led to a confrontation at the door between bouncers and officers. This was the conclusion of a day in which these officers, who were supposed to be at work, effectively ran amok in the town.

Back in the prison, they were down to the barest minimum of staff. Everybody was petrified that the prisoners would cop that so many were missing. Were that to occur, there is no doubt but they would have tried to take advantage of the situation. Violence of one form or another would surely have kicked off. Thankfully, they never got to know that their jailers were off on the beer.

You might expect that there would have been serious repercussions for Bloody Sunday. A chief officer was hopping mad about it and demanded, at the very least, that the Sunday allowance be deducted from these officers' pay. That didn't happen. The chief left the service not too long after that.

The one change that came out of it was that barbecues were organized for the staff for a number of Sundays in the year – in order, I suppose, to discourage them from going on the piss up the town.

That story goes to the heart of how the prison service is now run. If discipline had been meted out as it should have been, there would, in all likelihood, have been trouble with the Prison Officers' Association. That, in turn, would probably have meant word getting into the media about what had occurred. Controversy would be generated; the minister of the day would be cheesed off, and he or she would be the focus of attack from the opposition. Management of the Irish Prison Service would get it in the neck from both the department and the minister. For all involved, it's simply not worth the bother.

That incident demonstrates what everybody in the system knows – governors are no longer in charge. The real power lies in Longford, where the IPS headquarters are located. The prisons are effectively being run by civil servants, practically none of whom have ever worked in a prison. The priority in headquarters is that controversy of any sort must be avoided. Controversy puts prisons in the spotlight, which is the last place that politicians want to see it. They have that attitude simply because they know that issues relating to prisons are not vote-winners (unless in the context of being 'tough on crime') and therefore prisons are viewed as a negative on the political register.

A politician will talk until the cows come home about putting more gardaí on the street, because that is what interests voters. The approach to prisons is the total opposite: keep them out of sight and out of mind. John Lonergan, the former governor of Mountjoy, used to make a point that prisons and prisoners are part of society, that the prisons are *your* prisons, just as all public services are *your* services.

His point was well made, and he was making it simply because prisons and prisoners are not regarded in those terms by the public. And while that kind of detachment prevails, there is going to be an attitude at the political level that what goes on in prisons must be kept quiet because of the potential for bad publicity. It's no way to run a prison service.

The strong governors I worked under – people like Ned 'Nike' Whelan or John L. O'Sullivan – would not be tolerated under the current regime. They were managers who knew how to run a prison, who had worked their way up from the floor, knew everything there was to know, and took decisions based on their knowledge. Whether something was controversial or not didn't really enter their heads. Their main aim was to run the prison properly, in the best interests of staff and prisoners.

When I started out, a governor commanded total respect in the prison, usually because it was earned. That has changed for the worse. Staff don't respect the governors, because they know the governors don't have the power that they used to wield in the old days. That power now lies with managers in Longford who believe they can run the prisons by remote control. How anybody thinks that is a good idea is beyond me.

Most of the suits from Longford wouldn't know how to turn a key in a lock. Some of them have never actually been on a landing. Can you imagine a scenario in which, say, the top management in An Garda Síochána, the commissioner and his assistant commissioners, were all drawn from the ranks of the civil service, none of them having served a day as a cop? Yet that is now what you have in the prison service.

A few years before I retired, I and a few other ACOs and class officers were asked by the governor of training to go down to Longford and meet the management team and lay out our concerns and priorities. I think the idea was to provide a bit of an insight into what life on the landing was actually like.

We sat down and talked to them. One female class officer beside me in the meeting explained problems she was having in sourcing kettles. She told about having fifty prisoners on her landing and when she needed a kettle for one of the cells she had to wait for up to six weeks.

Now, anybody who knows anything about prisons knows that being short of kettles is a big deal. Prisoners have a few basic entitlements. The freedom to make a cup of tea might appear small but it is nothing of the sort. Depriving a man of that for an extended period can only lead to trouble. Yet the response my female colleague got from one of the suits was that the man in charge of kettles wasn't at the meeting. This woman looked at me and I looked at her and we didn't need to say anything. *They just haven't got a clue.*

At the same meeting, I suggested to the management people that they should familiarize themselves with prisons. There were five of them sitting opposite us and they all bristled and said, of course they knew about prisons, they'd often been in them. How many of you have been on a landing? I asked. One of them said he had. Was the landing unlocked at the time? Ah no, he said. The whole thing was farcical, but that is exactly how the system is being run. Even the most senior governors in the system are being sidelined, as if they are an irritant to efficient management.

I doubt that you will find anybody who has worked at management level within prisons in this country who believes all of this feeds back down into the system in a positive way. But that's how things are done today and where priorities lie.

None of it affects me any more, and I have no axe to grind. As I've said already, I had a good career. I was lucky both in my timing and in many of the colleagues and managers I worked with and under. Unfortunately, I doubt very much whether somebody entering the service today could look forward to the same prospects.

To conclude, I come back to what John Lonergan said, all those years ago. Until such time as there is a different attitude to prisons among society in general, then the priority at the top will remain to ensure that the prison system is kept in a dark corner of the public sector. Out of sight, and, as much as possible, out of mind.

Acknowledgements

Many thanks are due to those who contributed along the way. We would like to thank all past and present staff in the Irish Prison Service who provided information, insight and advice. They know who they are. We would also like to thank Faith O'Grady at the Lisa Richards Agency, and Patricia Deevy and Shân Morley Jones for Penguin.

Mick Clifford wishes to thank Pauline, Luke and Tom for their patience, love and support during this project.

David McDonald wants to offer special thanks for their love and support to the following people: my son Simon and his fiancée Maria. My daughter Róisín and her husband Keith, not forgetting the most important little dudes Kai and Ezra. Also my dad and friend Michael, who taught me never to give up. And lastly, my truly wonderful wife Valerie, my rock for the last thirty-five years. This book is dedicated to my childhood friend, younger brother and fellow prison officer Matthew McDonald, who died in a tragic road accident on his way to work in Mountjoy Prison.